GOD AND SCIENCE

FANTAGRAPHICS BOOKS
7563 Lake City Way NE
Seattle WA 98115

www.fantagraphics.com

Edited by Gary Groth
Designed by Jaime Hernandez
Production by Paul Baresh and Alexa Koenings
Additional Coloring by Joanne Bagge
Eric Reynolds, associate editor
Gary Groth and Kim Thompson, publishers

Portions of this graphic novel appeared in *Love and Rockets: New Stories* Vol. 1 and Vol. 2.
This edition contains 30 new pages.

Distributed in the U.S. by W.W. Norton and Company, Inc. (800-233-4830)
Distributed in Canada by Canadian Manda Group (800-452-6642 x862)
Distributed in the U.K. by Turnaround Distribution (44 020 8829-3002)
Distributed to comic book specialty stores by Diamond Comics Distributors (800-452-6642 x215)
First edition: April, 2012. Printed in China

ISBN: 978-1-60699-539-6

GOD AND SCIENCE
RETURN OF THE TI-GIRLS

JAIME HERNANDEZ

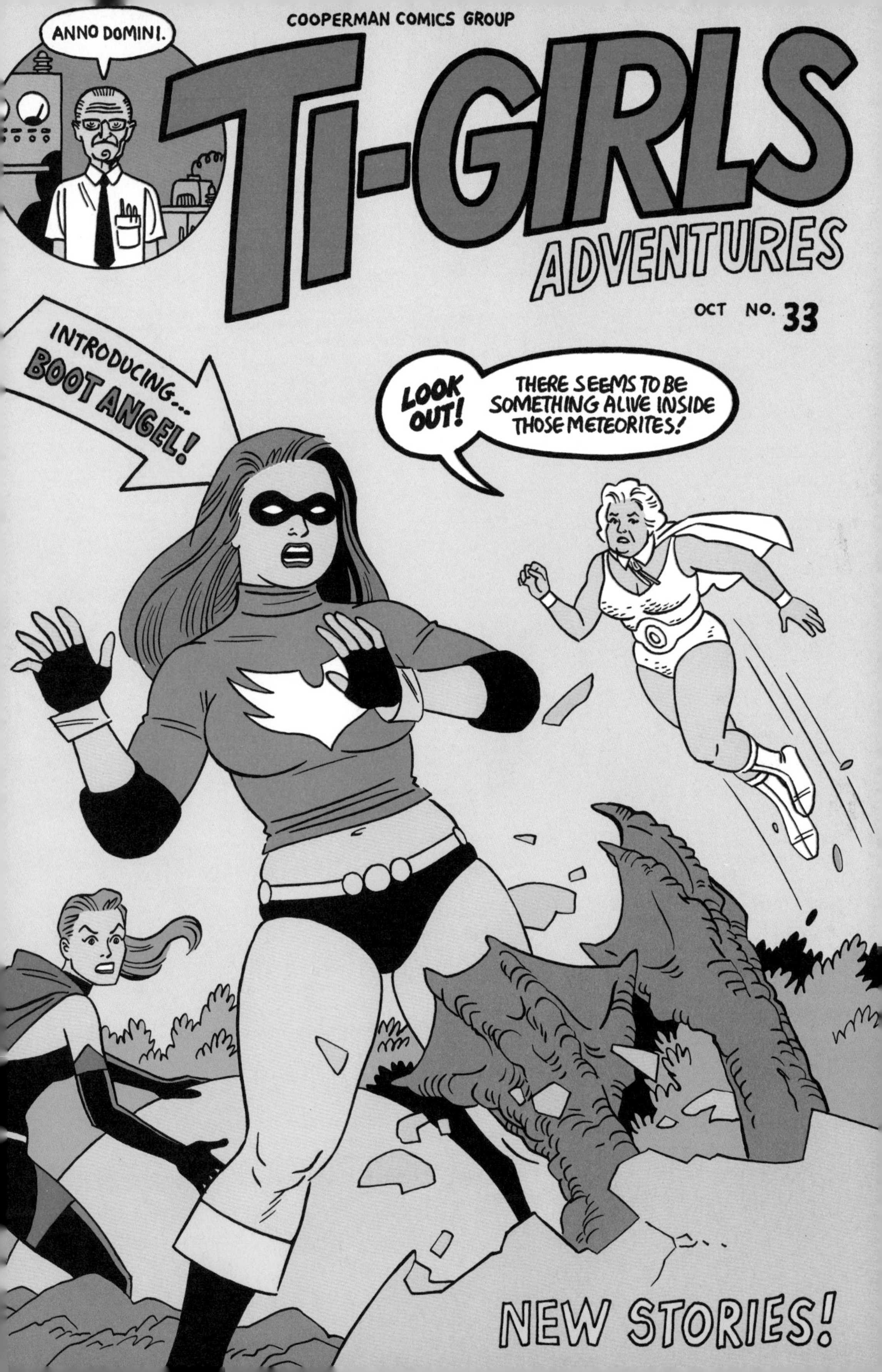
COOPERMAN COMICS GROUP
ANNO DOMINI.
TI-GIRLS
ADVENTURES
OCT NO. 33
INTRODUCING... BOOT ANGEL!
LOOK OUT!
THERE SEEMS TO BE SOMETHING ALIVE INSIDE THOSE METEORITES!
NEW STORIES!

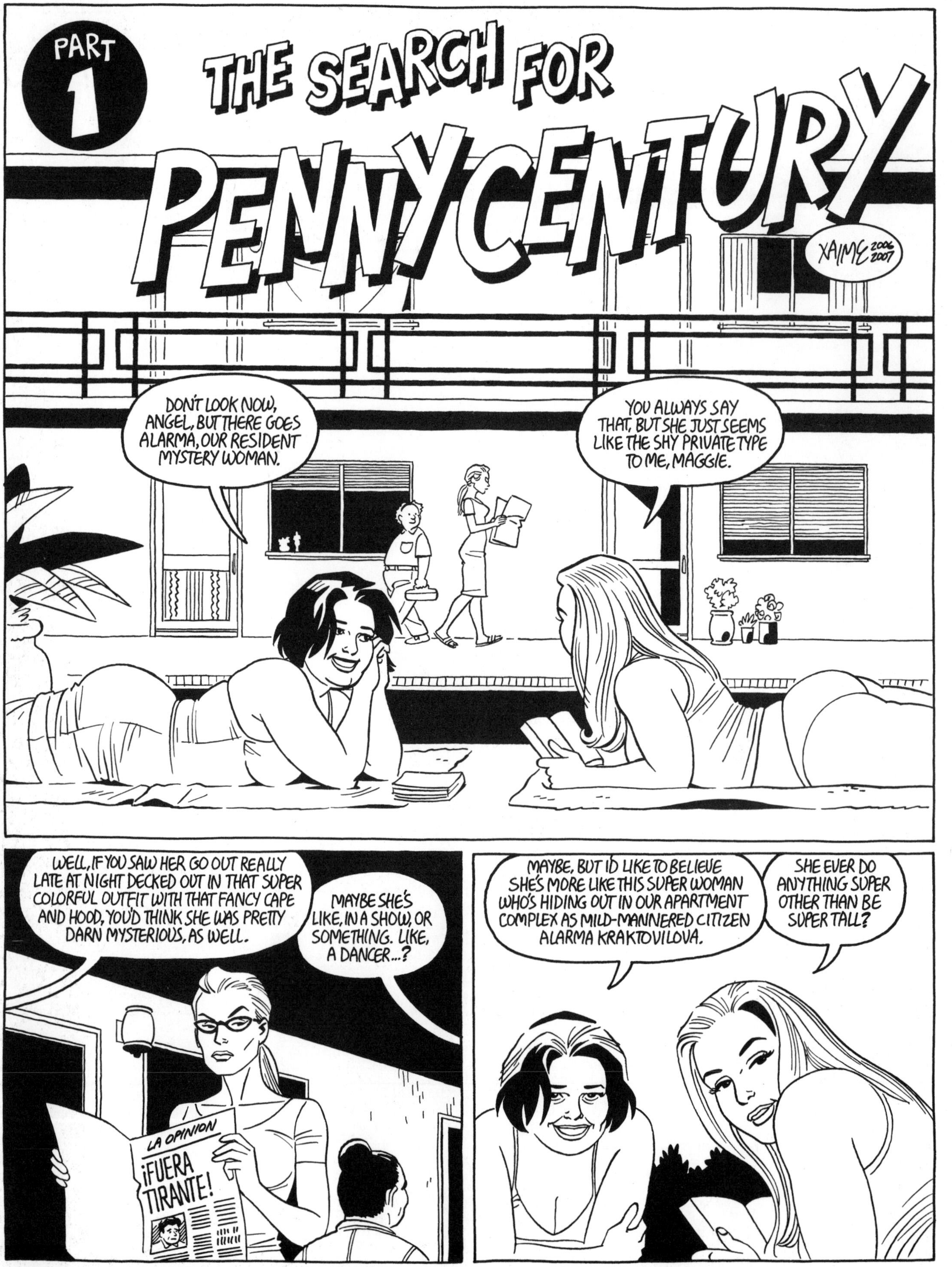
PART 1
THE SEARCH FOR PENNY CENTURY
XAIME 2006 2007
DON'T LOOK NOW, ANGEL, BUT THERE GOES ALARMA, OUR RESIDENT MYSTERY WOMAN.
YOU ALWAYS SAY THAT, BUT SHE JUST SEEMS LIKE THE SHY PRIVATE TYPE TO ME, MAGGIE.
WELL, IF YOU SAW HER GO OUT REALLY LATE AT NIGHT DECKED OUT IN THAT SUPER COLORFUL OUTFIT WITH THAT FANCY CAPE AND HOOD, YOU'D THINK SHE WAS PRETTY DARN MYSTERIOUS, AS WELL.
MAYBE SHE'S LIKE, IN A SHOW, OR SOMETHING. LIKE, A DANCER...?
LA OPINION
¡FUERA TIRANTE!
MAYBE, BUT I'D LIKE TO BELIEVE SHE'S MORE LIKE THIS SUPER WOMAN WHO'S HIDING OUT IN OUR APARTMENT COMPLEX AS MILD-MANNERED CITIZEN ALARMA KRAKTOVILOVA.
SHE EVER DO ANYTHING SUPER OTHER THAN BE SUPER TALL?

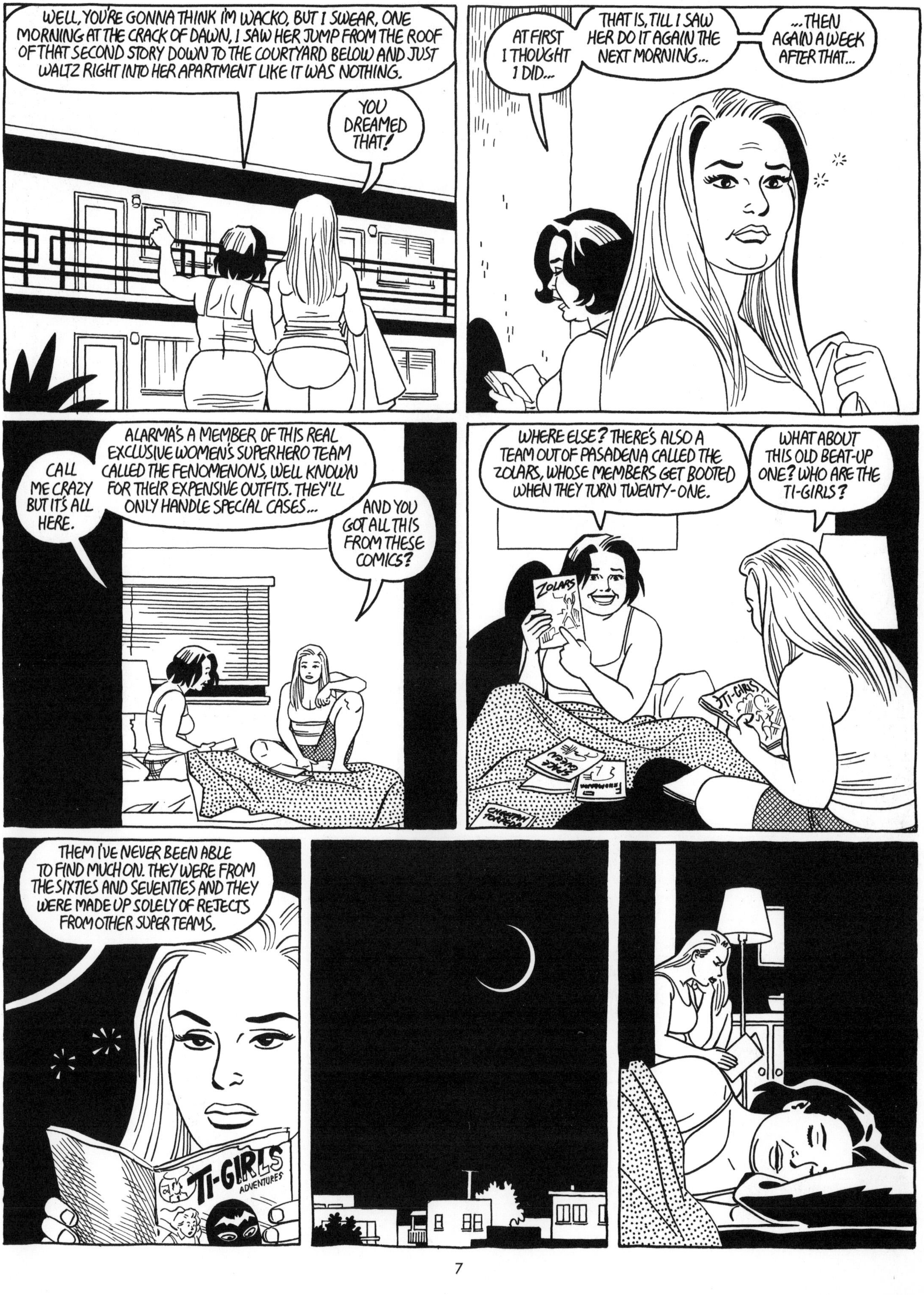

WELL, YOU'RE GONNA THINK I'M WACKO, BUT I SWEAR, ONE MORNING AT THE CRACK OF DAWN, I SAW HER JUMP FROM THE ROOF OF THAT SECOND STORY DOWN TO THE COURTYARD BELOW AND JUST WALTZ RIGHT INTO HER APARTMENT LIKE IT WAS NOTHING.
YOU DREAMED THAT!
AT FIRST I THOUGHT I DID...
THAT IS, TILL I SAW HER DO IT AGAIN THE NEXT MORNING...
...THEN AGAIN A WEEK AFTER THAT...
CALL ME CRAZY BUT IT'S ALL HERE.
ALARMA'S A MEMBER OF THIS REAL EXCLUSIVE WOMEN'S SUPERHERO TEAM CALLED THE FENOMENONS, WELL KNOWN FOR THEIR EXPENSIVE OUTFITS. THEY'LL ONLY HANDLE SPECIAL CASES...
AND YOU GOT ALL THIS FROM THESE COMICS?
WHERE ELSE? THERE'S ALSO A TEAM OUT OF PASADENA CALLED THE ZOLARS, WHOSE MEMBERS GET BOOTED WHEN THEY TURN TWENTY-ONE.
WHAT ABOUT THIS OLD BEAT-UP ONE? WHO ARE THE TI-GIRLS?
ZOLARS
TI-GIRLS
THEM I'VE NEVER BEEN ABLE TO FIND MUCH ON. THEY WERE FROM THE SIXTIES AND SEVENTIES AND THEY WERE MADE UP SOLELY OF REJECTS FROM OTHER SUPER TEAMS.
TI-GIRLS
ADVENTURES

LOOKING FOR ME?
OH JEEZ!
?!?!?
ZIIIP!

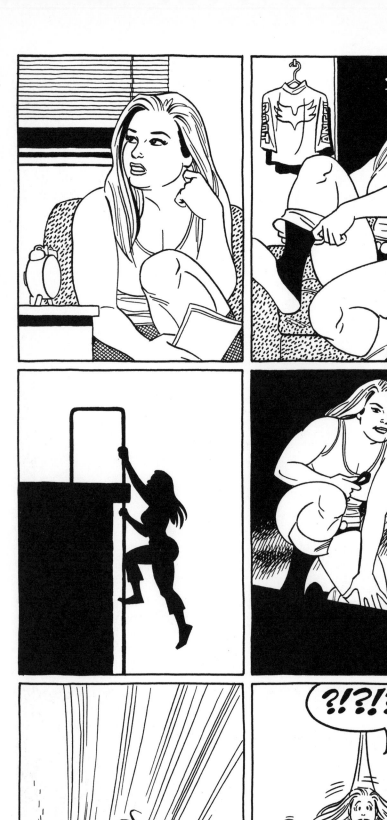

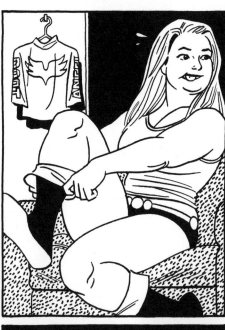

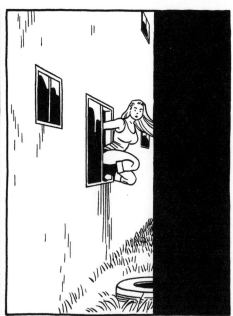

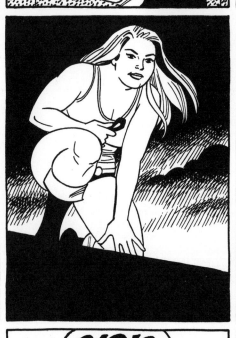

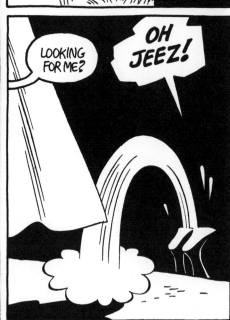

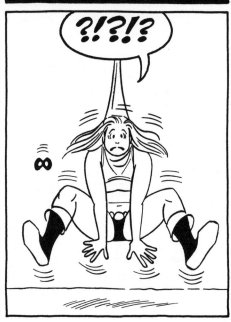

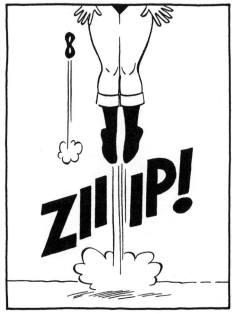

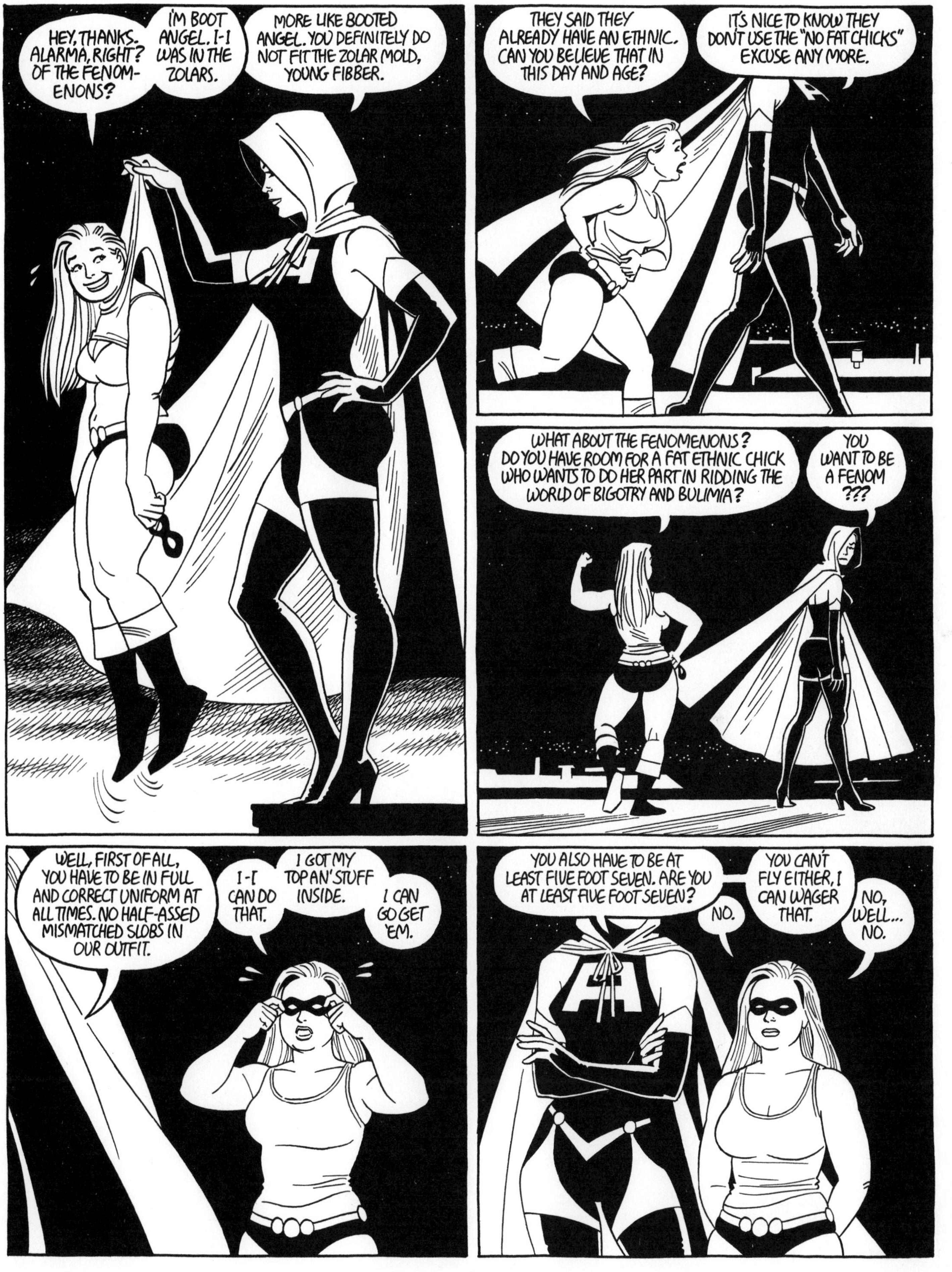
HEY, THANKS. ALARMA, RIGHT? OF THE FENOMENONS?
I'M BOOT ANGEL. I-I WAS IN THE ZOLARS.
MORE LIKE BOOTED ANGEL. YOU DEFINITELY DO NOT FIT THE ZOLAR MOLD, YOUNG FIBBER.
THEY SAID THEY ALREADY HAVE AN ETHNIC. CAN YOU BELIEVE THAT IN THIS DAY AND AGE?
IT'S NICE TO KNOW THEY DON'T USE THE "NO FAT CHICKS" EXCUSE ANY MORE.
WHAT ABOUT THE FENOMENONS? DO YOU HAVE ROOM FOR A FAT ETHNIC CHICK WHO WANTS TO DO HER PART IN RIDDING THE WORLD OF BIGOTRY AND BULIMIA?
YOU WANT TO BE A FENOM ???
WELL, FIRST OF ALL, YOU HAVE TO BE IN FULL AND CORRECT UNIFORM AT ALL TIMES. NO HALF-ASSED MISMATCHED SLOBS IN OUR OUTFIT.
I-I CAN DO THAT.
I GOT MY TOP AN' STUFF INSIDE.
I CAN GO GET 'EM.
YOU ALSO HAVE TO BE AT LEAST FIVE FOOT SEVEN. ARE YOU AT LEAST FIVE FOOT SEVEN?
NO.
YOU CAN'T FLY EITHER, I CAN WAGER THAT.
NO, WELL... NO.

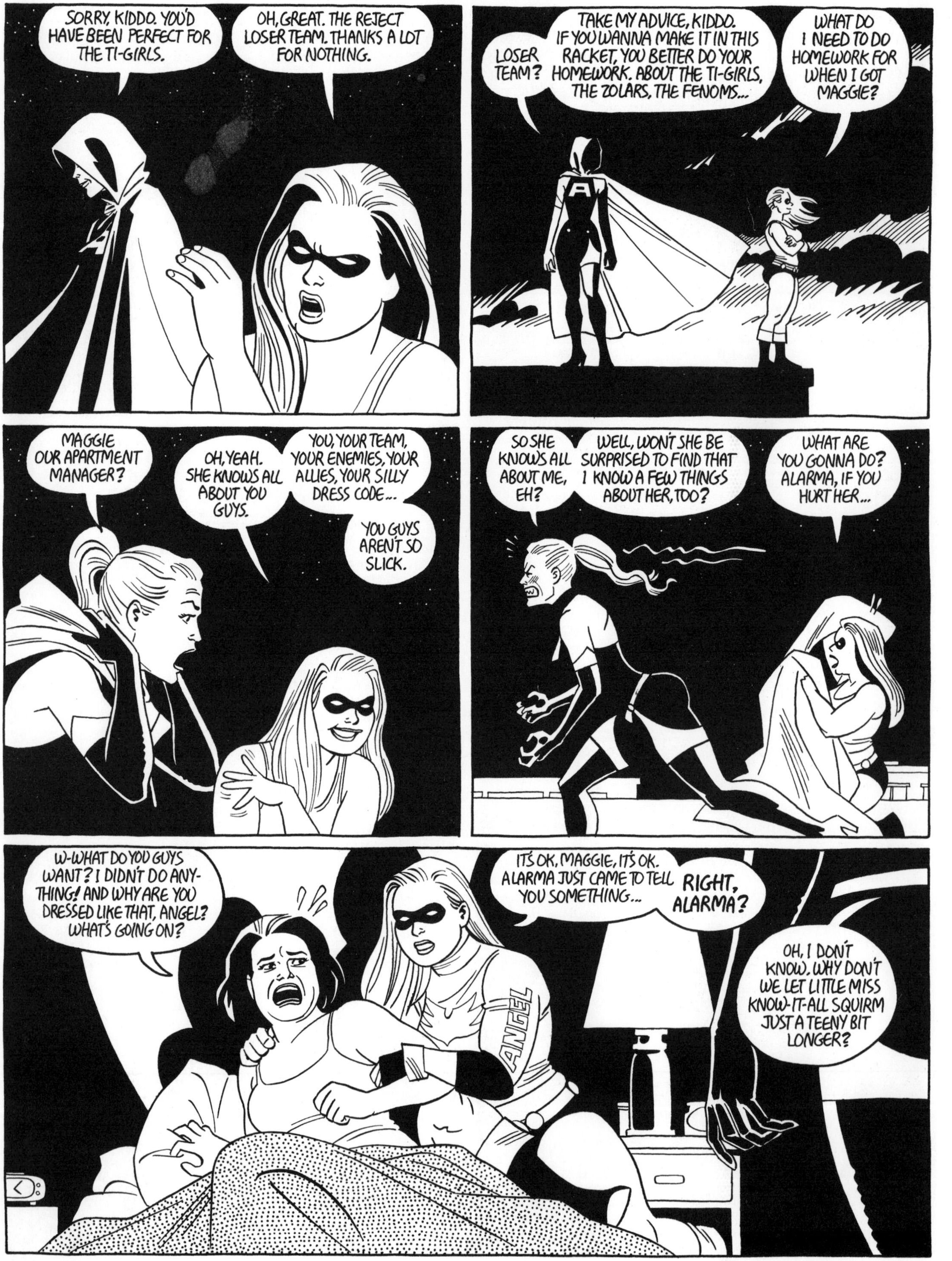
SORRY, KIDDO. YOU'D HAVE BEEN PERFECT FOR THE TI-GIRLS.
OH, GREAT. THE REJECT LOSER TEAM. THANKS A LOT FOR NOTHING.
LOSER TEAM?
TAKE MY ADVICE, KIDDO. IF YOU WANNA MAKE IT IN THIS RACKET, YOU BETTER DO YOUR HOMEWORK. ABOUT THE TI-GIRLS, THE ZOLARS, THE FENOMS...
WHAT DO I NEED TO DO HOMEWORK FOR WHEN I GOT MAGGIE?
MAGGIE OUR APARTMENT MANAGER?
OH, YEAH. SHE KNOWS ALL ABOUT YOU GUYS.
YOU, YOUR TEAM, YOUR ENEMIES, YOUR ALLIES, YOUR SILLY DRESS CODE...
YOU GUYS AREN'T SO SLICK.
SO SHE KNOWS ALL ABOUT ME, EH?
WELL, WON'T SHE BE SURPRISED TO FIND THAT I KNOW A FEW THINGS ABOUT HER, TOO?
WHAT ARE YOU GONNA DO? ALARMA, IF YOU HURT HER...
W-WHAT DO YOU GUYS WANT? I DIDN'T DO ANYTHING! AND WHY ARE YOU DRESSED LIKE THAT, ANGEL? WHAT'S GOING ON?
IT'S OK, MAGGIE, IT'S OK. ALARMA JUST CAME TO TELL YOU SOMETHING...
RIGHT, ALARMA?
ANGEL
OH, I DON'T KNOW. WHY DON'T WE LET LITTLE MISS KNOW-IT-ALL SQUIRM JUST A TEENY BIT LONGER?

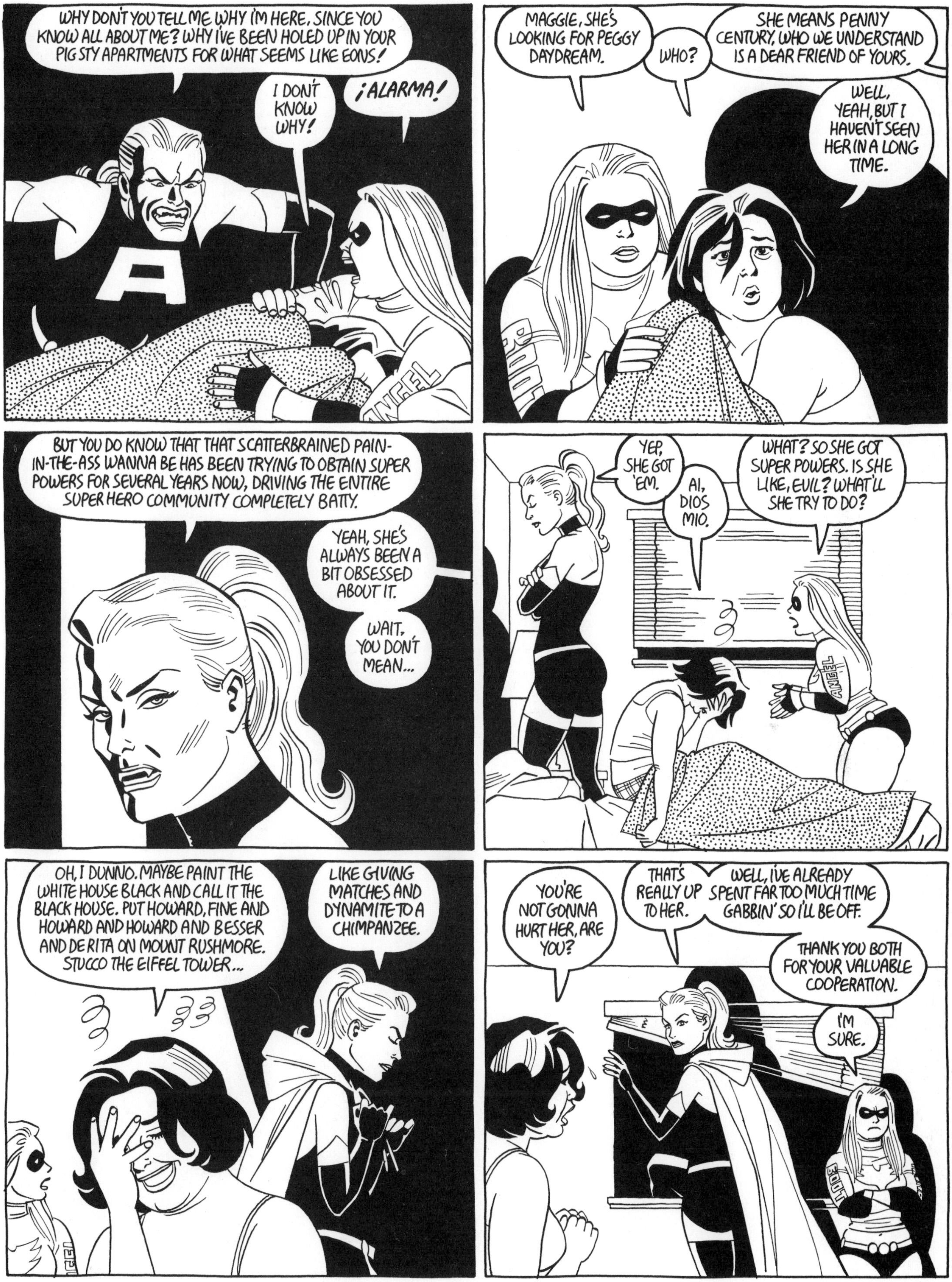
WHY DON'T YOU TELL ME WHY I'M HERE, SINCE YOU KNOW ALL ABOUT ME? WHY I'VE BEEN HOLED UP IN YOUR PIG STY APARTMENTS FOR WHAT SEEMS LIKE EONS!
I DON'T KNOW WHY!
¡ALARMA!
ANGEL
MAGGIE, SHE'S LOOKING FOR PEGGY DAYDREAM.
WHO?
SHE MEANS PENNY CENTURY, WHO WE UNDERSTAND IS A DEAR FRIEND OF YOURS.
WELL, YEAH, BUT I HAVEN'T SEEN HER IN A LONG TIME.
BUT YOU DO KNOW THAT THAT SCATTERBRAINED PAIN-IN-THE-ASS WANNA BE HAS BEEN TRYING TO OBTAIN SUPER POWERS FOR SEVERAL YEARS NOW, DRIVING THE ENTIRE SUPER HERO COMMUNITY COMPLETELY BATTY.
YEAH, SHE'S ALWAYS BEEN A BIT OBSESSED ABOUT IT.
WAIT, YOU DON'T MEAN...
YEP, SHE GOT 'EM.
AI, DIOS MIO.
WHAT? SO SHE GOT SUPER POWERS. IS SHE LIKE, EVIL? WHAT'LL SHE TRY TO DO?
ANGEL
OH, I DUNNO. MAYBE PAINT THE WHITE HOUSE BLACK AND CALL IT THE BLACK HOUSE. PUT HOWARD, FINE AND HOWARD AND HOWARD AND BESSER AND DE RITA ON MOUNT RUSHMORE. STUCCO THE EIFFEL TOWER...
LIKE GIVING MATCHES AND DYNAMITE TO A CHIMPANZEE.
YOU'RE NOT GONNA HURT HER, ARE YOU?
THAT'S REALLY UP TO HER.
WELL, I'VE ALREADY SPENT FAR TOO MUCH TIME GABBIN' SO I'LL BE OFF.
THANK YOU BOTH FOR YOUR VALUABLE COOPERATION.
I'M SURE.

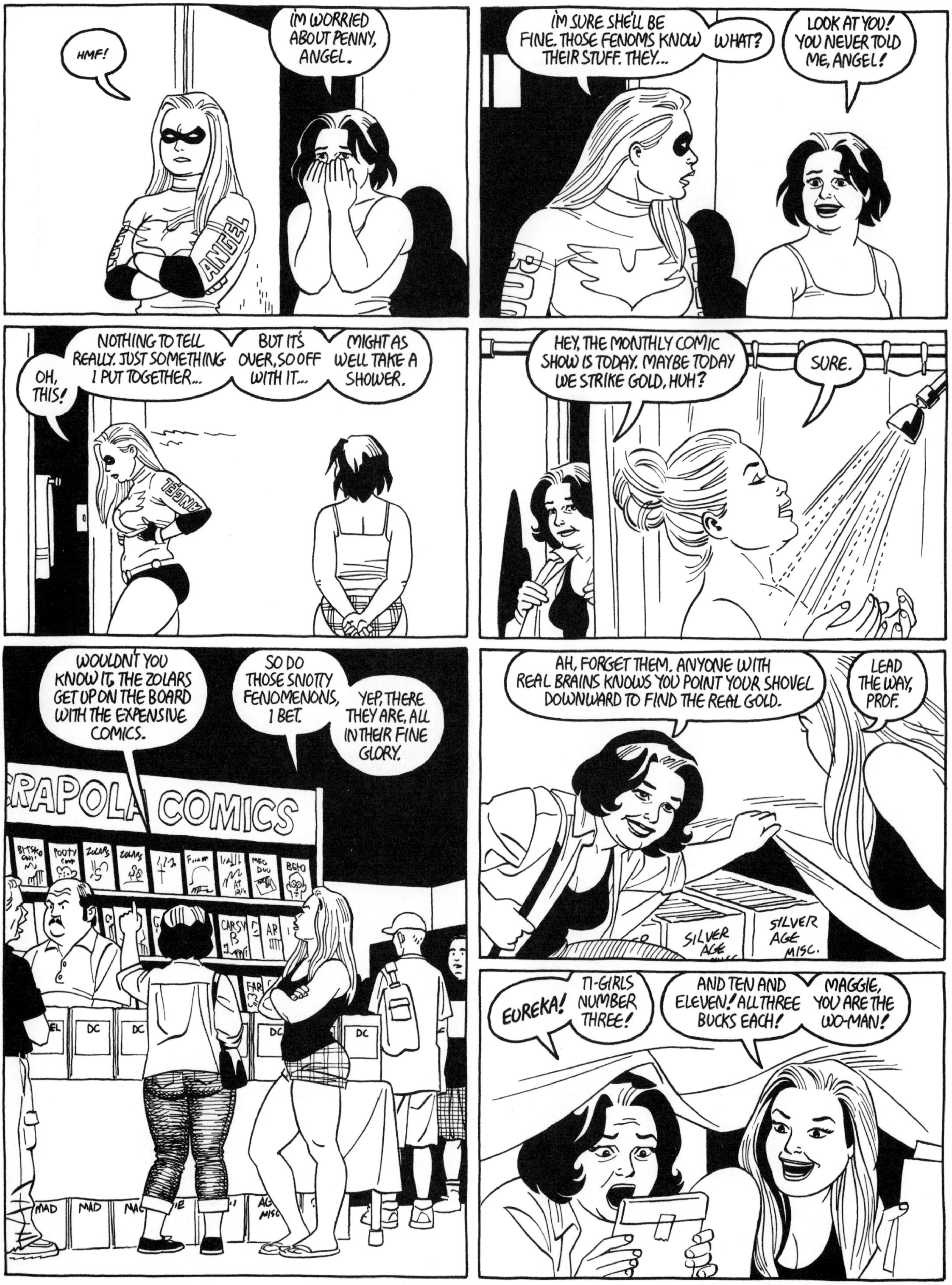
HMF!
I'M WORRIED ABOUT PENNY, ANGEL.
I'M SURE SHE'LL BE FINE. THOSE FENOMS KNOW THEIR STUFF. THEY...
WHAT?
LOOK AT YOU! YOU NEVER TOLD ME, ANGEL!
OH, THIS!
NOTHING TO TELL REALLY. JUST SOMETHING I PUT TOGETHER...
BUT IT'S OVER, SO OFF WITH IT...
MIGHT AS WELL TAKE A SHOWER.
HEY, THE MONTHLY COMIC SHOW IS TODAY. MAYBE TODAY WE STRIKE GOLD, HUH?
SURE.
WOULDN'T YOU KNOW IT, THE ZOLARS GET UP ON THE BOARD WITH THE EXPENSIVE COMICS.
SO DO THOSE SNOTTY FENOMENONS, I BET.
YEP, THERE THEY ARE, ALL IN THEIR FINE GLORY.
COMICS
AH, FORGET THEM. ANYONE WITH REAL BRAINS KNOWS YOU POINT YOUR SHOVEL DOWNWARD TO FIND THE REAL GOLD.
LEAD THE WAY, PROF.
SILVER AGE
SILVER AGE MISC.
EUREKA!
TI-GIRLS NUMBER THREE!
AND TEN AND ELEVEN! ALL THREE BUCKS EACH!
MAGGIE, YOU ARE THE WO-MAN!

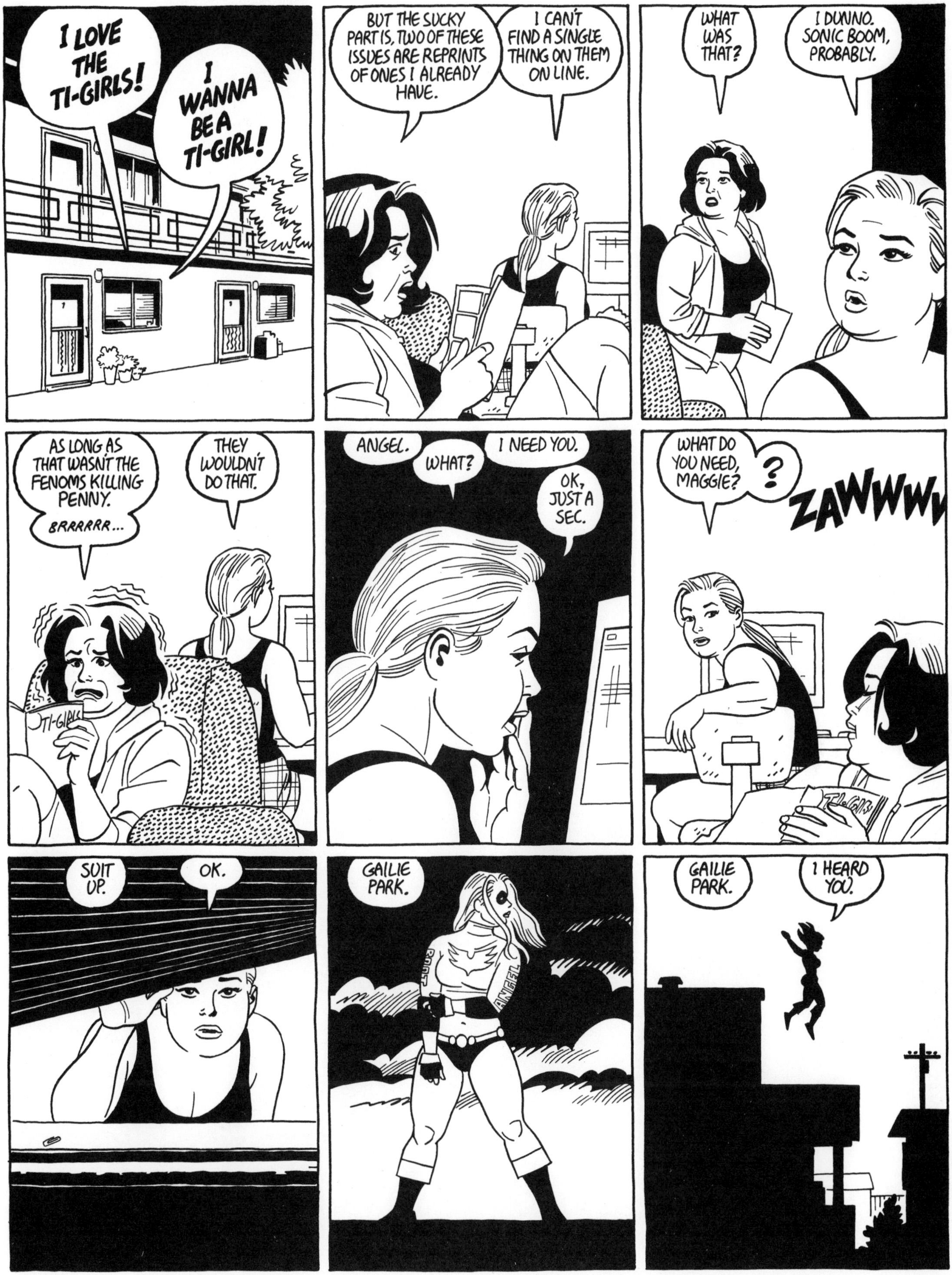
I LOVE THE TI-GIRLS!
I WANNA BE A TI-GIRL!
BUT THE SUCKY PART IS, TWO OF THESE ISSUES ARE REPRINTS OF ONES I ALREADY HAVE.
I CAN'T FIND A SINGLE THING ON THEM ON LINE.
WHAT WAS THAT?
I DUNNO. SONIC BOOM, PROBABLY.
AS LONG AS THAT WASN'T THE FENOMS KILLING PENNY.
BRRRRRR...
THEY WOULDN'T DO THAT.
ANGEL.
WHAT?
I NEED YOU.
OK, JUST A SEC.
WHAT DO YOU NEED, MAGGIE?
?
ZAWWWW
TI-GIRLS
SUIT UP.
OK.
GAILIE PARK.
ANGEL
GAILIE PARK.
I HEARD YOU.

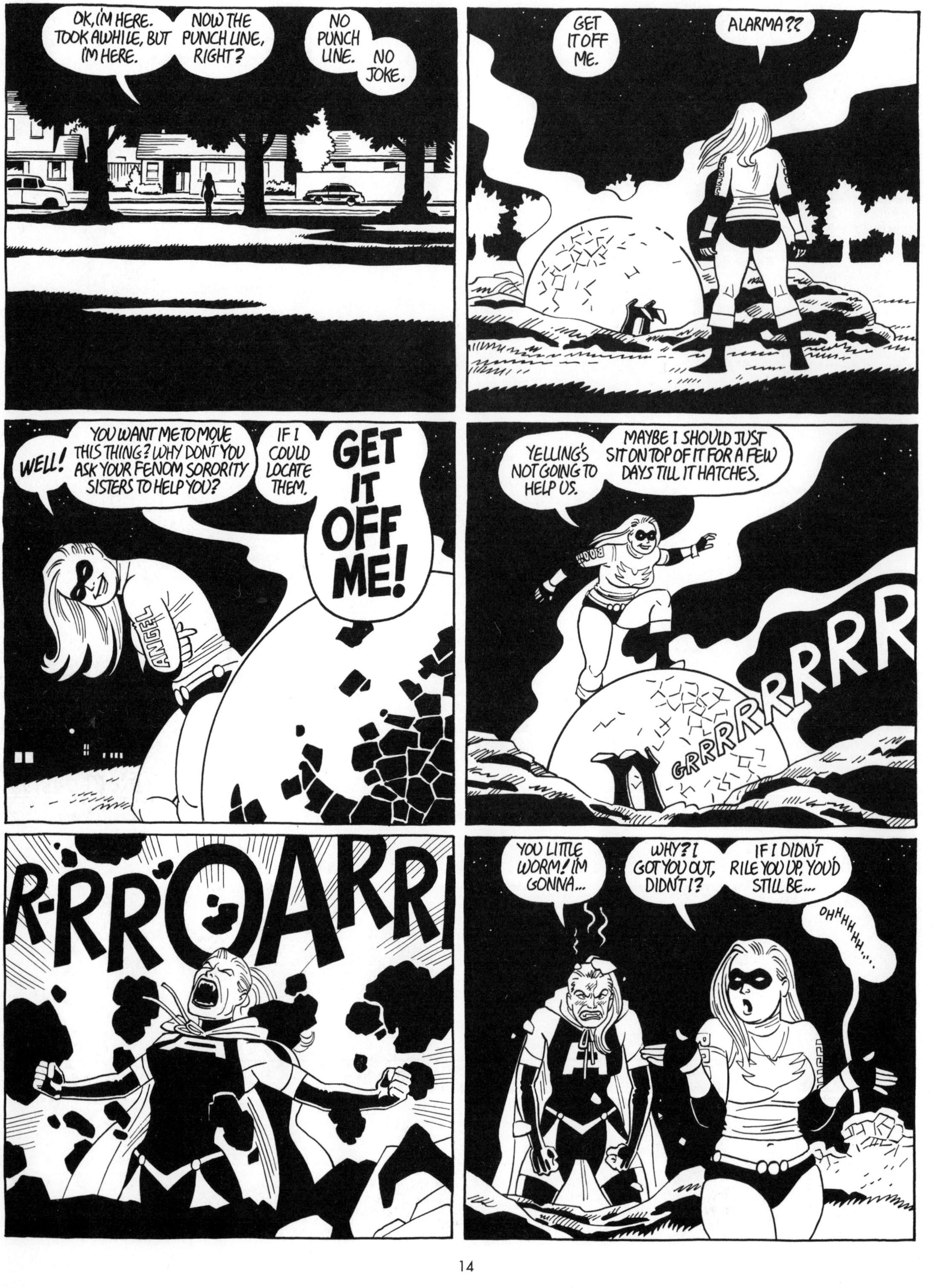
OK, I'M HERE. TOOK AWHILE, BUT I'M HERE.
NOW THE PUNCH LINE, RIGHT?
NO PUNCH LINE.
NO JOKE.
GET IT OFF ME.
ALARMA??
WELL!
YOU WANT ME TO MOVE THIS THING? WHY DONT YOU ASK YOUR FENOM SORORITY SISTERS TO HELP YOU?
IF I COULD LOCATE THEM.
GET IT OFF ME!
ANGEL
YELLING'S NOT GOING TO HELP US.
MAYBE I SHOULD JUST SIT ON TOP OF IT FOR A FEW DAYS TILL IT HATCHES.
GRRRRRRRRRRRRR
R-RROARR
YOU LITTLE WORM! I'M GONNA...
WHY?! I GOT YOU OUT, DIDN'T I?
IF I DIDN'T RILE YOU UP, YOU'D STILL BE...
OHHHHHH....

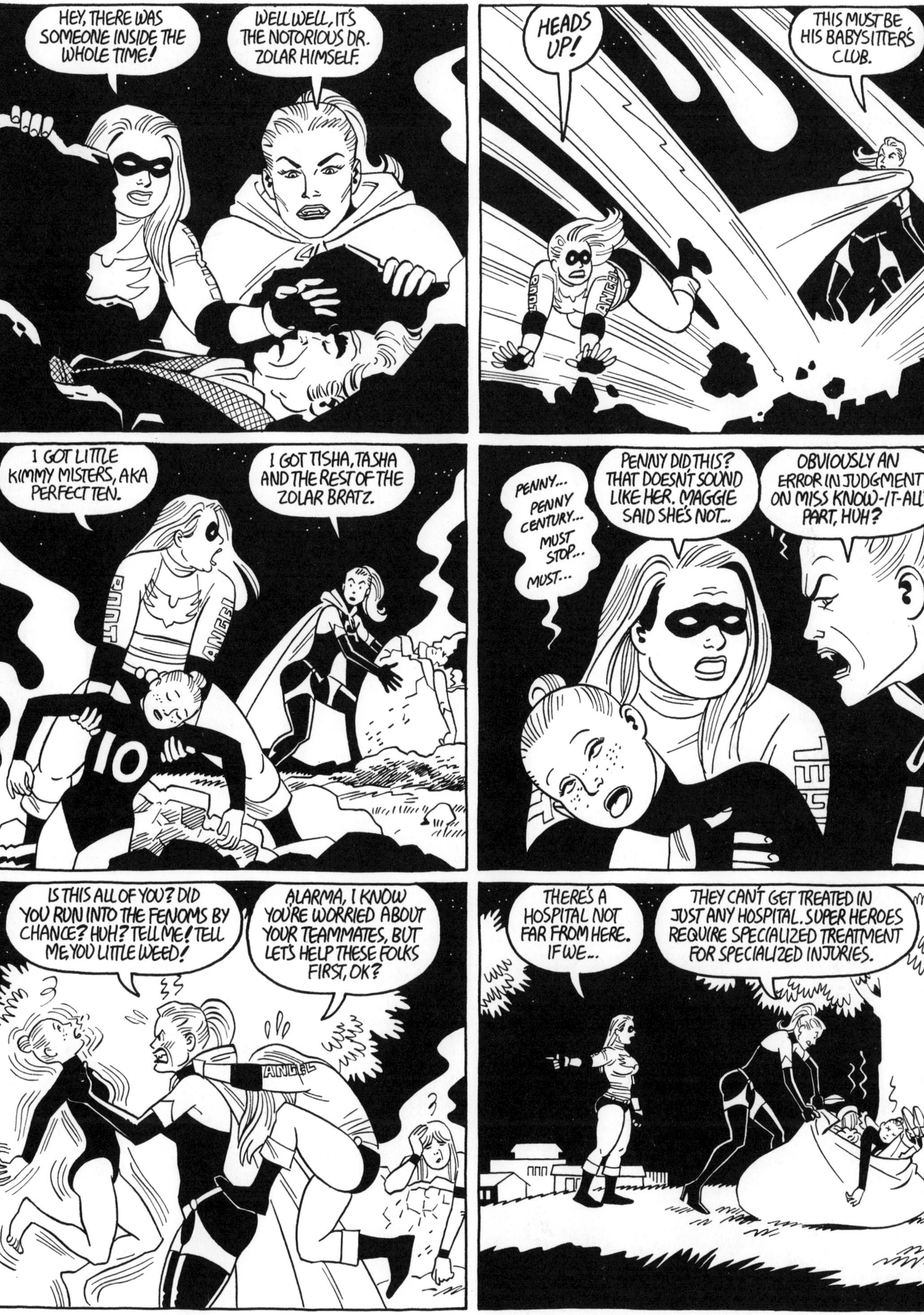
HEY, THERE WAS SOMEONE INSIDE THE WHOLE TIME!
WELL WELL, IT'S THE NOTORIOUS DR. ZOLAR HIMSELF.
HEADS UP!
THIS MUST BE HIS BABYSITTER'S CLUB.
I GOT LITTLE KIMMY MISTERS, AKA PERFECT TEN.
I GOT TISHA, TASHA AND THE REST OF THE ZOLAR BRATZ.
PENNY... PENNY CENTURY... MUST STOP... MUST...
PENNY DID THIS? THAT DOESN'T SOUND LIKE HER. MAGGIE SAID SHE'S NOT...
OBVIOUSLY AN ERROR IN JUDGMENT ON MISS KNOW-IT-ALL'S PART, HUH?
IS THIS ALL OF YOU? DID YOU RUN INTO THE FENOMS BY CHANCE? HUH? TELL ME! TELL ME, YOU LITTLE WEED!
ALARMA, I KNOW YOU'RE WORRIED ABOUT YOUR TEAMMATES, BUT LET'S HELP THESE FOLKS FIRST, OK?
THERE'S A HOSPITAL NOT FAR FROM HERE. IF WE...
THEY CAN'T GET TREATED IN JUST ANY HOSPITAL. SUPER HEROES REQUIRE SPECIALIZED TREATMENT FOR SPECIALIZED INJURIES.

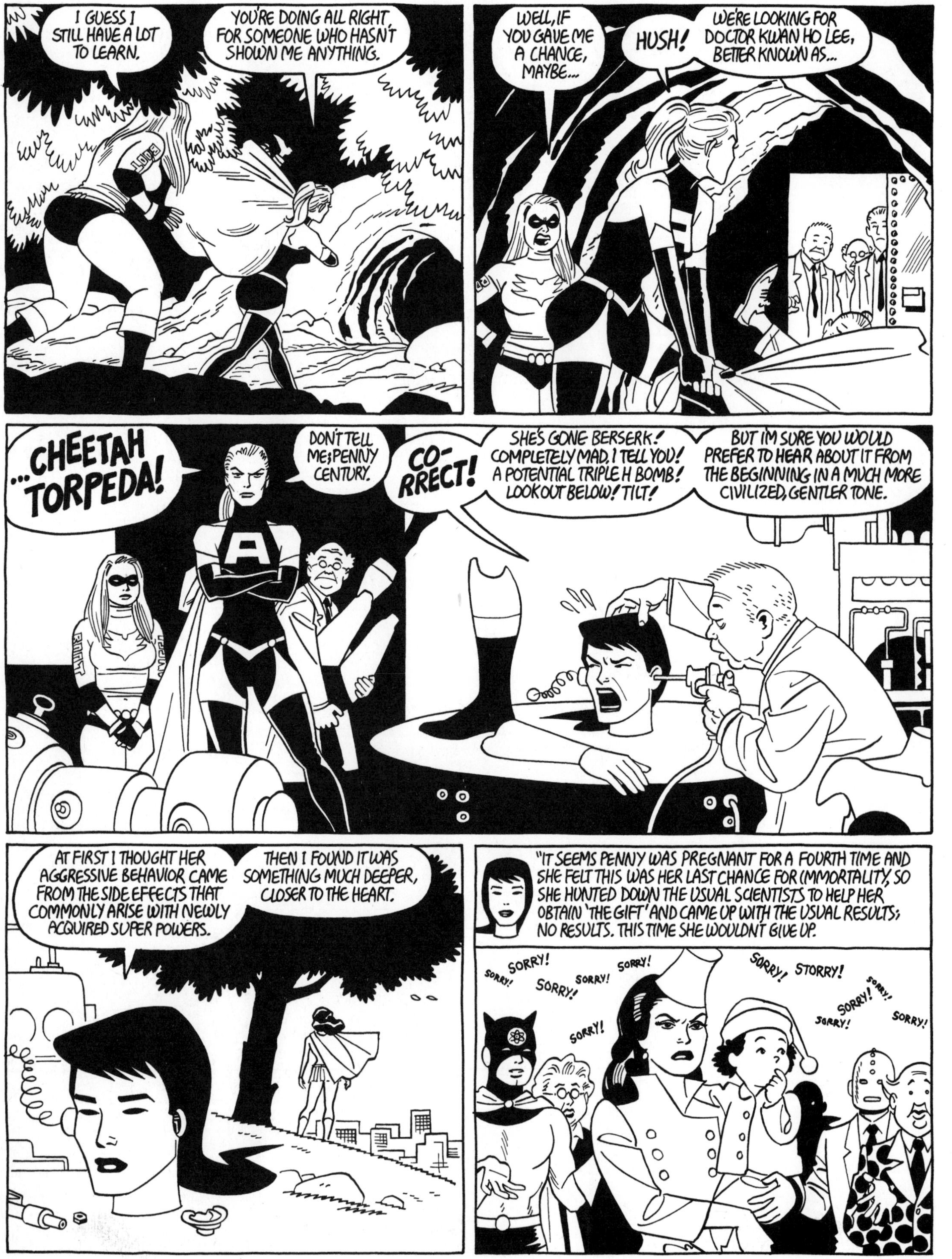
I GUESS I STILL HAVE A LOT TO LEARN.
YOU'RE DOING ALL RIGHT, FOR SOMEONE WHO HASN'T SHOWN ME ANYTHING.
WELL, IF YOU GAVE ME A CHANCE, MAYBE...
HUSH!
WE'RE LOOKING FOR DOCTOR KWAN HO LEE, BETTER KNOWN AS...
...CHEETAH TORPEDA!
DON'T TELL ME; PENNY CENTURY.
CO-RRECT!
SHE'S GONE BERSERK! COMPLETELY MAD, I TELL YOU! A POTENTIAL TRIPLE H BOMB! LOOKOUT BELOW! TILT!
BUT I'M SURE YOU WOULD PREFER TO HEAR ABOUT IT FROM THE BEGINNING IN A MUCH MORE CIVILIZED, GENTLER TONE.
AT FIRST I THOUGHT HER AGGRESSIVE BEHAVIOR CAME FROM THE SIDE EFFECTS THAT COMMONLY ARISE WITH NEWLY ACQUIRED SUPER POWERS.
THEN I FOUND IT WAS SOMETHING MUCH DEEPER, CLOSER TO THE HEART.
"IT SEEMS PENNY WAS PREGNANT FOR A FOURTH TIME AND SHE FELT THIS WAS HER LAST CHANCE FOR IMMORTALITY, SO SHE HUNTED DOWN THE USUAL SCIENTISTS TO HELP HER OBTAIN 'THE GIFT' AND CAME UP WITH THE USUAL RESULTS; NO RESULTS. THIS TIME SHE WOULDN'T GIVE UP.
SORRY! SORRY! SORRY! SORRY! SORRY!
SORRY!
SORRY! STORRY!
SORRY! SORRY! SORRY! SORRY!

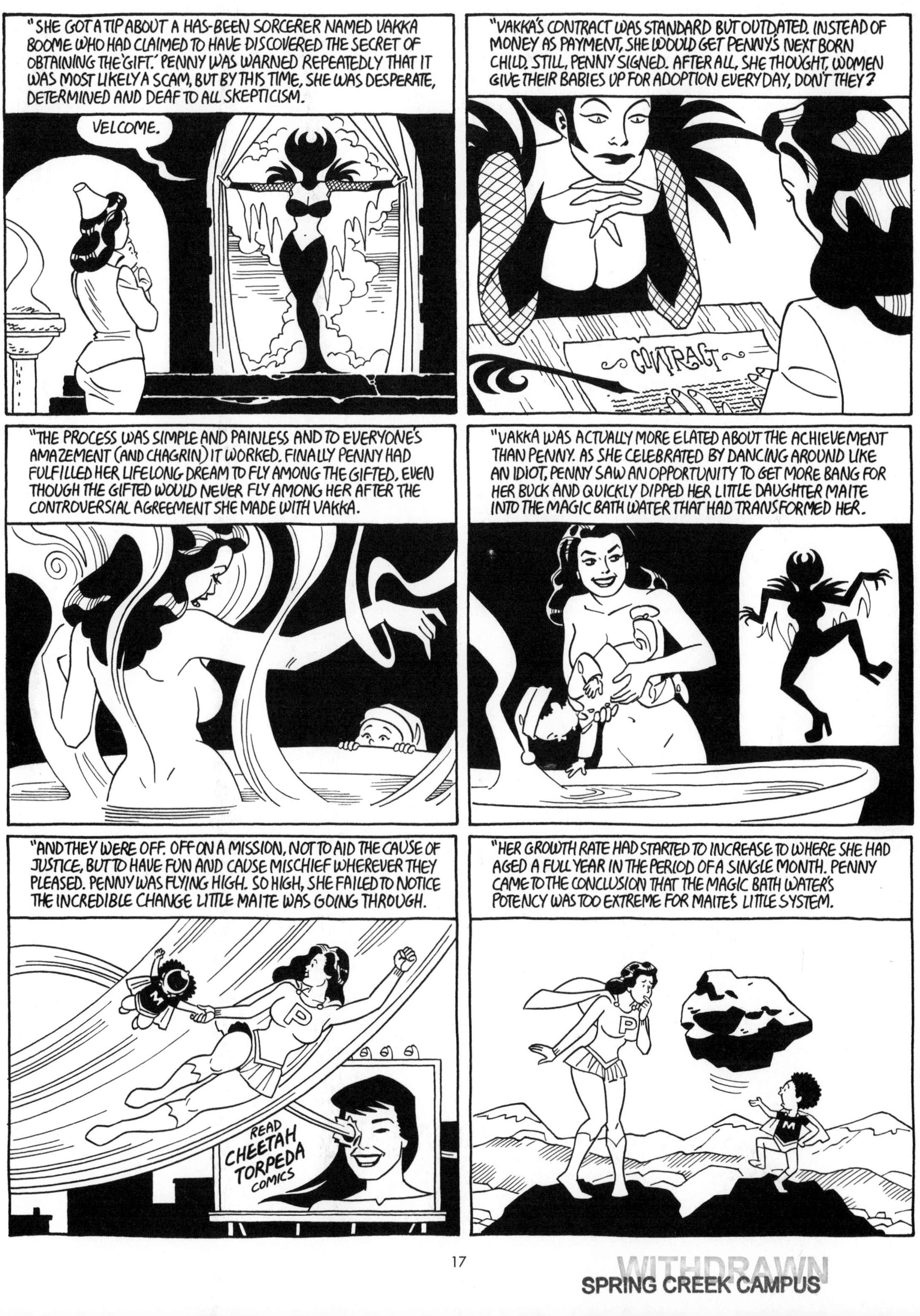
"SHE GOT A TIP ABOUT A HAS-BEEN SORCERER NAMED VAKKA BOOME WHO HAD CLAIMED TO HAVE DISCOVERED THE SECRET OF OBTAINING THE 'GIFT.' PENNY WAS WARNED REPEATEDLY THAT IT WAS MOST LIKELY A SCAM, BUT BY THIS TIME, SHE WAS DESPERATE, DETERMINED AND DEAF TO ALL SKEPTICISM.
VELCOME.
"VAKKA'S CONTRACT WAS STANDARD BUT OUTDATED. INSTEAD OF MONEY AS PAYMENT, SHE WOULD GET PENNY'S NEXT BORN CHILD. STILL, PENNY SIGNED. AFTER ALL, SHE THOUGHT, WOMEN GIVE THEIR BABIES UP FOR ADOPTION EVERY DAY, DON'T THEY?
CONTRACT
"THE PROCESS WAS SIMPLE AND PAINLESS AND TO EVERYONE'S AMAZEMENT (AND CHAGRIN) IT WORKED. FINALLY PENNY HAD FULFILLED HER LIFELONG DREAM TO FLY AMONG THE GIFTED, EVEN THOUGH THE GIFTED WOULD NEVER FLY AMONG HER AFTER THE CONTROVERSIAL AGREEMENT SHE MADE WITH VAKKA.
"VAKKA WAS ACTUALLY MORE ELATED ABOUT THE ACHIEVEMENT THAN PENNY. AS SHE CELEBRATED BY DANCING AROUND LIKE AN IDIOT, PENNY SAW AN OPPORTUNITY TO GET MORE BANG FOR HER BUCK AND QUICKLY DIPPED HER LITTLE DAUGHTER MAITE INTO THE MAGIC BATH WATER THAT HAD TRANSFORMED HER.
"AND THEY WERE OFF. OFF ON A MISSION, NOT TO AID THE CAUSE OF JUSTICE, BUT TO HAVE FUN AND CAUSE MISCHIEF WHEREVER THEY PLEASED. PENNY WAS FLYING HIGH. SO HIGH, SHE FAILED TO NOTICE THE INCREDIBLE CHANGE LITTLE MAITE WAS GOING THROUGH.
READ CHEETAH TORPEDA COMICS
"HER GROWTH RATE HAD STARTED TO INCREASE TO WHERE SHE HAD AGED A FULL YEAR IN THE PERIOD OF A SINGLE MONTH. PENNY CAME TO THE CONCLUSION THAT THE MAGIC BATH WATER'S POTENCY WAS TOO EXTREME FOR MAITE'S LITTLE SYSTEM.

"AN OUTRAGED PENNY ACCUSED VAKKA OF FOUL PLAY. VAKKA BLAMED IT ON PENNY'S SELFISHNESS. AN INTENSE FEUD BEGAN THAT ESCALATED INTO AN ALL-OUT WAR. IT BECAME SO INTENSE, THAT SIX MONTHS INTO IT, PENNY FAILED TO NOTICE A CHANGE SHE HERSELF HAD GONE THROUGH.

"PENNY WAS NEARLY NINE MONTHS PREGNANT, YET SHE WAS NOT SHOWING. DOCTORS CONFIRMED THAT HER BABY WAS IN PERFECT HEALTH, BUT THAT AT BIRTH, IT WOULD BE A MERE ONE INCH IN SIZE. PERHAPS ONE MORE VICTIM OF THE MYSTERIOUS MAGICAL BATH WATER.

"ONE MORNING BETWEEN BATTLES, HER BABY WAS BORN. NOW, WHETHER IT WAS IN WRITING OR NOT, IN NO WAY WAS PENNY GIVING IT UP TO VAKKA BOOME. SHE NAMED HER THIMBELINA AND KEPT HER SAFE INSIDE A CHARM ATTACHED TO HER BELT.

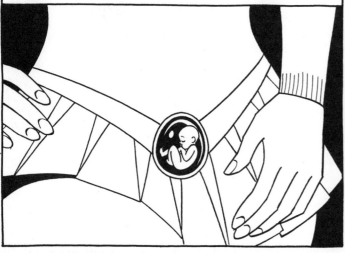

"THIS INFURIATED VAKKA EVEN MORE AND THE WAR ESCALATED TO GALACTIC PROPORTIONS, AS IT BECAME TOO BIG FOR EARTH. TEN MORE GRUELLING MONTHS OF INTENSE GIVE AND TAKE HAD PASSED WHEN THE TIDE FINALLY SHIFTED TO THE ADVANTAGE OF THE MORE EXPERIENCED VAKKA.

"AN EXHAUSTED PENNY WAS DOWN FOR THE COUNT AND VAKKA WAS ZEROING IN FOR THE KILL, WHEN A NOW TEENAGED MAITE CAME TO HER MOTHER'S RESCUE AND FINISHED OFF THE EQUALLY EXHAUSTED VAKKA WITH A SUPER RIGHT CROSS THAT SENT HER SAILING OFF INTO ETERNITY.

"PENNY WAS SO PROUD AND WANTED TO CELEBRATE WITH HER TWO DAUGHTERS WHEN MAITE DEALT A CRUSHING BLOW. SHE WAS LEAVING PENNY FOREVER, OFF TO SEE THE UNIVERSE. AFTER ALL, SHE ONLY HAD A GOOD SIX OR SEVEN YEARS BEFORE SHE WOULD DIE OF OLD AGE.

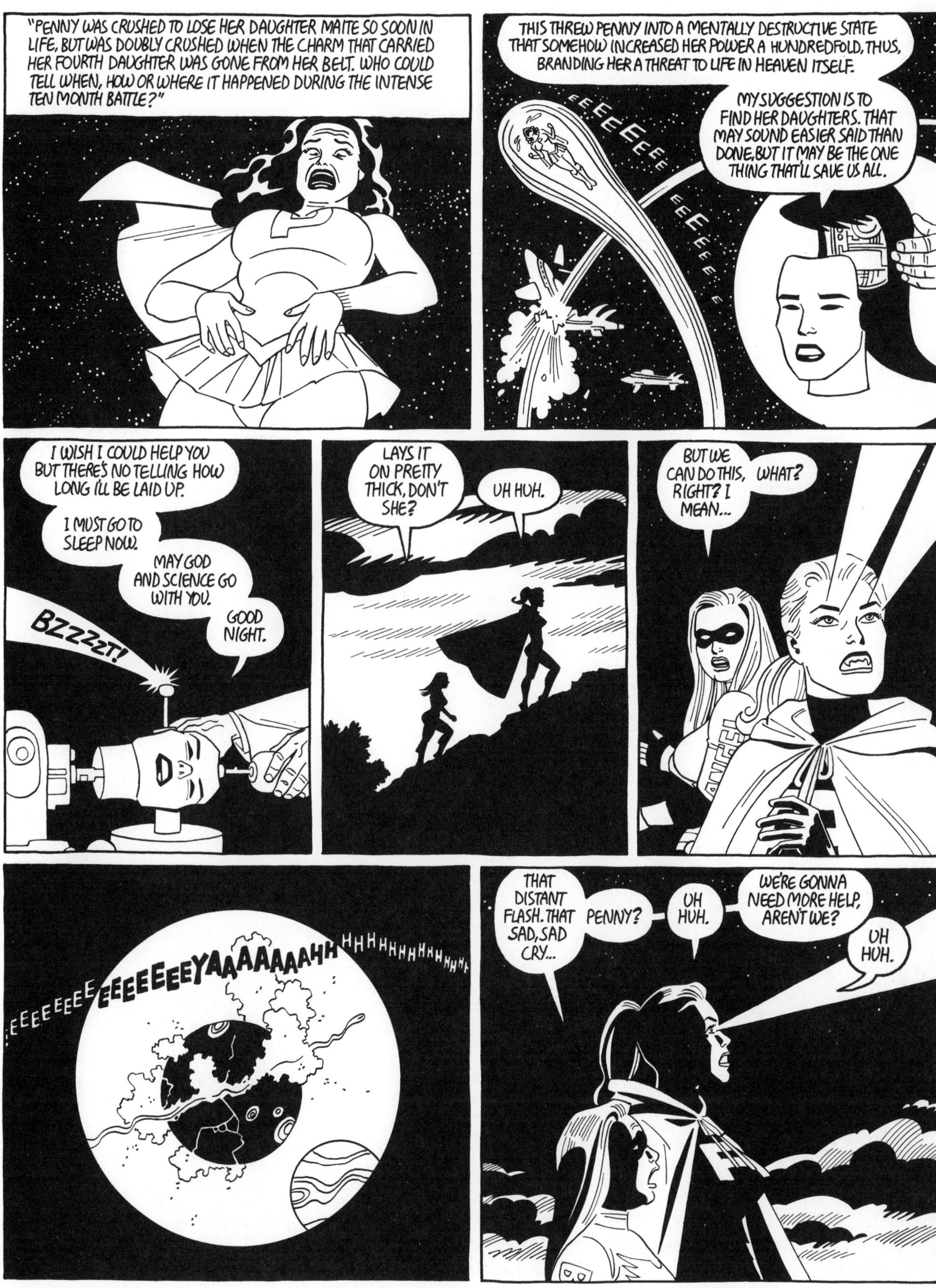

"PENNY WAS CRUSHED TO LOSE HER DAUGHTER MAITE SO SOON IN LIFE, BUT WAS DOUBLY CRUSHED WHEN THE CHARM THAT CARRIED HER FOURTH DAUGHTER WAS GONE FROM HER BELT. WHO COULD TELL WHEN, HOW OR WHERE IT HAPPENED DURING THE INTENSE TEN MONTH BATTLE?"
THIS THREW PENNY INTO A MENTALLY DESTRUCTIVE STATE THAT SOMEHOW INCREASED HER POWER A HUNDREDFOLD, THUS, BRANDING HER A THREAT TO LIFE IN HEAVEN ITSELF.
EEEEEEEEE
EEEEEEEE
MY SUGGESTION IS TO FIND HER DAUGHTERS. THAT MAY SOUND EASIER SAID THAN DONE, BUT IT MAY BE THE ONE THING THAT'LL SAVE US ALL.
I WISH I COULD HELP YOU BUT THERE'S NO TELLING HOW LONG I'LL BE LAID UP.
I MUST GO TO SLEEP NOW.
MAY GOD AND SCIENCE GO WITH YOU.
GOOD NIGHT.
BZZZZT!
LAYS IT ON PRETTY THICK, DON'T SHE?
UH HUH.
BUT WE CAN DO THIS, RIGHT? I MEAN...
WHAT?
EEEEEEEEEEEEEEEEYAAAAAAAHHHHHHHHHHHHHH
THAT DISTANT FLASH. THAT SAD, SAD CRY...
PENNY?
UH HUH.
WE'RE GONNA NEED MORE HELP, AREN'T WE?
UH HUH.

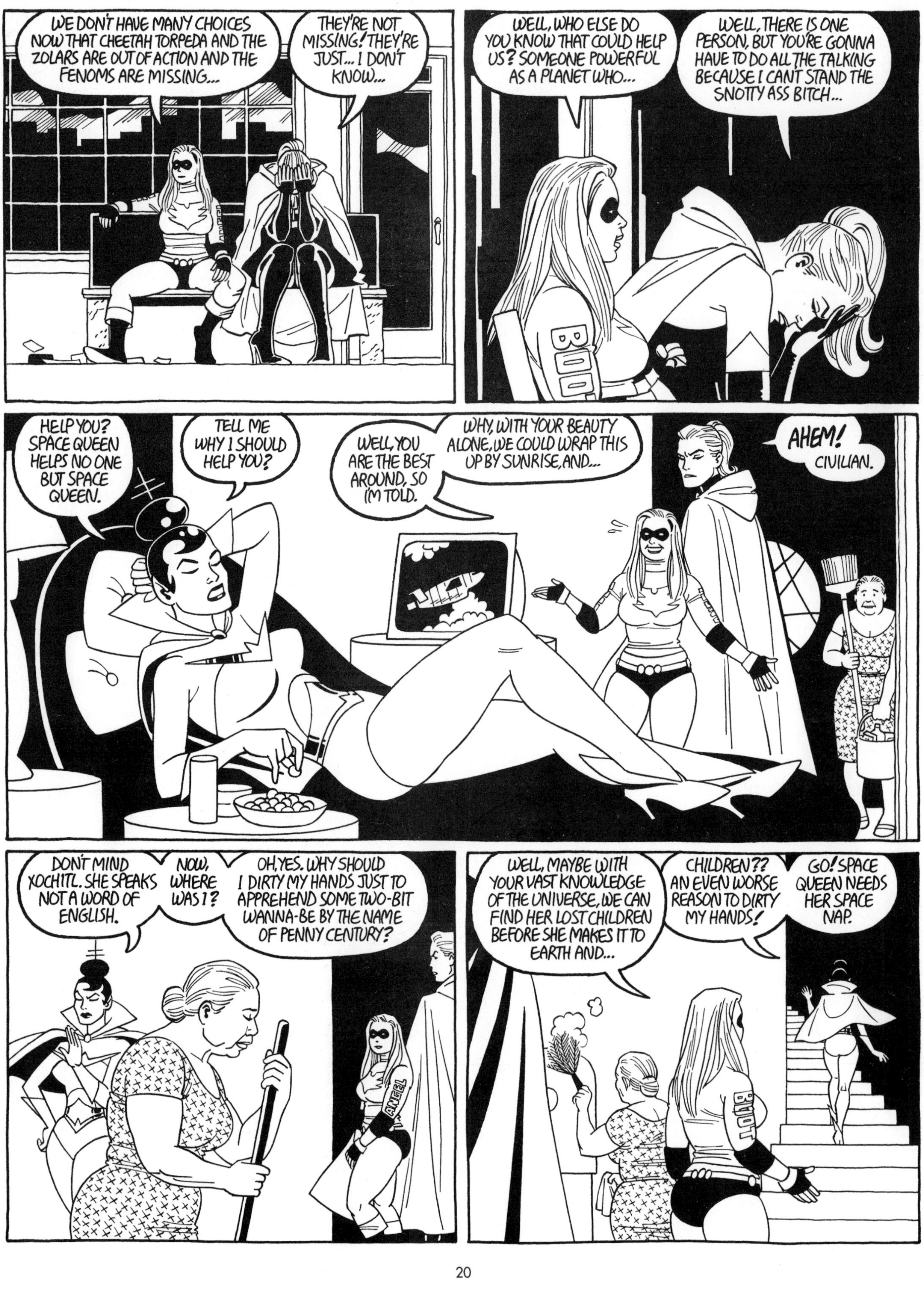
WE DON'T HAVE MANY CHOICES NOW THAT CHEETAH TORPEDA AND THE ZOLARS ARE OUT OF ACTION AND THE FENOMS ARE MISSING...
THEY'RE NOT MISSING! THEY'RE JUST... I DON'T KNOW...
WELL, WHO ELSE DO YOU KNOW THAT COULD HELP US? SOMEONE POWERFUL AS A PLANET WHO...
WELL, THERE IS ONE PERSON, BUT YOU'RE GONNA HAVE TO DO ALL THE TALKING BECAUSE I CAN'T STAND THE SNOTTY ASS BITCH...
HELP YOU? SPACE QUEEN HELPS NO ONE BUT SPACE QUEEN.
TELL ME WHY I SHOULD HELP YOU?
WELL, YOU ARE THE BEST AROUND, SO I'M TOLD.
WHY, WITH YOUR BEAUTY ALONE, WE COULD WRAP THIS UP BY SUNRISE, AND...
AHEM! CIVILIAN.
DON'T MIND XOCHITL. SHE SPEAKS NOT A WORD OF ENGLISH.
NOW, WHERE WAS I?
OH, YES. WHY SHOULD I DIRTY MY HANDS JUST TO APPREHEND SOME TWO-BIT WANNA-BE BY THE NAME OF PENNY CENTURY?
ANGEL
WELL, MAYBE WITH YOUR VAST KNOWLEDGE OF THE UNIVERSE, WE CAN FIND HER LOST CHILDREN BEFORE SHE MAKES IT TO EARTH AND...
CHILDREN?? AN EVEN WORSE REASON TO DIRTY MY HANDS!
GO! SPACE QUEEN NEEDS HER SPACE NAP.

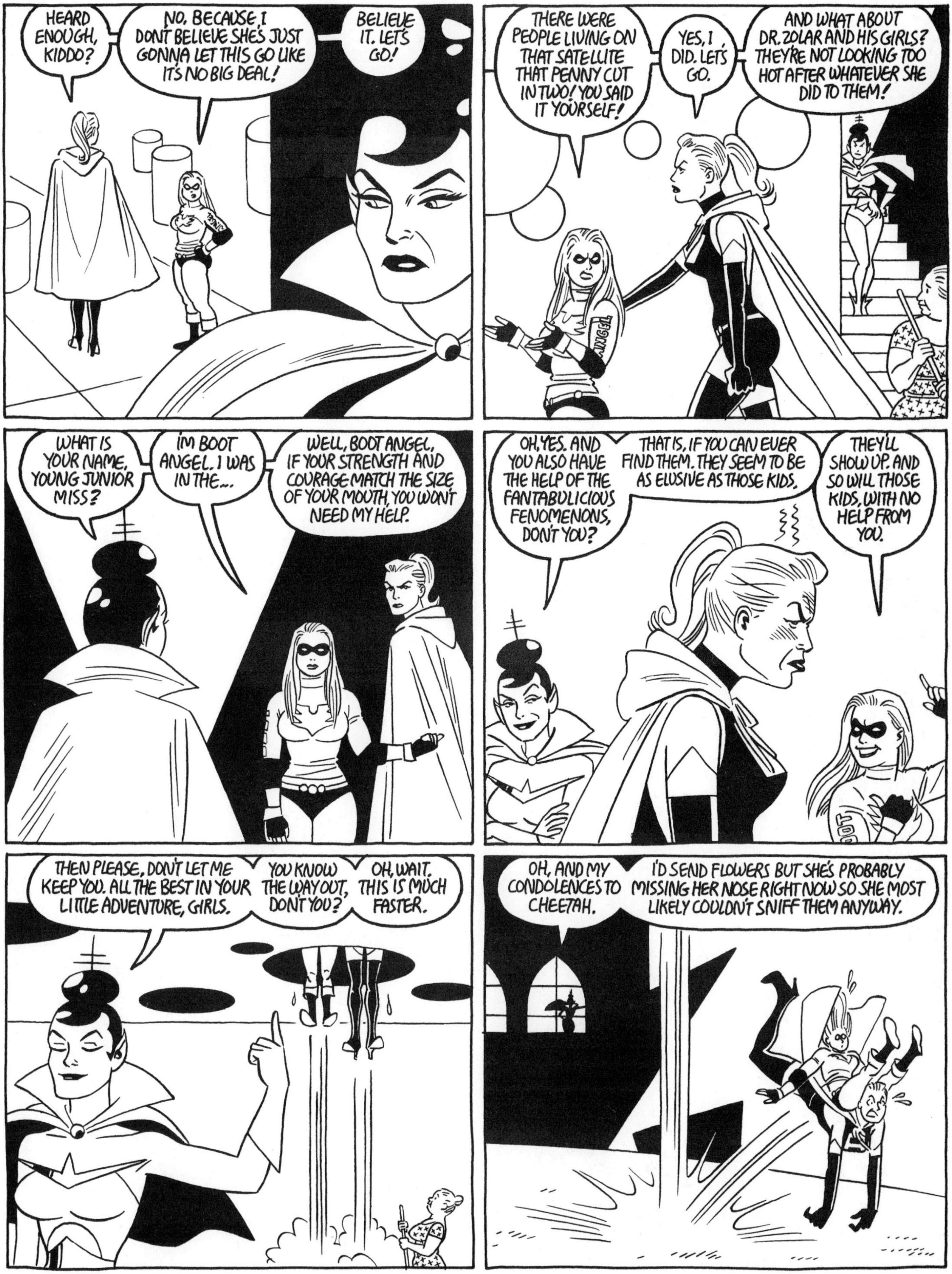

HEARD ENOUGH, KIDDO?
NO. BECAUSE I DON'T BELIEVE SHE'S JUST GONNA LET THIS GO LIKE IT'S NO BIG DEAL!
BELIEVE IT. LET'S GO!
THERE WERE PEOPLE LIVING ON THAT SATELLITE THAT PENNY CUT IN TWO! YOU SAID IT YOURSELF!
YES, I DID. LET'S GO.
AND WHAT ABOUT DR. ZOLAR AND HIS GIRLS? THEY'RE NOT LOOKING TOO HOT AFTER WHATEVER SHE DID TO THEM!
WHAT IS YOUR NAME, YOUNG JUNIOR MISS?
I'M BOOT ANGEL. I WAS IN THE...
WELL, BOOT ANGEL, IF YOUR STRENGTH AND COURAGE MATCH THE SIZE OF YOUR MOUTH, YOU WON'T NEED MY HELP.
OH, YES. AND YOU ALSO HAVE THE HELP OF THE FANTABULICIOUS FENOMENONS, DON'T YOU?
THAT IS, IF YOU CAN EVER FIND THEM. THEY SEEM TO BE AS ELUSIVE AS THOSE KIDS.
THEY'LL SHOW UP. AND SO WILL THOSE KIDS, WITH NO HELP FROM YOU.
THEN PLEASE, DON'T LET ME KEEP YOU. ALL THE BEST IN YOUR LITTLE ADVENTURE, GIRLS.
YOU KNOW THE WAY OUT, DON'T YOU?
OH, WAIT. THIS IS MUCH FASTER.
OH, AND MY CONDOLENCES TO CHEETAH.
I'D SEND FLOWERS BUT SHE'S PROBABLY MISSING HER NOSE RIGHT NOW SO SHE MOST LIKELY COULDN'T SNIFF THEM ANYWAY.

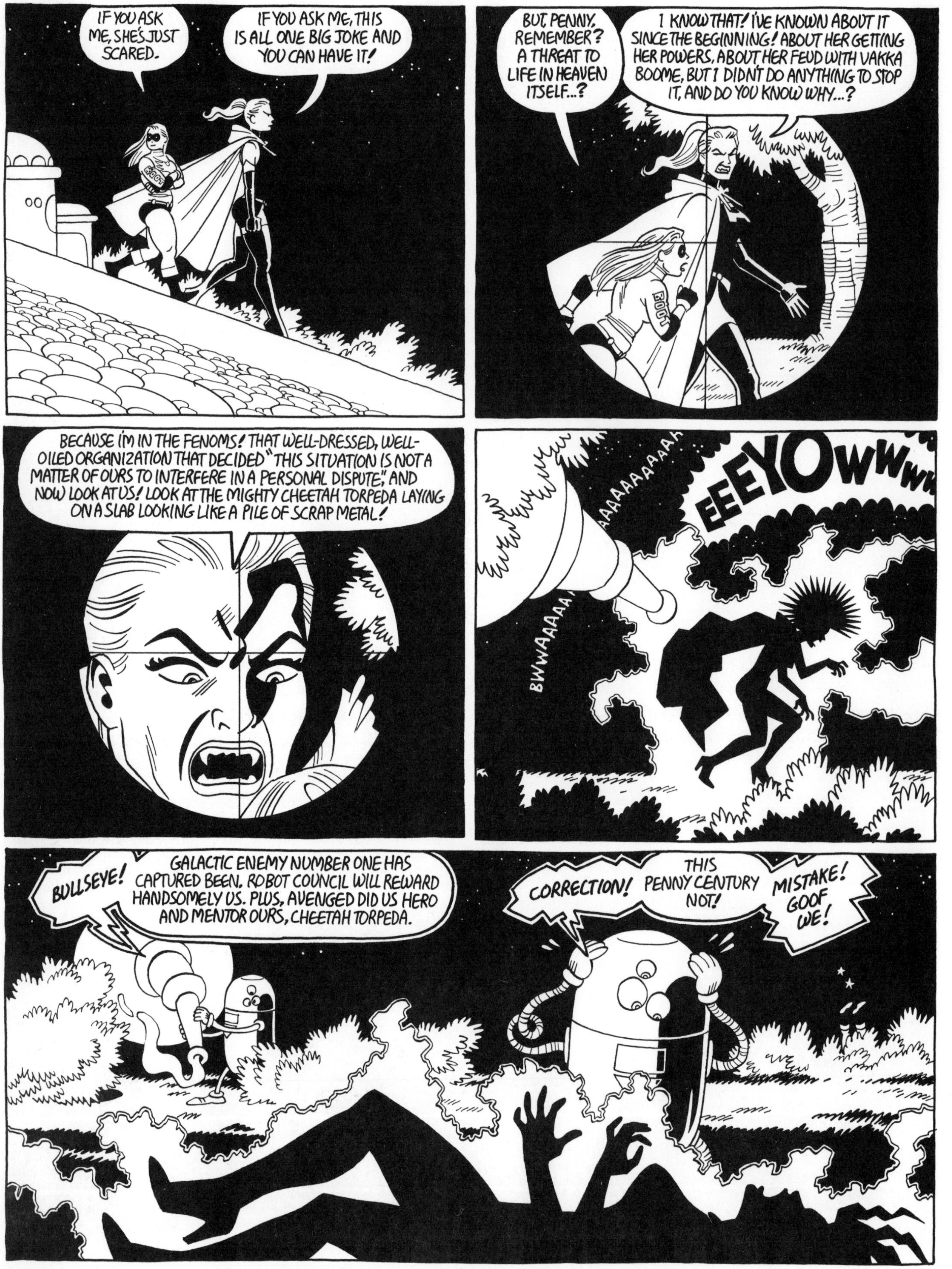
IF YOU ASK ME, SHE'S JUST SCARED.
IF YOU ASK ME, THIS IS ALL ONE BIG JOKE AND YOU CAN HAVE IT!
BUT, PENNY, REMEMBER? A THREAT TO LIFE IN HEAVEN ITSELF...?
I KNOW THAT! I'VE KNOWN ABOUT IT SINCE THE BEGINNING! ABOUT HER GETTING HER POWERS, ABOUT HER FEUD WITH VAKKA BOOME, BUT I DIDN'T DO ANYTHING TO STOP IT, AND DO YOU KNOW WHY...?
BECAUSE I'M IN THE FENOMS! THAT WELL-DRESSED, WELL-OILED ORGANIZATION THAT DECIDED "THIS SITUATION IS NOT A MATTER OF OURS TO INTERFERE IN A PERSONAL DISPUTE," AND NOW LOOK AT US! LOOK AT THE MIGHTY CHEETAH TORPEDA LAYING ON A SLAB LOOKING LIKE A PILE OF SCRAP METAL!
EEEYOWWW
BWWAAAAAAAAAAAAAAAAAAAAH
BULLSEYE!
GALACTIC ENEMY NUMBER ONE HAS CAPTURED BEEN. ROBOT COUNCIL WILL REWARD HANDSOMELY US. PLUS, AVENGED DID US HERO AND MENTOR OURS, CHEETAH TORPEDA.
CORRECTION!
THIS PENNY CENTURY NOT!
MISTAKE! GOOF WE!

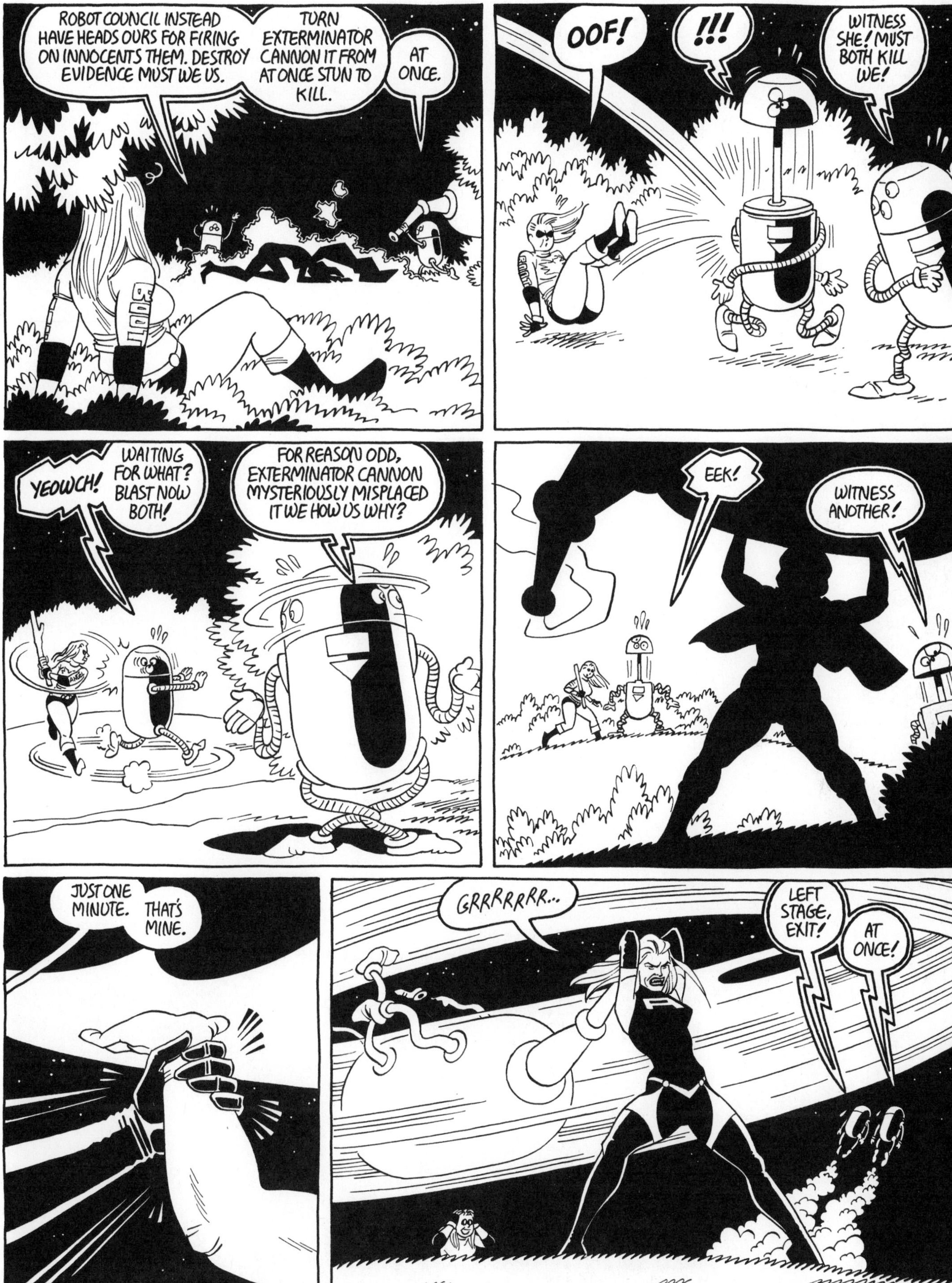

ROBOT COUNCIL INSTEAD HAVE HEADS OURS FOR FIRING ON INNOCENTS THEM. DESTROY EVIDENCE MUST WE US.
TURN EXTERMINATOR CANNON IT FROM AT ONCE STUN TO KILL.
AT ONCE.
OOF!
!!!
WITNESS SHE! MUST BOTH KILL WE!
YEOWCH!
WAITING FOR WHAT? BLAST NOW BOTH!
FOR REASON ODD, EXTERMINATOR CANNON MYSTERIOUSLY MISPLACED IT WE HOW US WHY?
EEK!
WITNESS ANOTHER!
JUST ONE MINUTE.
THAT'S MINE.
GRRRRRRR...
LEFT STAGE, EXIT!
AT ONCE!

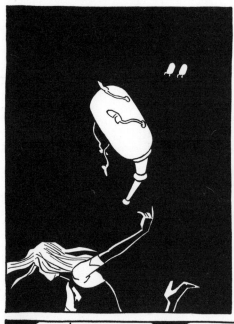

THAT'S WHAT SUCKERS YOU GET FOR THINKING I WAS TWO-BIT WANNA-BE PSYCHO THAT SHE!

YOU KNOW, ALARMA, I HAD A DREAM ONCE WHERE I WAS RESCUED BY A SPANISH SPEAKING MAID...

...IN WHITE TIGHTS YET.

MAID, MY ASS. THAT'S ESPECTRA, LEADER OF THE TI-GIRLS.

BUT ONLY AFTER WE AXED DR. ZOLAR.

STILL, I'M FLATTERED YOU RECOGNIZE ME. I HAVE BEEN AWAY.

SPACE QUEEN SENT YOU?

NO, TO THE HIGHNESS OF CLUELESSNESS I'M STILL JUST A HOUSEKEEPER, WHICH UP TILL NOW WAS THE BASIC TRUTH FOR THIRTY YEARS SINCE THE TI-GIRLS CALLED IT QUITS.

OK, SO WHY NOW?

NOBODY POPS OUT OF THIRTY YEARS RETIREMENT JUST TO SMASH UP CHEAP ROBOT TRASH.

YOU TWO WERE ABOUT TO BE KILLED. HOW COULD I STAY AWAY?

THAT WAS COOL TIMING, TOO!

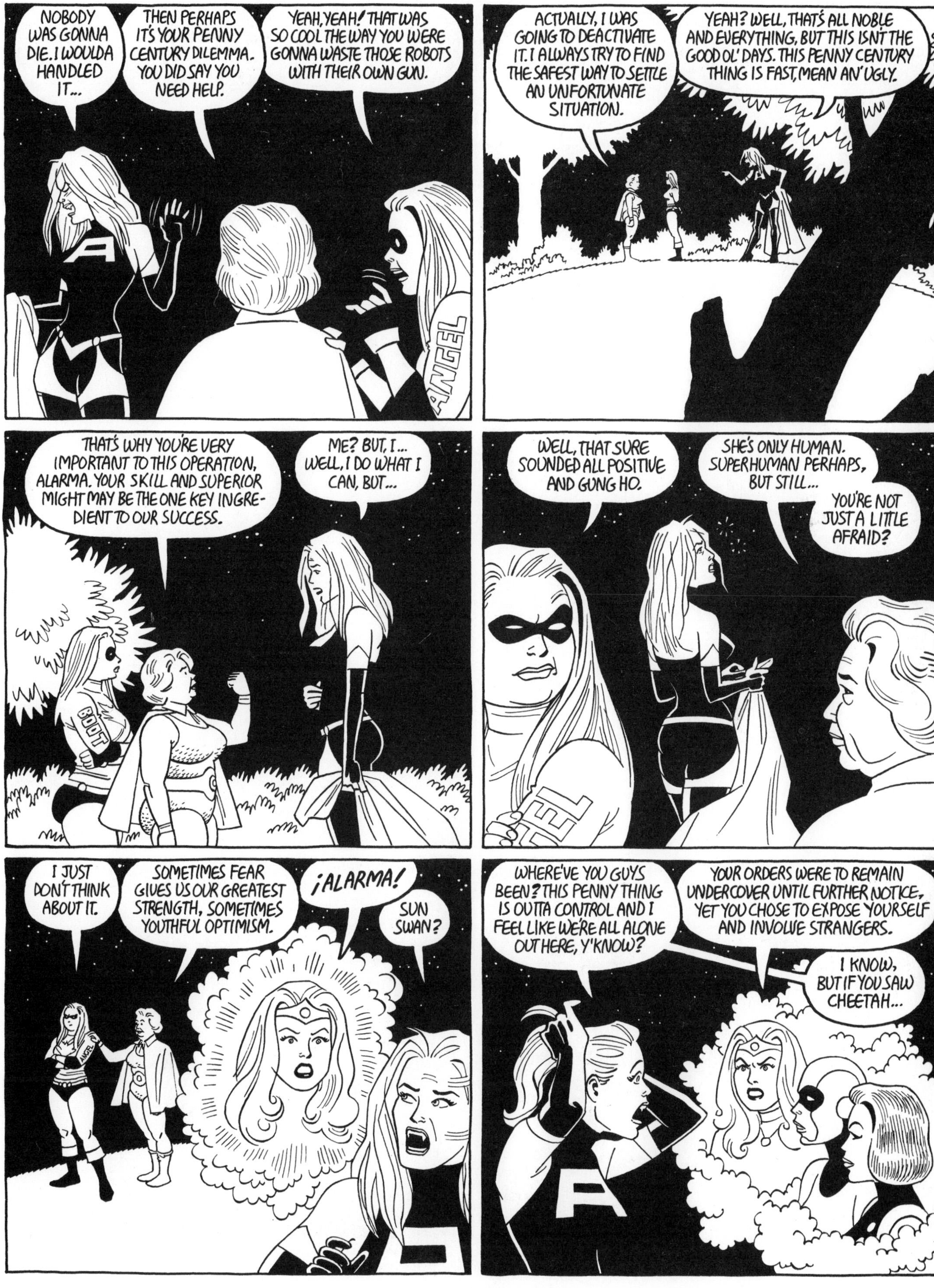

NOBODY WAS GONNA DIE. I WOULDA HANDLED IT...
THEN PERHAPS IT'S YOUR PENNY CENTURY DILEMMA. YOU DID SAY YOU NEED HELP.
YEAH, YEAH! THAT WAS SO COOL THE WAY YOU WERE GONNA WASTE THOSE ROBOTS WITH THEIR OWN GUN.
ANGEL
ACTUALLY, I WAS GOING TO DEACTIVATE IT. I ALWAYS TRY TO FIND THE SAFEST WAY TO SETTLE AN UNFORTUNATE SITUATION.
YEAH? WELL, THAT'S ALL NOBLE AND EVERYTHING, BUT THIS ISN'T THE GOOD OL' DAYS. THIS PENNY CENTURY THING IS FAST, MEAN AN' UGLY.
THAT'S WHY YOU'RE VERY IMPORTANT TO THIS OPERATION, ALARMA. YOUR SKILL AND SUPERIOR MIGHT MAY BE THE ONE KEY INGREDIENT TO OUR SUCCESS.
ME? BUT, I... WELL, I DO WHAT I CAN, BUT...
WELL, THAT SURE SOUNDED ALL POSITIVE AND GUNG HO.
SHE'S ONLY HUMAN. SUPERHUMAN PERHAPS, BUT STILL...
YOU'RE NOT JUST A LITTLE AFRAID?
I JUST DON'T THINK ABOUT IT.
SOMETIMES FEAR GIVES US OUR GREATEST STRENGTH, SOMETIMES YOUTHFUL OPTIMISM.
¡ALARMA!
SUN SWAN?
WHERE'VE YOU GUYS BEEN? THIS PENNY THING IS OUTTA CONTROL AND I FEEL LIKE WE'RE ALL ALONE OUT HERE, Y'KNOW?
YOUR ORDERS WERE TO REMAIN UNDERCOVER UNTIL FURTHER NOTICE, YET YOU CHOSE TO EXPOSE YOURSELF AND INVOLVE STRANGERS.
I KNOW, BUT IF YOU SAW CHEETAH...

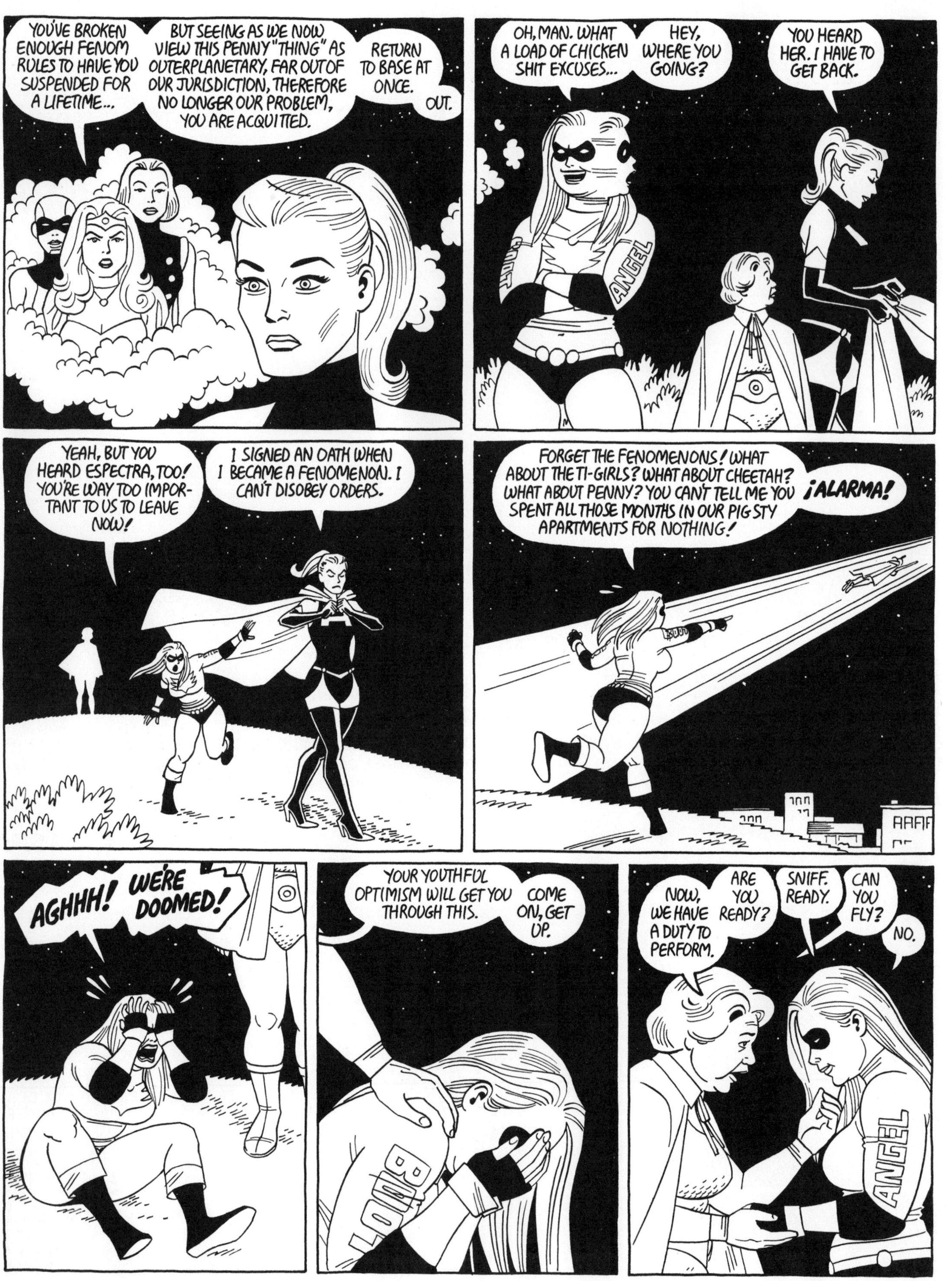
YOU'VE BROKEN ENOUGH FENOM RULES TO HAVE YOU SUSPENDED FOR A LIFETIME...
BUT SEEING AS WE NOW VIEW THIS PENNY "THING" AS OUTERPLANETARY, FAR OUT OF OUR JURISDICTION, THEREFORE NO LONGER OUR PROBLEM, YOU ARE ACQUITTED.
RETURN TO BASE AT ONCE.
OUT.
OH, MAN. WHAT A LOAD OF CHICKEN SHIT EXCUSES...
HEY, WHERE YOU GOING?
YOU HEARD HER. I HAVE TO GET BACK.
ANGEL
YEAH, BUT YOU HEARD ESPECTRA, TOO! YOU'RE WAY TOO IMPORTANT TO US TO LEAVE NOW!
I SIGNED AN OATH WHEN I BECAME A FENOMENON. I CAN'T DISOBEY ORDERS.
FORGET THE FENOMENONS! WHAT ABOUT THE TI-GIRLS? WHAT ABOUT CHEETAH? WHAT ABOUT PENNY? YOU CAN'T TELL ME YOU SPENT ALL THOSE MONTHS IN OUR PIG STY APARTMENTS FOR NOTHING!
¡ALARMA!
AGHHH! WE'RE DOOMED!
YOUR YOUTHFUL OPTIMISM WILL GET YOU THROUGH THIS.
COME ON, GET UP.
NOW, WE HAVE A DUTY TO PERFORM.
ARE YOU READY?
SNIFF. READY.
CAN YOU FLY?
NO.
ANGEL

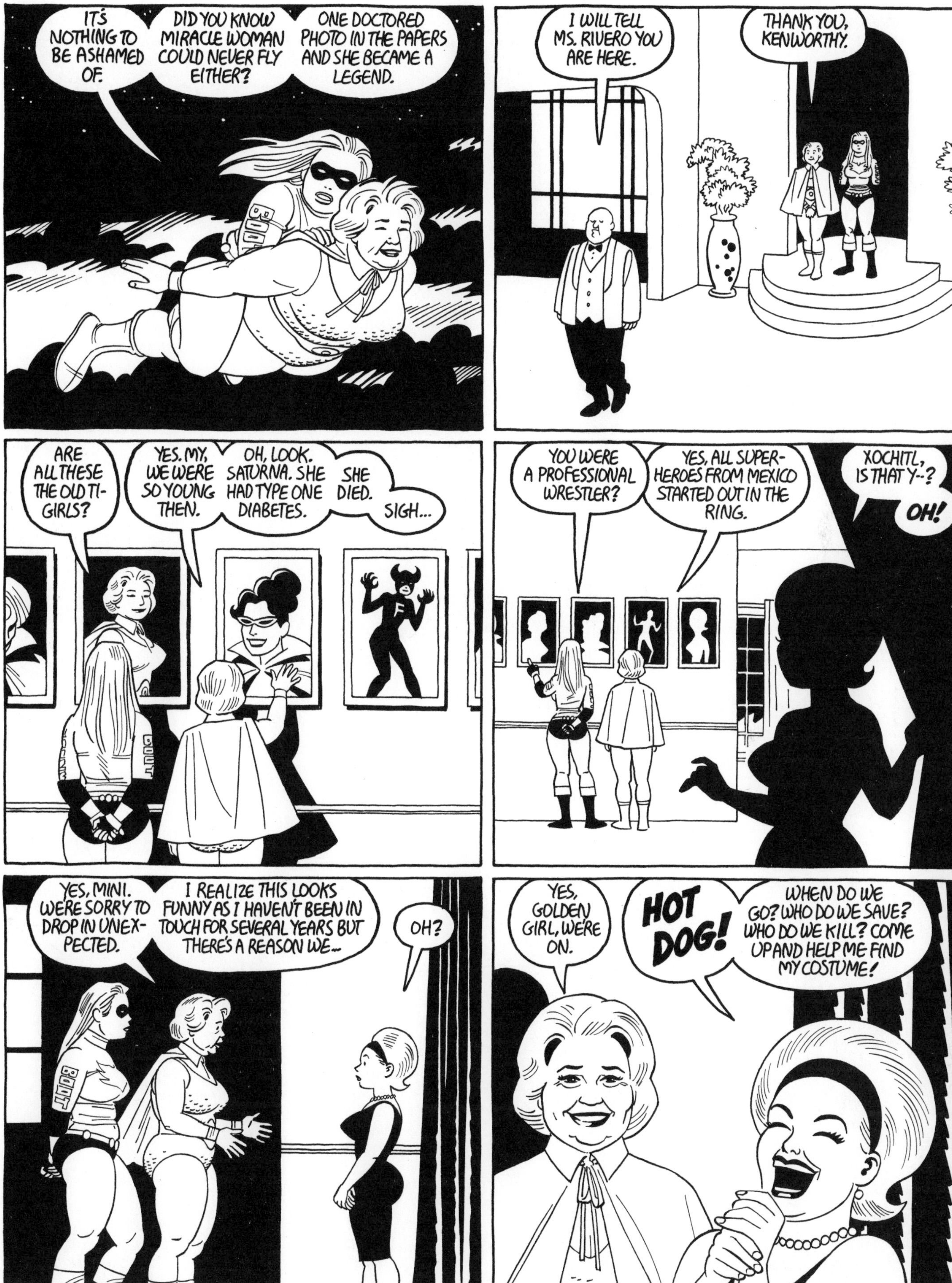
IT'S NOTHING TO BE ASHAMED OF.
DID YOU KNOW MIRACLE WOMAN COULD NEVER FLY EITHER?
ONE DOCTORED PHOTO IN THE PAPERS AND SHE BECAME A LEGEND.
I WILL TELL MS. RIVERO YOU ARE HERE.
THANK YOU, KENWORTHY.
ARE ALL THESE THE OLD TI-GIRLS?
YES. MY, WE WERE SO YOUNG THEN.
OH, LOOK. SATURNA. SHE HAD TYPE ONE DIABETES.
SHE DIED.
SIGH...
YOU WERE A PROFESSIONAL WRESTLER?
YES, ALL SUPER-HEROES FROM MEXICO STARTED OUT IN THE RING.
XOCHITL, IS THAT Y--?
OH!
YES, MINI. WE'RE SORRY TO DROP IN UNEX-PECTED.
I REALIZE THIS LOOKS FUNNY AS I HAVEN'T BEEN IN TOUCH FOR SEVERAL YEARS BUT THERE'S A REASON WE...
OH?
YES, GOLDEN GIRL, WE'RE ON.
HOT DOG!
WHEN DO WE GO? WHO DO WE SAVE? WHO DO WE KILL? COME UP AND HELP ME FIND MY COSTUME!

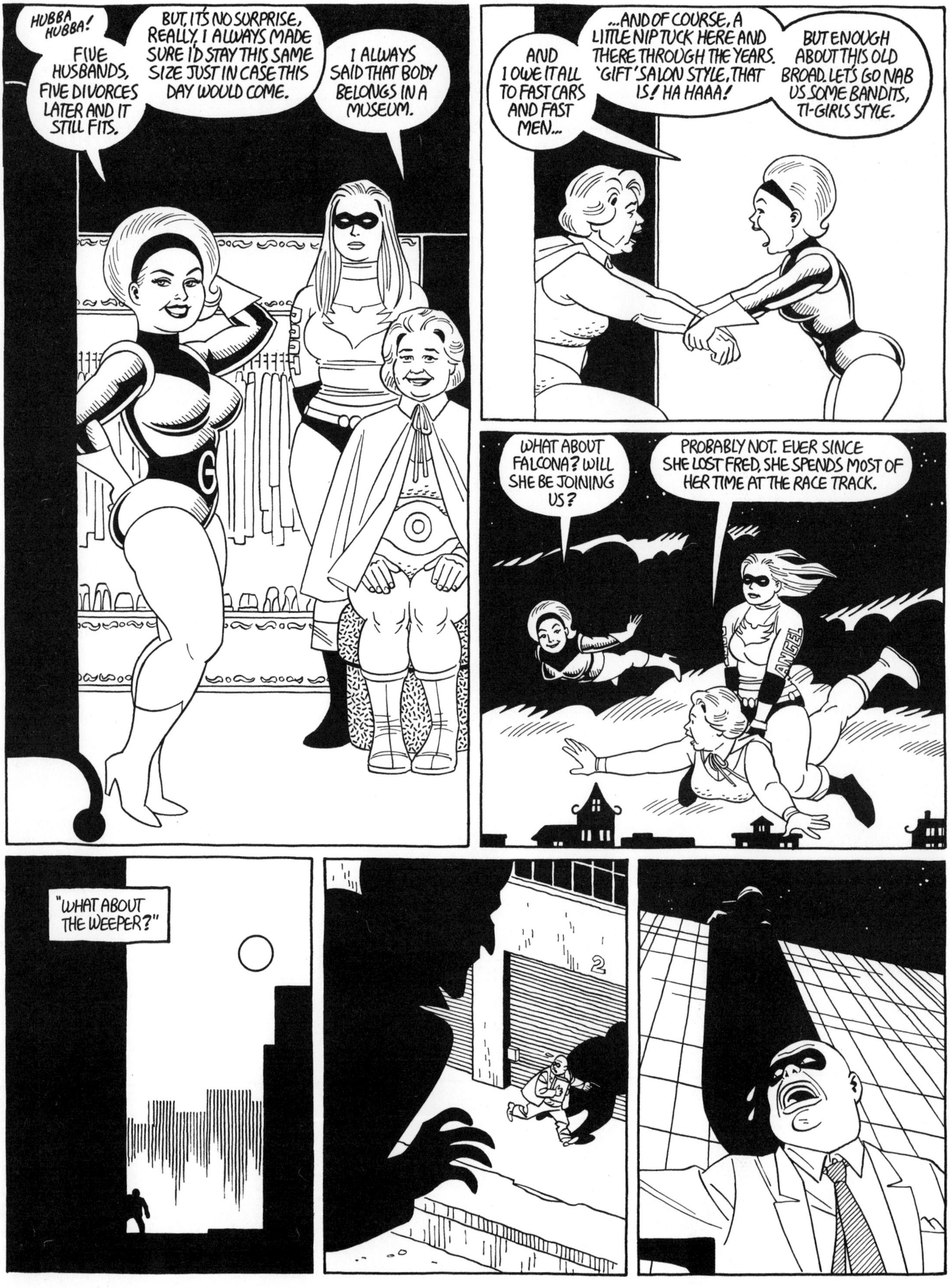
HUBBA HUBBA! FIVE HUSBANDS, FIVE DIVORCES LATER AND IT STILL FITS.
BUT, IT'S NO SURPRISE, REALLY, I ALWAYS MADE SURE I'D STAY THIS SAME SIZE JUST IN CASE THIS DAY WOULD COME.
I ALWAYS SAID THAT BODY BELONGS IN A MUSEUM.
AND I OWE IT ALL TO FAST CARS AND FAST MEN...
...AND OF COURSE, A LITTLE NIP TUCK HERE AND THERE THROUGH THE YEARS. 'GIFT' SALON STYLE, THAT IS! HA HAAA!
BUT ENOUGH ABOUT THIS OLD BROAD. LET'S GO NAB US SOME BANDITS, TI-GIRLS STYLE.
WHAT ABOUT FALCONA? WILL SHE BE JOINING US?
PROBABLY NOT. EVER SINCE SHE LOST FRED, SHE SPENDS MOST OF HER TIME AT THE RACE TRACK.
ANGEL
"WHAT ABOUT THE WEEPER?"
2

12
13
STOP, OR I'LL SHOOT!
GIRL, PUT THAT DOWN.
ROCKY, IT'S US.

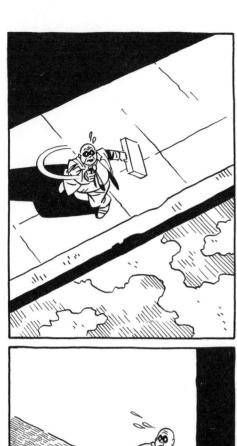

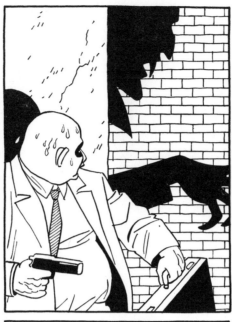

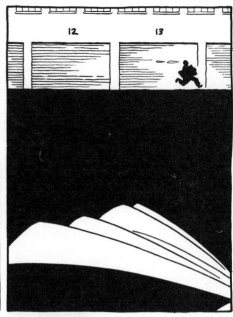

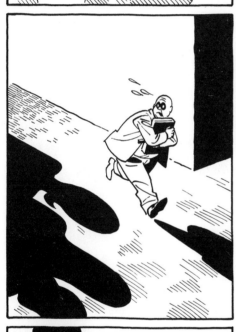

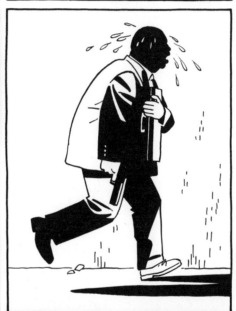

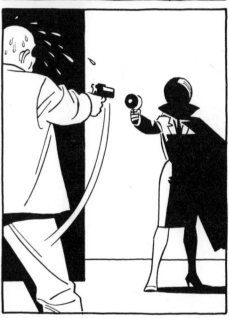

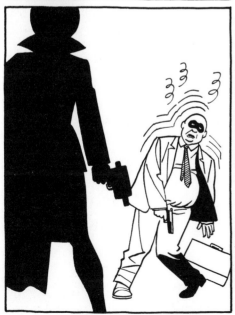

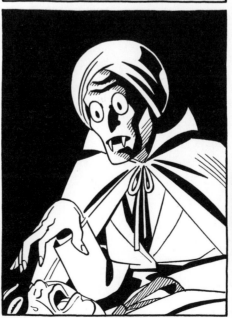

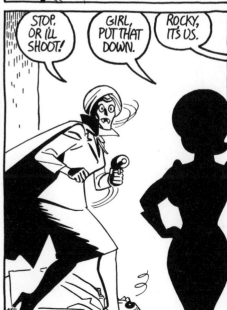

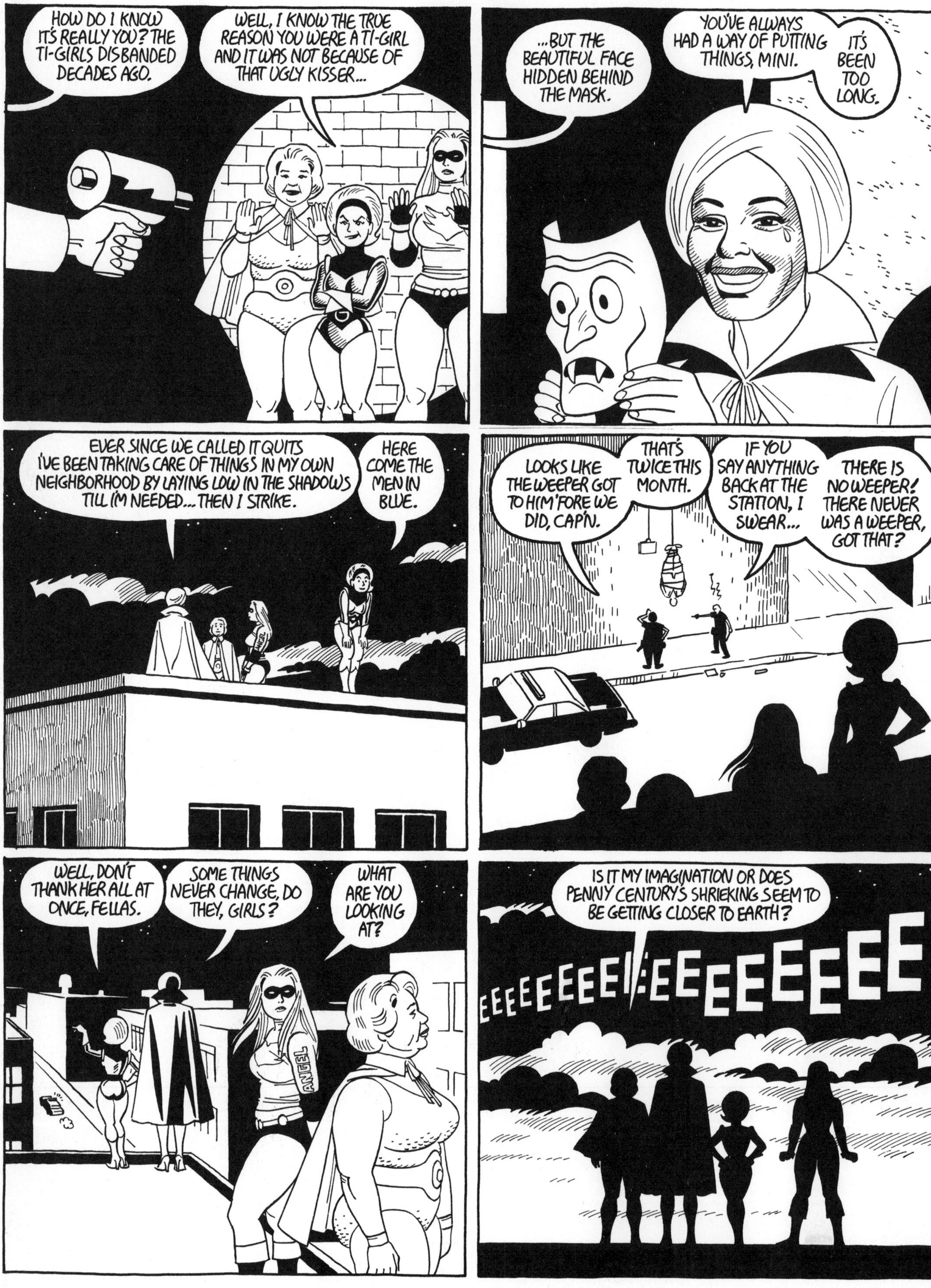
HOW DO I KNOW IT'S REALLY YOU? THE TI-GIRLS DISBANDED DECADES AGO.
WELL, I KNOW THE TRUE REASON YOU WERE A TI-GIRL AND IT WAS NOT BECAUSE OF THAT UGLY KISSER...
...BUT THE BEAUTIFUL FACE HIDDEN BEHIND THE MASK.
YOU'VE ALWAYS HAD A WAY OF PUTTING THINGS, MINI.
IT'S BEEN TOO LONG.
EVER SINCE WE CALLED IT QUITS I'VE BEEN TAKING CARE OF THINGS IN MY OWN NEIGHBORHOOD BY LAYING LOW IN THE SHADOWS TILL I'M NEEDED... THEN I STRIKE.
HERE COME THE MEN IN BLUE.
LOOKS LIKE THE WEEPER GOT TO HIM 'FORE WE DID, CAP'N.
THAT'S TWICE THIS MONTH.
IF YOU SAY ANYTHING BACK AT THE STATION, I SWEAR...
THERE IS NO WEEPER! THERE NEVER WAS A WEEPER, GOT THAT?
WELL, DON'T THANK HER ALL AT ONCE, FELLAS.
SOME THINGS NEVER CHANGE, DO THEY, GIRLS?
WHAT ARE YOU LOOKING AT?
IS IT MY IMAGINATION OR DOES PENNY CENTURY'S SHRIEKING SEEM TO BE GETTING CLOSER TO EARTH?
EEEEEEEEI!EEEEEEEI

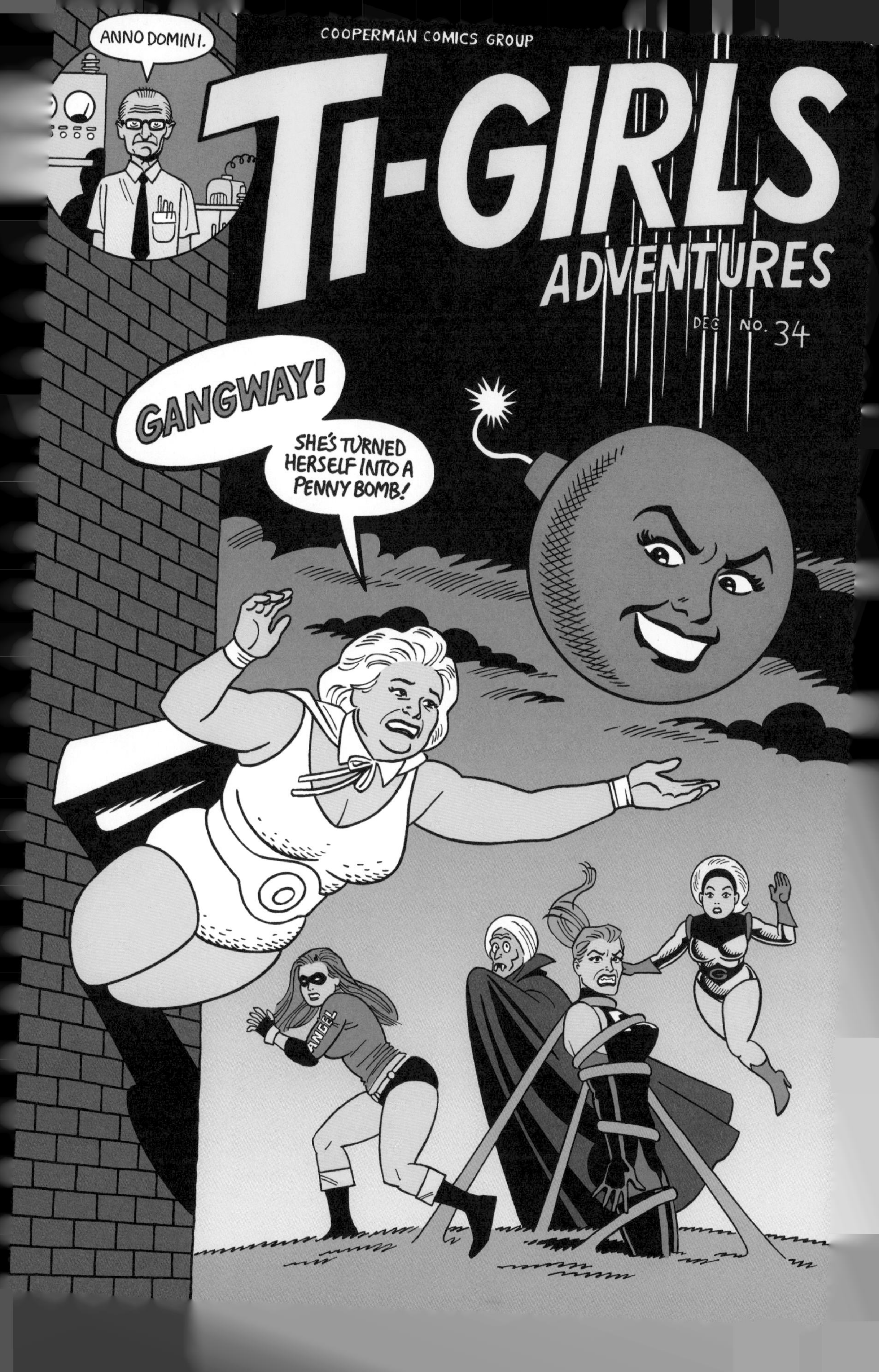

ANNO DOMINI.
COOPERMAN COMICS GROUP
TI-GIRLS
ADVENTURES
DEC NO. 34
GANGWAY!
SHE'S TURNED HERSELF INTO A PENNY BOMB!
ANGEL

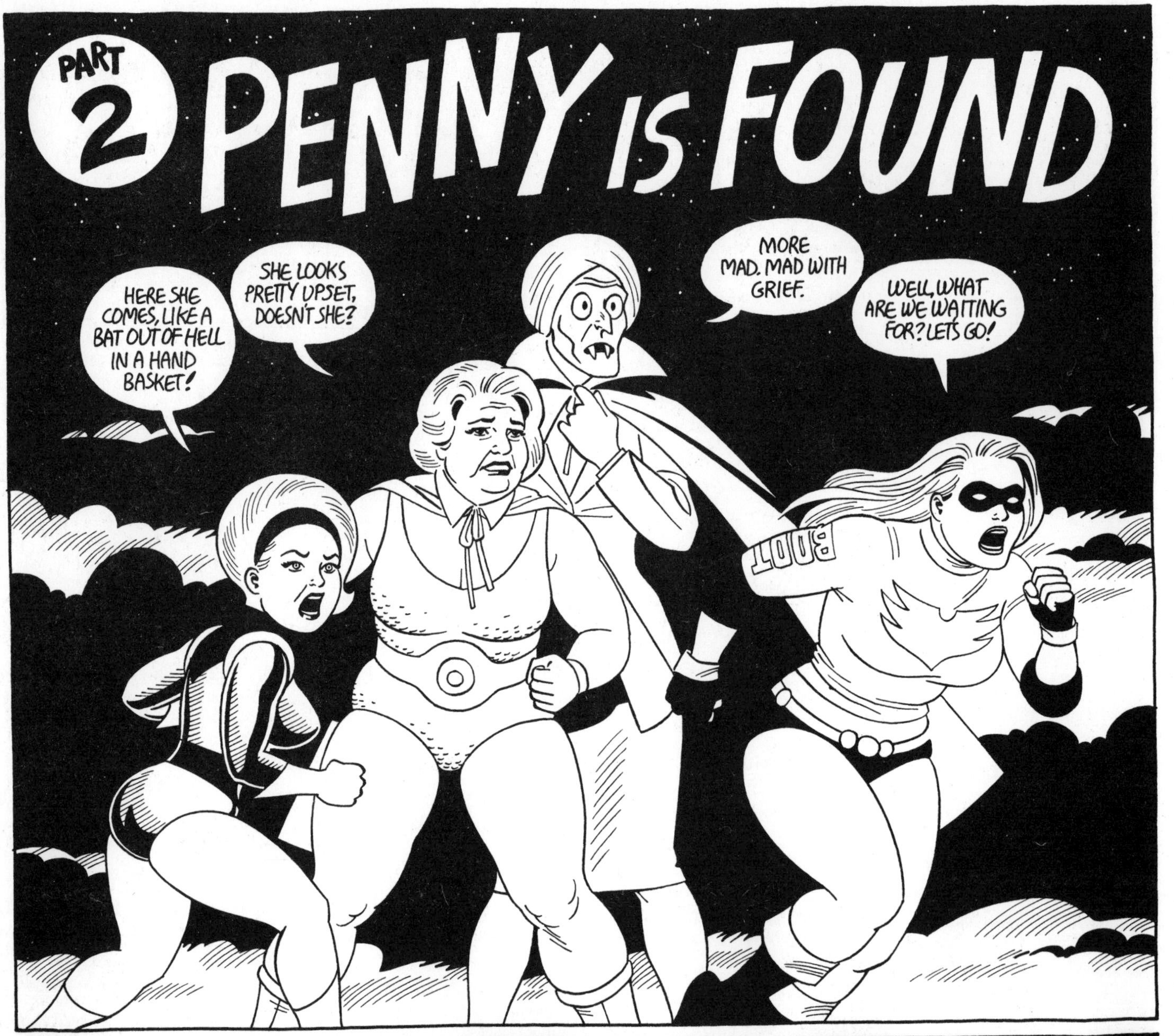
PART 2 PENNY IS FOUND
HERE SHE COMES, LIKE A BAT OUT OF HELL IN A HAND BASKET!
SHE LOOKS PRETTY UPSET, DOESN'T SHE?
MORE MAD. MAD WITH GRIEF.
WELL, WHAT ARE WE WAITING FOR? LET'S GO!
BOOT

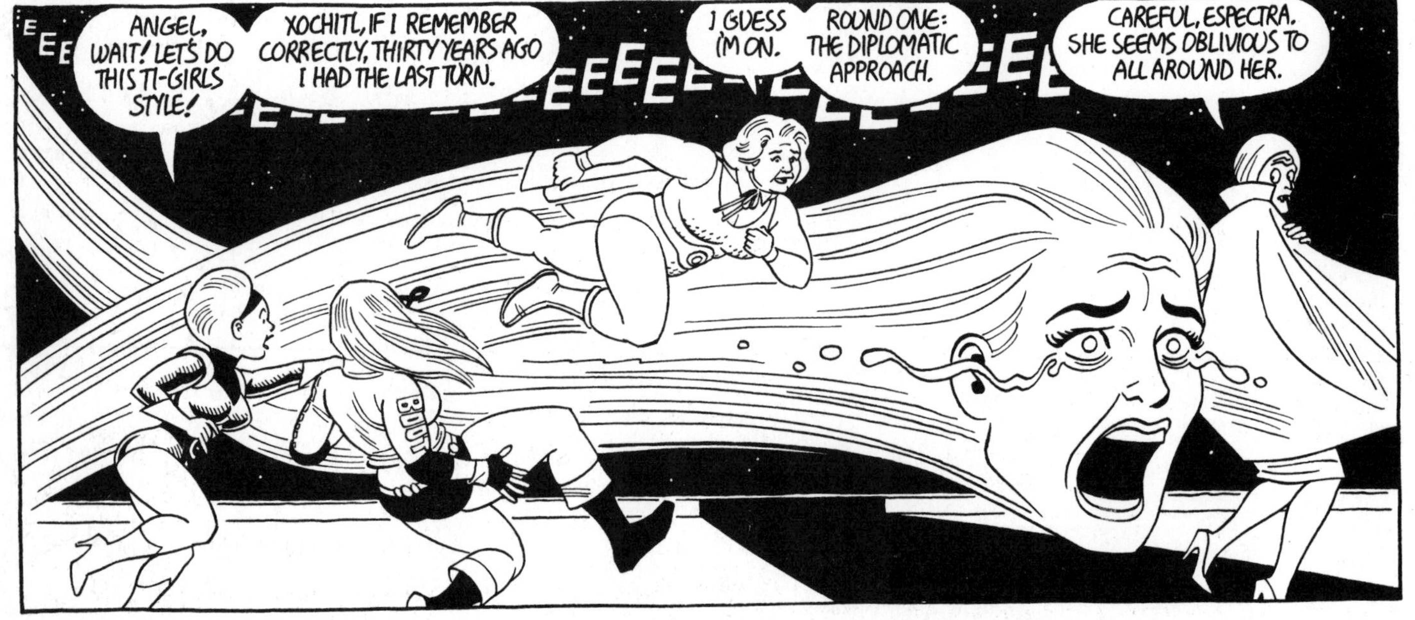
ANGEL, WAIT! LET'S DO THIS TI-GIRLS STYLE!
XOCHITL, IF I REMEMBER CORRECTLY, THIRTY YEARS AGO I HAD THE LAST TURN.
I GUESS I'M ON.
ROUND ONE: THE DIPLOMATIC APPROACH.
CAREFUL, ESPECTRA. SHE SEEMS OBLIVIOUS TO ALL AROUND HER.
EEEEEEEEEEEEE
BOOT

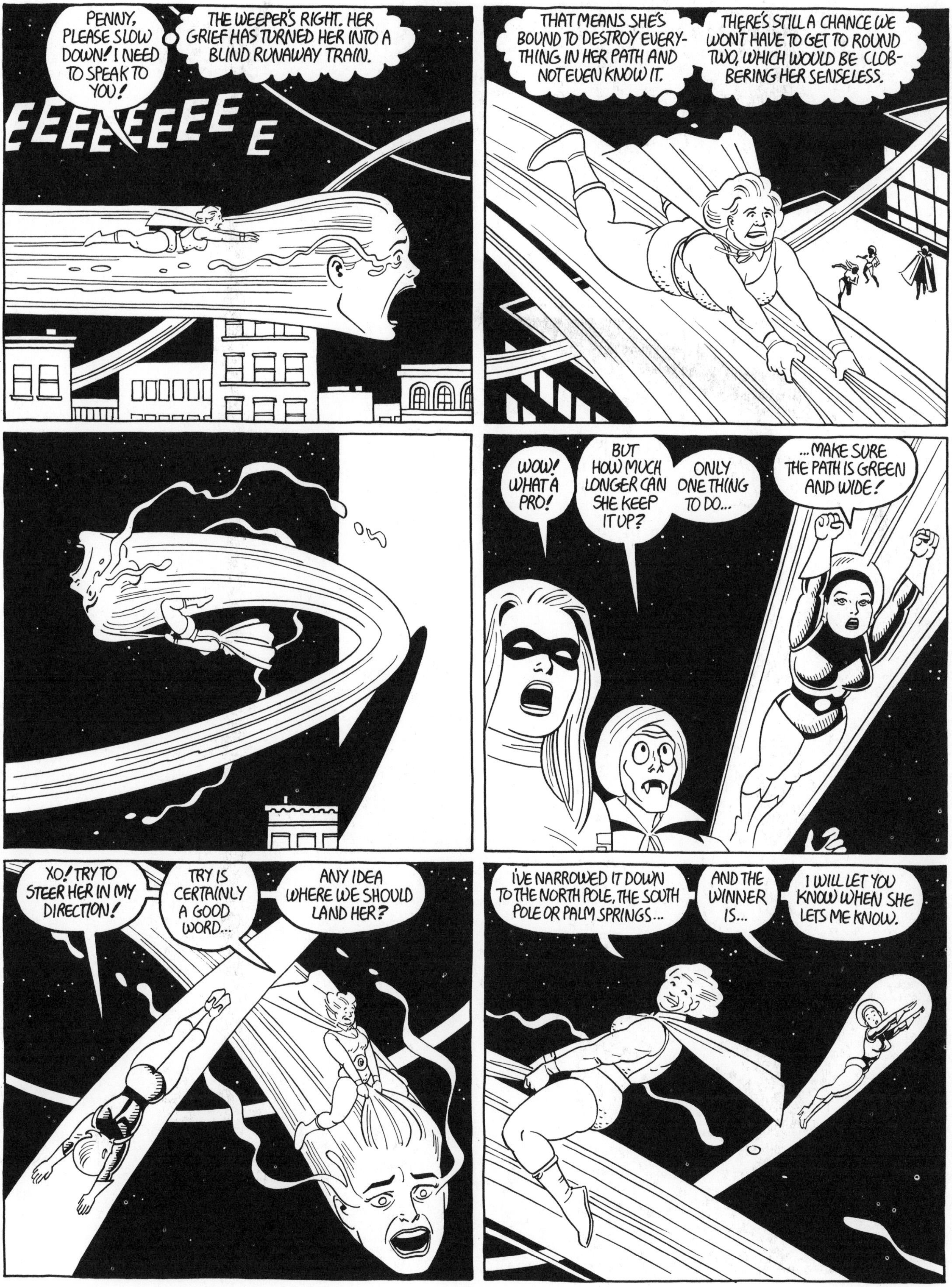
PENNY, PLEASE SLOW DOWN! I NEED TO SPEAK TO YOU!
THE WEEPER'S RIGHT. HER GRIEF HAS TURNED HER INTO A BLIND RUNAWAY TRAIN.
EEEEEEEEE E
THAT MEANS SHE'S BOUND TO DESTROY EVERY-THING IN HER PATH AND NOT EVEN KNOW IT.
THERE'S STILL A CHANCE WE WON'T HAVE TO GET TO ROUND TWO, WHICH WOULD BE CLOB-BERING HER SENSELESS.
WOW! WHAT A PRO!
BUT HOW MUCH LONGER CAN SHE KEEP IT UP?
ONLY ONE THING TO DO...
...MAKE SURE THE PATH IS GREEN AND WIDE!
XO! TRY TO STEER HER IN MY DIRECTION!
TRY IS CERTAINLY A GOOD WORD...
ANY IDEA WHERE WE SHOULD LAND HER?
I'VE NARROWED IT DOWN TO THE NORTH POLE, THE SOUTH POLE OR PALM SPRINGS...
AND THE WINNER IS...
I WILL LET YOU KNOW WHEN SHE LETS ME KNOW.

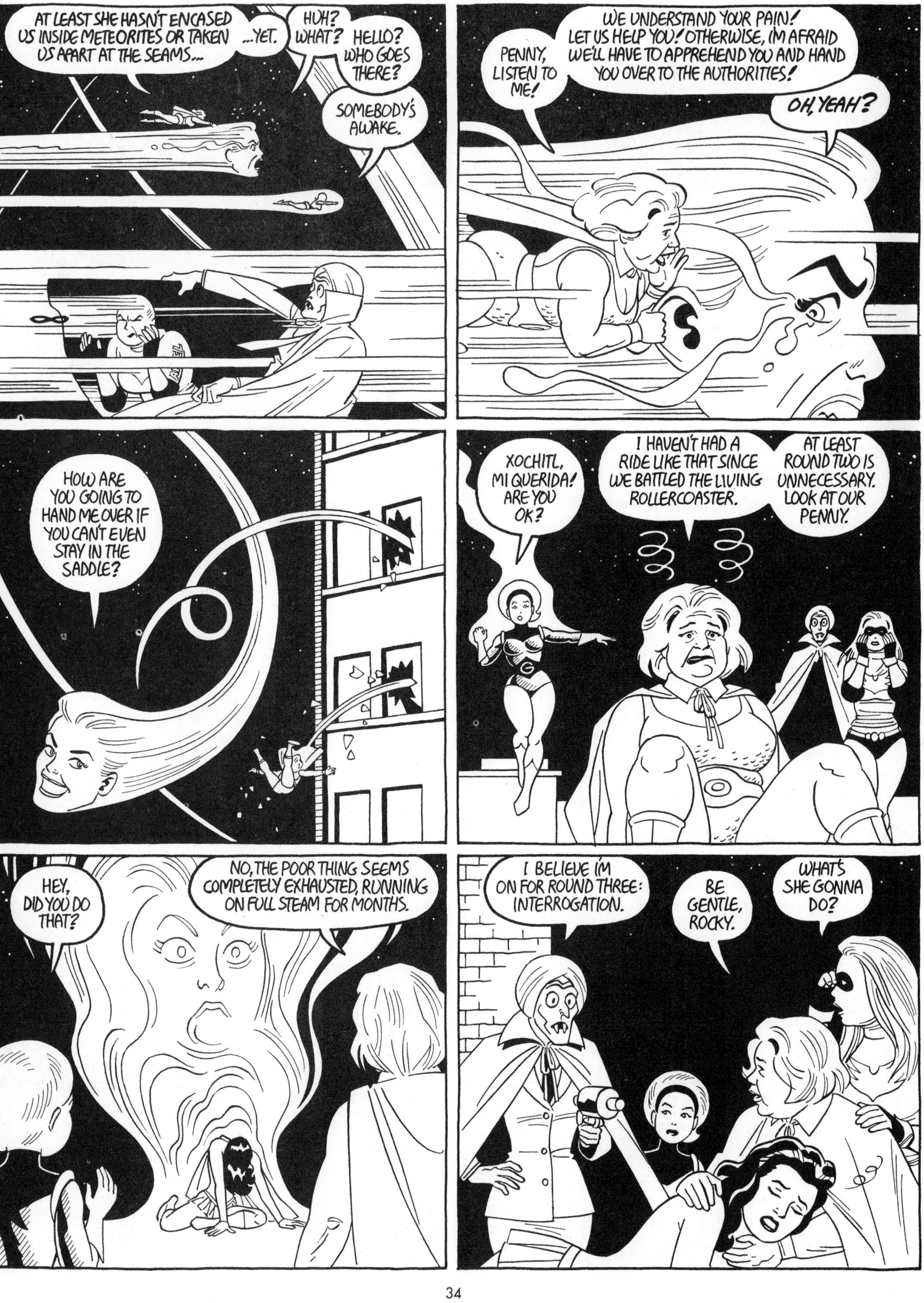
AT LEAST SHE HASN'T ENCASED US INSIDE METEORITES OR TAKEN US APART AT THE SEAMS...
...YET.
HUH? WHAT?
HELLO? WHO GOES THERE?
SOMEBODY'S AWAKE.
PENNY, LISTEN TO ME!
WE UNDERSTAND YOUR PAIN! LET US HELP YOU! OTHERWISE, I'M AFRAID WE'LL HAVE TO APPREHEND YOU AND HAND YOU OVER TO THE AUTHORITIES!
OH, YEAH?
HOW ARE YOU GOING TO HAND ME OVER IF YOU CAN'T EVEN STAY IN THE SADDLE?
XOCHITL, MI QUERIDA! ARE YOU OK?
I HAVEN'T HAD A RIDE LIKE THAT SINCE WE BATTLED THE LIVING ROLLERCOASTER.
AT LEAST ROUND TWO IS UNNECESSARY. LOOK AT OUR PENNY.
HEY, DID YOU DO THAT?
NO, THE POOR THING SEEMS COMPLETELY EXHAUSTED, RUNNING ON FULL STEAM FOR MONTHS.
I BELIEVE I'M ON FOR ROUND THREE: INTERROGATION.
BE GENTLE, ROCKY.
WHAT'S SHE GONNA DO?

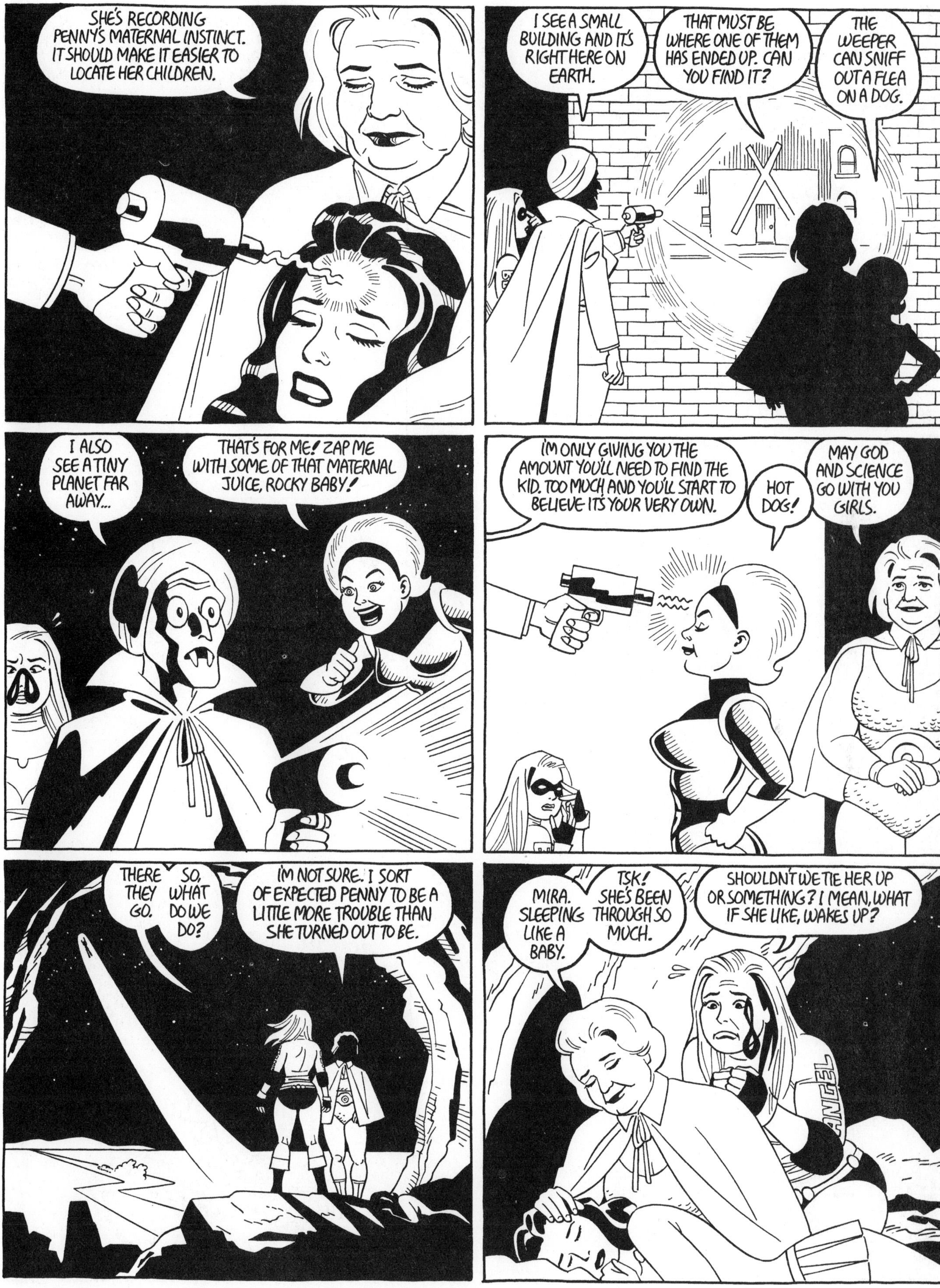
SHE'S RECORDING PENNY'S MATERNAL INSTINCT. IT SHOULD MAKE IT EASIER TO LOCATE HER CHILDREN.
I SEE A SMALL BUILDING AND IT'S RIGHT HERE ON EARTH.
THAT MUST BE WHERE ONE OF THEM HAS ENDED UP. CAN YOU FIND IT?
THE WEEPER CAN SNIFF OUT A FLEA ON A DOG.
I ALSO SEE A TINY PLANET FAR AWAY...
THAT'S FOR ME! ZAP ME WITH SOME OF THAT MATERNAL JUICE, ROCKY BABY!
I'M ONLY GIVING YOU THE AMOUNT YOU'LL NEED TO FIND THE KID. TOO MUCH AND YOU'LL START TO BELIEVE IT'S YOUR VERY OWN.
HOT DOG!
MAY GOD AND SCIENCE GO WITH YOU GIRLS.
THERE THEY GO.
SO, WHAT DO WE DO?
I'M NOT SURE. I SORT OF EXPECTED PENNY TO BE A LITTLE MORE TROUBLE THAN SHE TURNED OUT TO BE.
MIRA. SLEEPING LIKE A BABY.
TSK! SHE'S BEEN THROUGH SO MUCH.
SHOULDN'T WE TIE HER UP OR SOMETHING? I MEAN, WHAT IF SHE LIKE, WAKES UP?
ANGEL

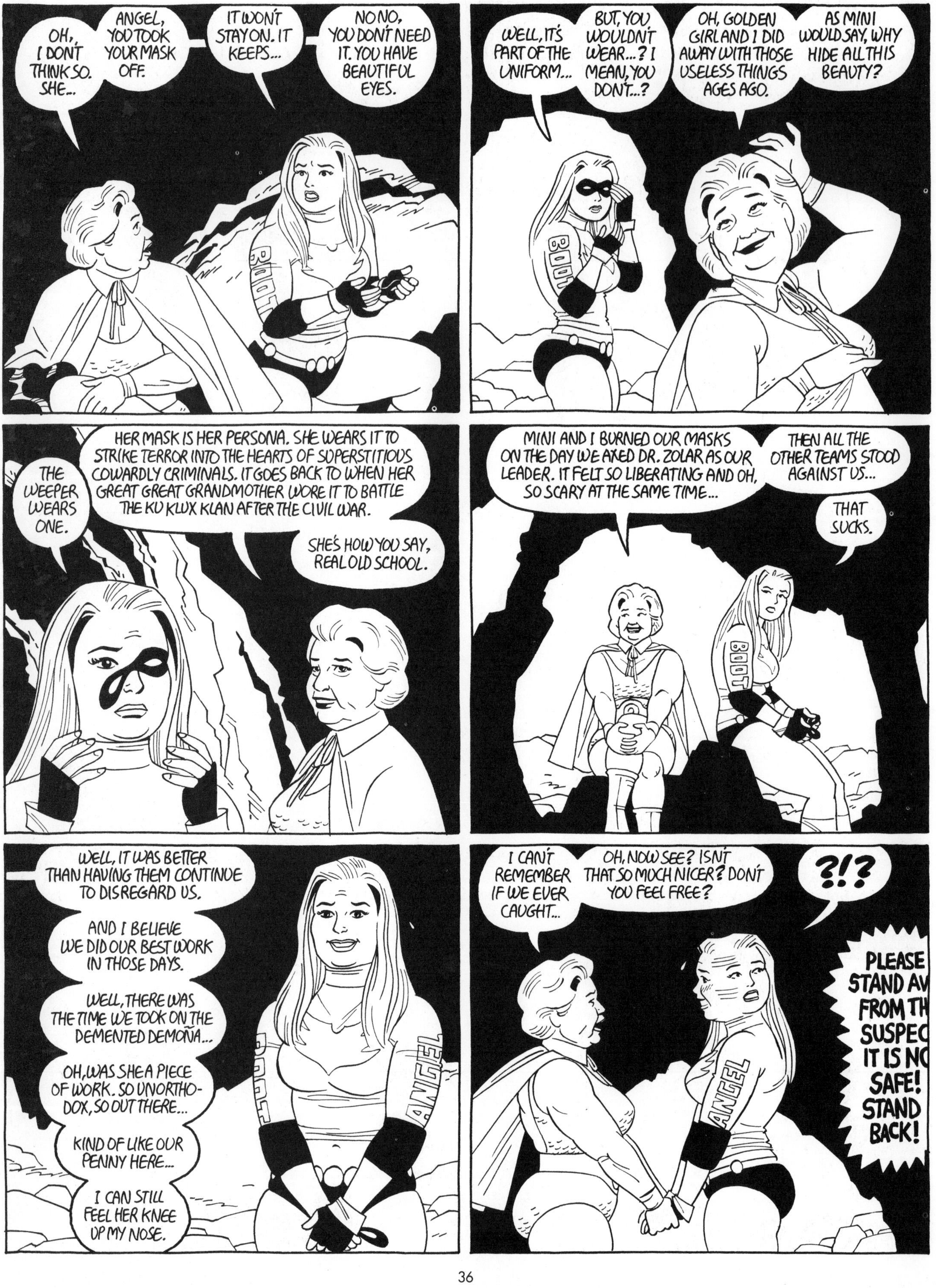
OH, I DON'T THINK SO. SHE...
ANGEL, YOU TOOK YOUR MASK OFF.
IT WON'T STAY ON. IT KEEPS...
NO NO, YOU DON'T NEED IT. YOU HAVE BEAUTIFUL EYES.
BOOT
WELL, IT'S PART OF THE UNIFORM...
BUT, YOU WOULDN'T WEAR...? I MEAN, YOU DON'T...?
OH, GOLDEN GIRL AND I DID AWAY WITH THOSE USELESS THINGS AGES AGO.
AS MINI WOULD SAY, WHY HIDE ALL THIS BEAUTY?
BOOT
THE WEEPER WEARS ONE.
HER MASK IS HER PERSONA. SHE WEARS IT TO STRIKE TERROR INTO THE HEARTS OF SUPERSTITIOUS COWARDLY CRIMINALS. IT GOES BACK TO WHEN HER GREAT GREAT GRANDMOTHER WORE IT TO BATTLE THE KU KLUX KLAN AFTER THE CIVIL WAR.
SHE'S HOW YOU SAY, REAL OLD SCHOOL.
MINI AND I BURNED OUR MASKS ON THE DAY WE AXED DR. ZOLAR AS OUR LEADER. IT FELT SO LIBERATING AND OH, SO SCARY AT THE SAME TIME...
THEN ALL THE OTHER TEAMS STOOD AGAINST US...
THAT SUCKS.
BOOT
WELL, IT WAS BETTER THAN HAVING THEM CONTINUE TO DISREGARD US.
AND I BELIEVE WE DID OUR BEST WORK IN THOSE DAYS.
WELL, THERE WAS THE TIME WE TOOK ON THE DEMENTED DEMOÑA...
OH, WAS SHE A PIECE OF WORK. SO UNORTHODOX, SO OUT THERE...
KIND OF LIKE OUR PENNY HERE...
I CAN STILL FEEL HER KNEE UP MY NOSE.
ANGEL
I CAN'T REMEMBER IF WE EVER CAUGHT...
OH, NOW SEE? ISN'T THAT SO MUCH NICER? DON'T YOU FEEL FREE?
?!?
PLEASE STAND AV FROM TH SUSPEC IT IS NO SAFE! STAND BACK!
ANGEL

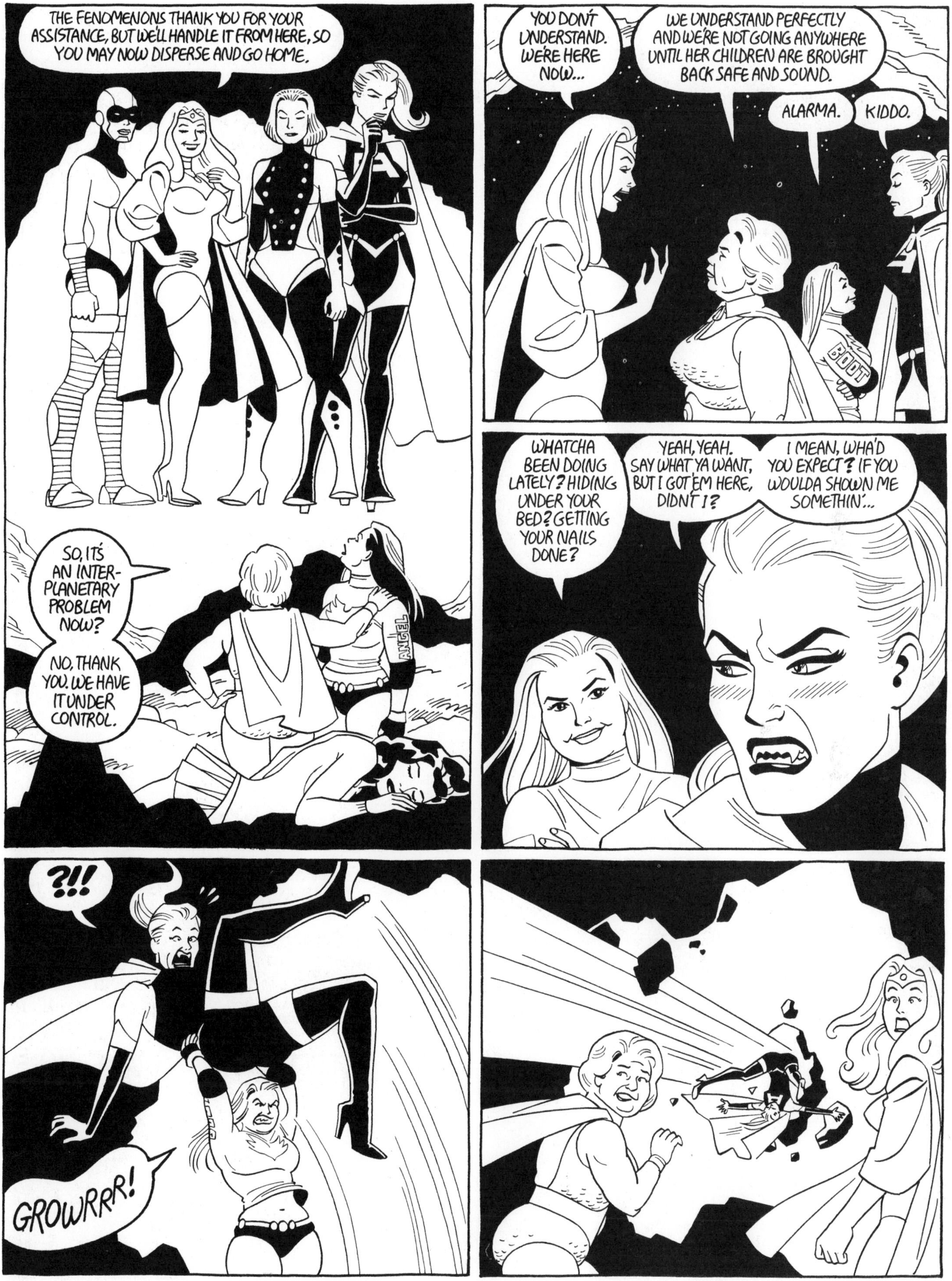
THE FENOMENONS THANK YOU FOR YOUR ASSISTANCE, BUT WE'LL HANDLE IT FROM HERE, SO YOU MAY NOW DISPERSE AND GO HOME.
YOU DON'T UNDERSTAND. WE'RE HERE NOW...
WE UNDERSTAND PERFECTLY AND WE'RE NOT GOING ANYWHERE UNTIL HER CHILDREN ARE BROUGHT BACK SAFE AND SOUND.
ALARMA.
KIDDO.
BOOT
SO, IT'S AN INTER-PLANETARY PROBLEM NOW?
NO, THANK YOU. WE HAVE IT UNDER CONTROL.
ANGEL
WHATCHA BEEN DOING LATELY? HIDING UNDER YOUR BED? GETTING YOUR NAILS DONE?
YEAH, YEAH. SAY WHAT YA WANT, BUT I GOT 'EM HERE, DIDN'T I?
I MEAN, WHA'D YOU EXPECT? IF YOU WOULDA SHOWN ME SOMETHIN'...
?!!
GROWRRR!

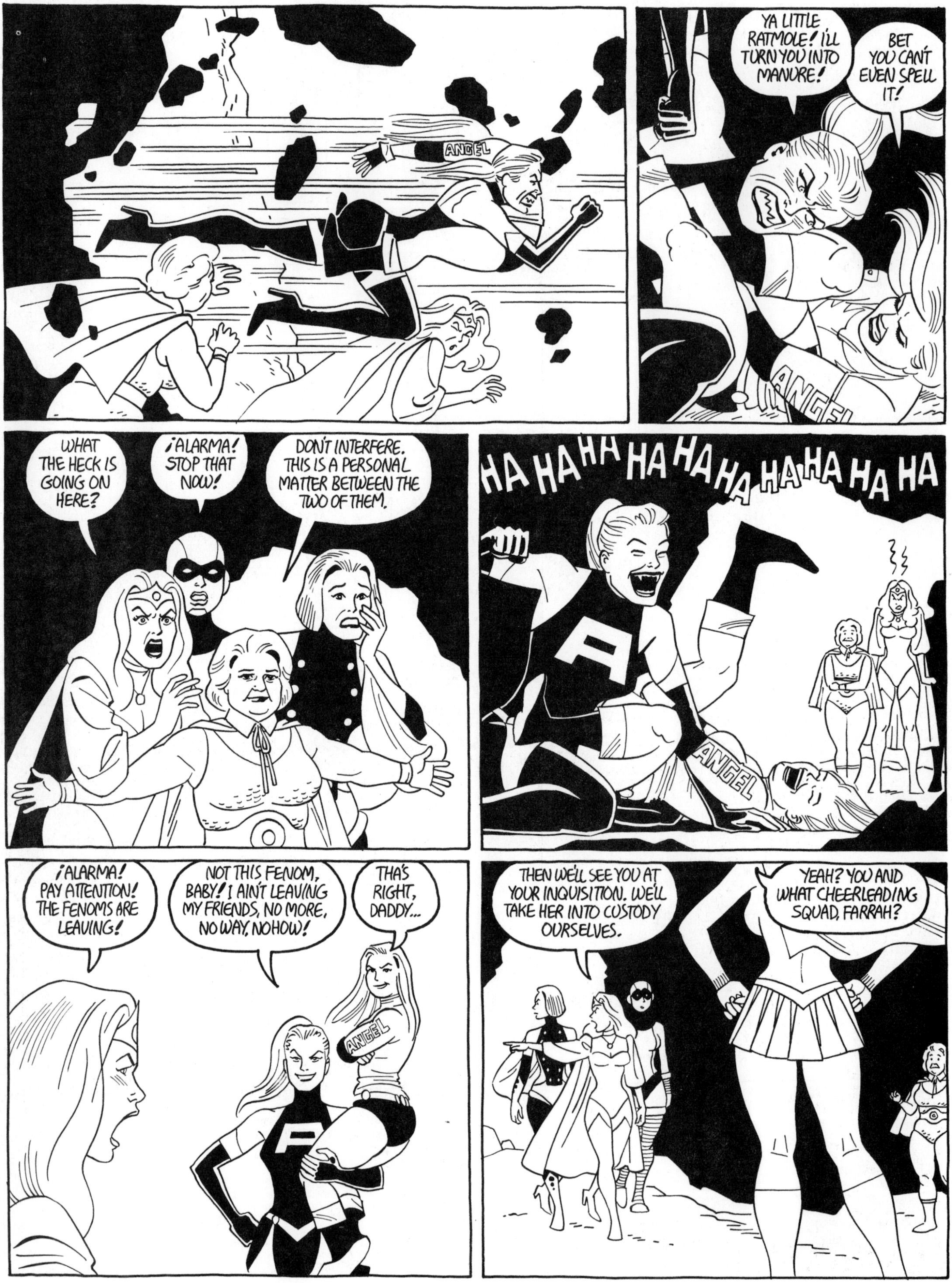

ANGEL
YA LITTLE RATMOLE! I'LL TURN YOU INTO MANURE!
BET YOU CAN'T EVEN SPELL IT!
ANGEL
WHAT THE HECK IS GOING ON HERE?
¡ALARMA! STOP THAT NOW!
DON'T INTERFERE. THIS IS A PERSONAL MATTER BETWEEN THE TWO OF THEM.
HA HA HA HA HA HA HA HA HA HA HA
A
ANGEL
¡ALARMA! PAY ATTENTION! THE FENOMS ARE LEAVING!
NOT THIS FENOM, BABY! I AIN'T LEAVING MY FRIENDS, NO MORE, NO WAY, NOHOW!
THA'S RIGHT, DADDY...
ANGEL
THEN WE'LL SEE YOU AT YOUR INQUISITION. WE'LL TAKE HER INTO CUSTODY OURSELVES.
YEAH? YOU AND WHAT CHEERLEADING SQUAD, FARRAH?

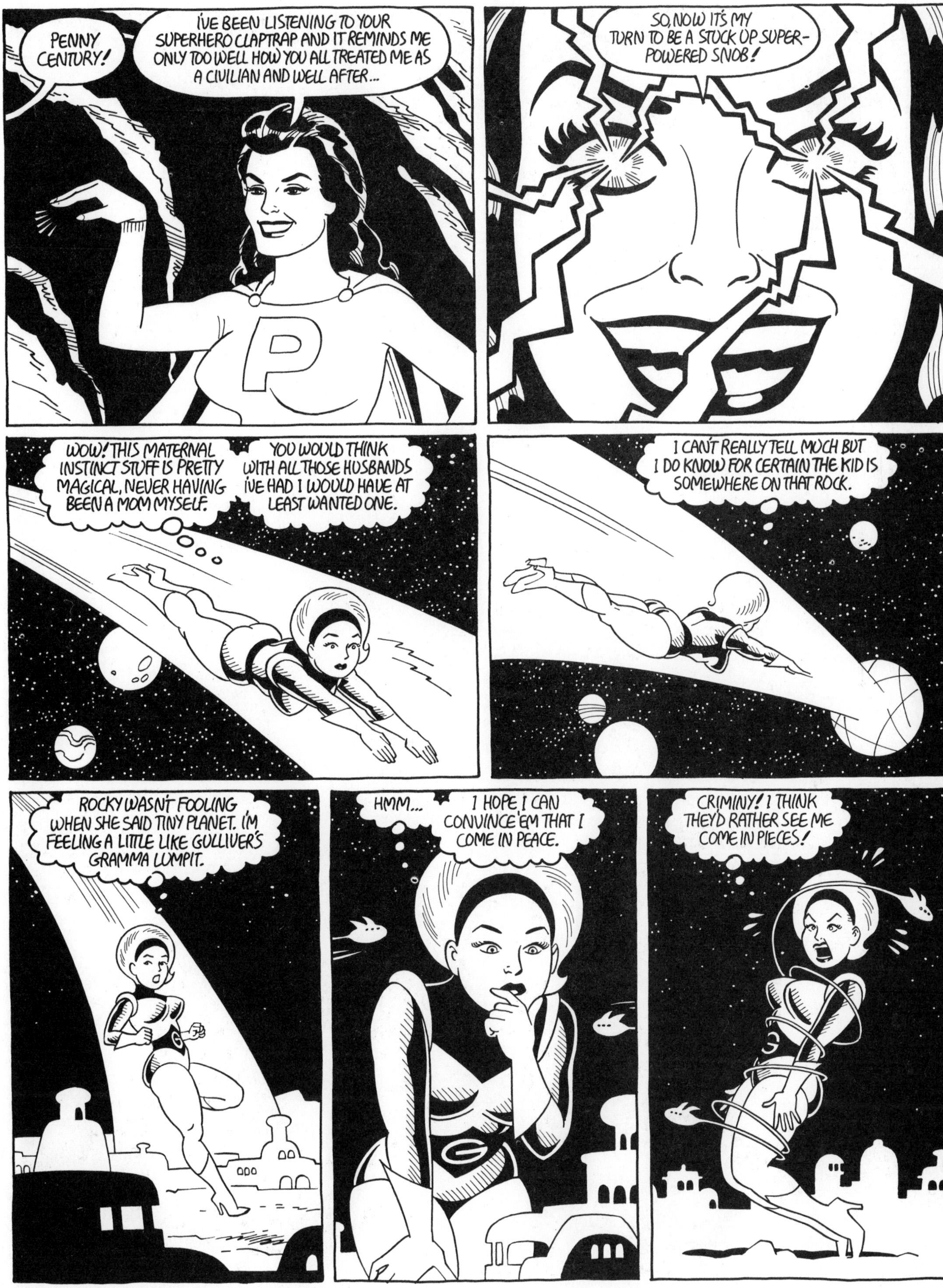
PENNY CENTURY!
I'VE BEEN LISTENING TO YOUR SUPERHERO CLAPTRAP AND IT REMINDS ME ONLY TOO WELL HOW YOU ALL TREATED ME AS A CIVILIAN AND WELL AFTER...
SO, NOW IT'S MY TURN TO BE A STUCK UP SUPER-POWERED SNOB!
WOW! THIS MATERNAL INSTINCT STUFF IS PRETTY MAGICAL, NEVER HAVING BEEN A MOM MYSELF.
YOU WOULD THINK WITH ALL THOSE HUSBANDS I'VE HAD I WOULD HAVE AT LEAST WANTED ONE.
I CAN'T REALLY TELL MUCH BUT I DO KNOW FOR CERTAIN THE KID IS SOMEWHERE ON THAT ROCK.
ROCKY WASN'T FOOLING WHEN SHE SAID TINY PLANET. I'M FEELING A LITTLE LIKE GULLIVER'S GRAMMA LUMPIT.
HMM...
I HOPE I CAN CONVINCE 'EM THAT I COME IN PEACE.
CRIMINY! I THINK THEY'D RATHER SEE ME COME IN PIECES!

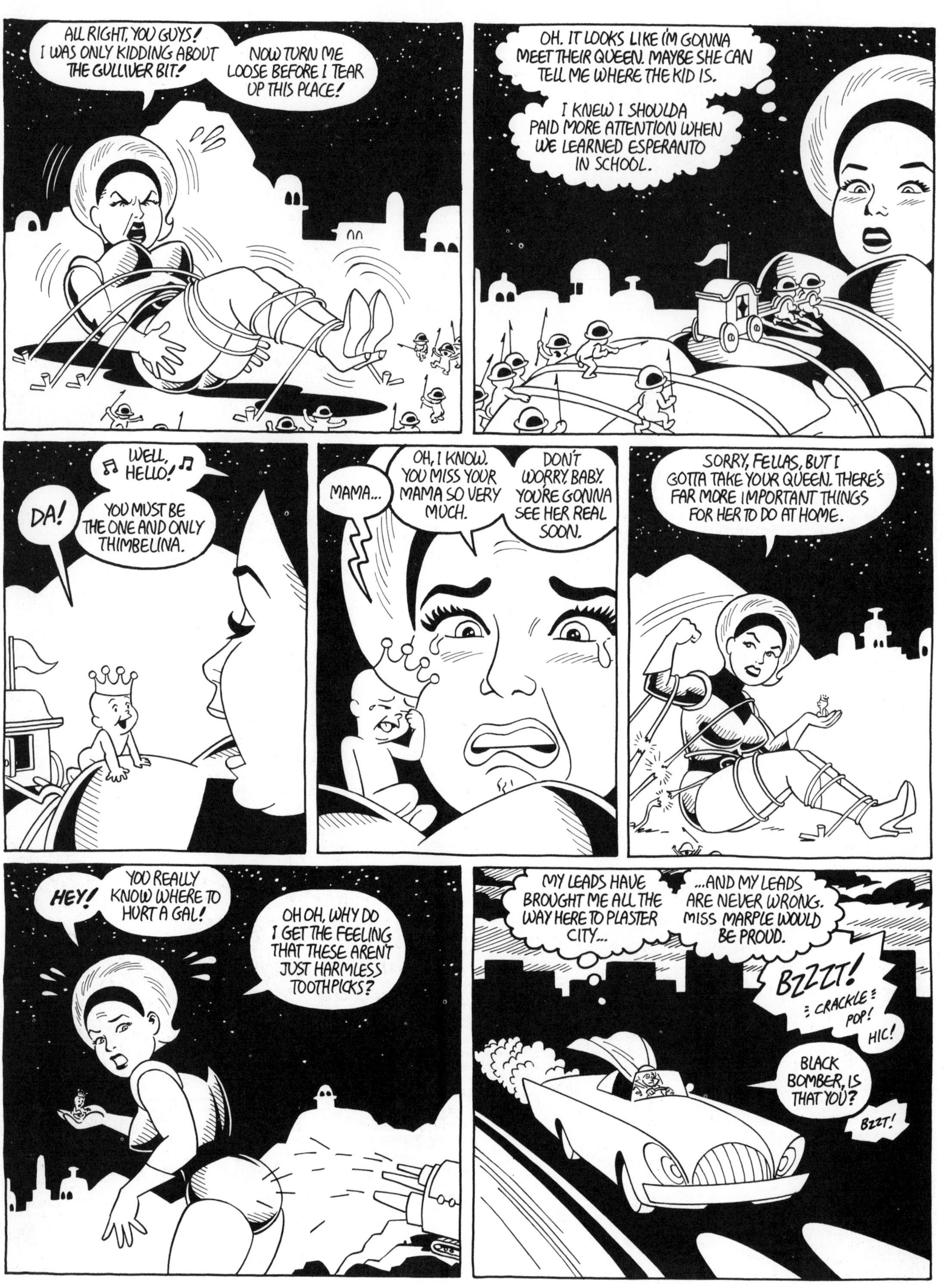
ALL RIGHT, YOU GUYS! I WAS ONLY KIDDING ABOUT THE GULLIVER BIT!
NOW TURN ME LOOSE BEFORE I TEAR UP THIS PLACE!
OH. IT LOOKS LIKE I'M GONNA MEET THEIR QUEEN. MAYBE SHE CAN TELL ME WHERE THE KID IS.
I KNEW I SHOULDA PAID MORE ATTENTION WHEN WE LEARNED ESPERANTO IN SCHOOL.
♫ WELL, HELLO! ♫
DA!
YOU MUST BE THE ONE AND ONLY THIMBELINA.
MAMA...
OH, I KNOW. YOU MISS YOUR MAMA SO VERY MUCH.
DON'T WORRY, BABY. YOU'RE GONNA SEE HER REAL SOON.
SORRY, FELLAS, BUT I GOTTA TAKE YOUR QUEEN. THERE'S FAR MORE IMPORTANT THINGS FOR HER TO DO AT HOME.
HEY!
YOU REALLY KNOW WHERE TO HURT A GAL!
OH OH, WHY DO I GET THE FEELING THAT THESE AREN'T JUST HARMLESS TOOTHPICKS?
MY LEADS HAVE BROUGHT ME ALL THE WAY HERE TO PLASTER CITY...
...AND MY LEADS ARE NEVER WRONG. MISS MARPLE WOULD BE PROUD.
BZZZT!
CRACKLE
POP!
HIC!
BLACK BOMBER, IS THAT YOU?
BZZT!

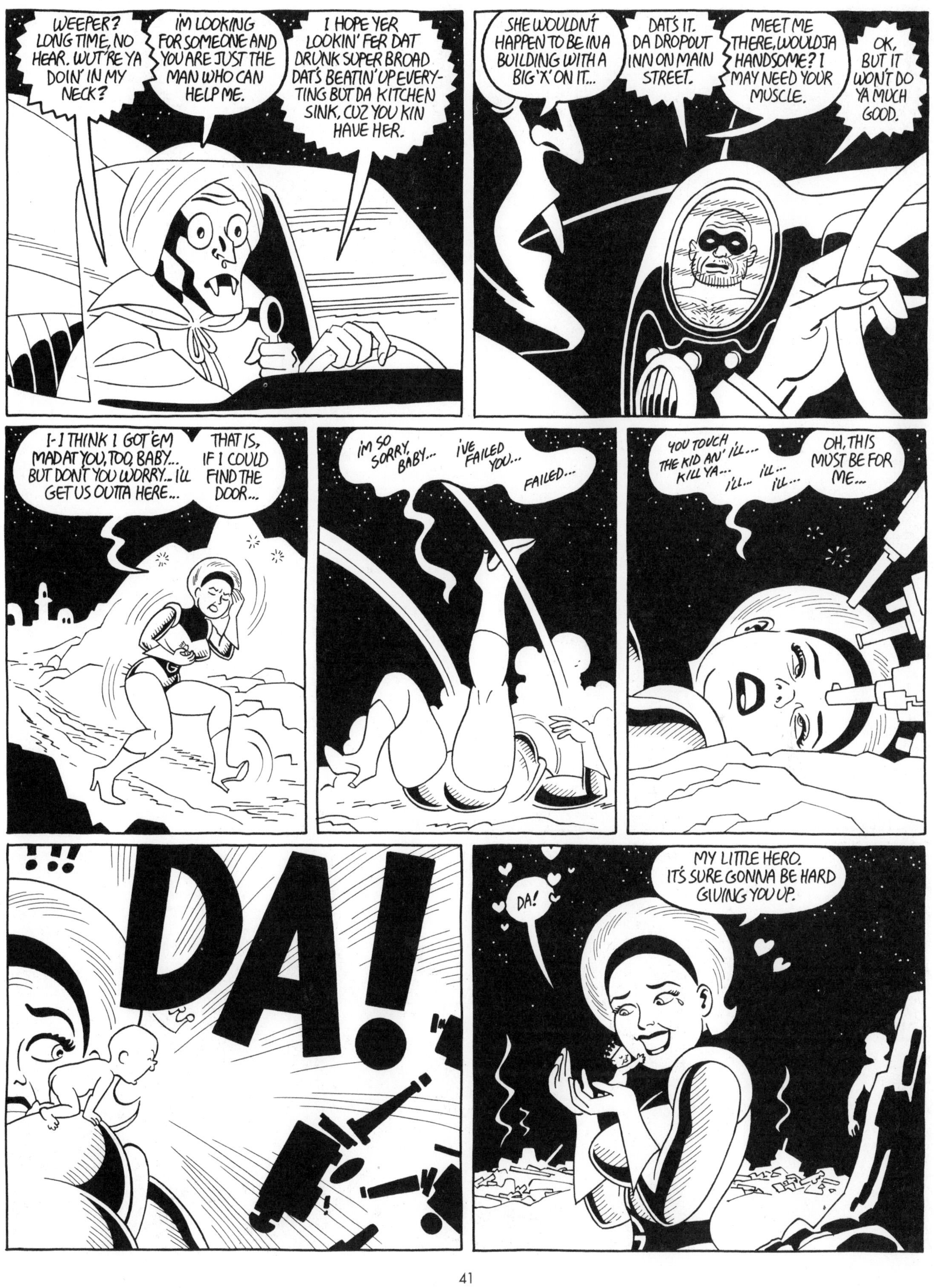

WEEPER? LONG TIME, NO HEAR. WUT'RE YA DOIN' IN MY NECK?
I'M LOOKING FOR SOMEONE AND YOU ARE JUST THE MAN WHO CAN HELP ME.
I HOPE YER LOOKIN' FER DAT DRUNK SUPER BROAD DAT'S BEATIN' UP EVERY-TING BUT DA KITCHEN SINK, CUZ YOU KIN HAVE HER.
SHE WOULDN'T HAPPEN TO BE IN A BUILDING WITH A BIG 'X' ON IT...
DAT'S IT. DA DROPOUT INN ON MAIN STREET.
MEET ME THERE, WOULDJA HANDSOME? I MAY NEED YOUR MUSCLE.
OK, BUT IT WON'T DO YA MUCH GOOD.
I-I THINK I GOT 'EM MAD AT YOU, TOO, BABY... BUT DON'T YOU WORRY... I'LL GET US OUTTA HERE...
THAT IS, IF I COULD FIND THE DOOR...
I'M SO SORRY, BABY... I'VE FAILED YOU... FAILED...
YOU TOUCH THE KID AN' I'LL... KILL YA... I'LL... I'LL... I'LL...
OH, THIS MUST BE FOR ME...
!!!
DA!
DA!
MY LITTLE HERO. IT'S SURE GONNA BE HARD GIVING YOU UP.

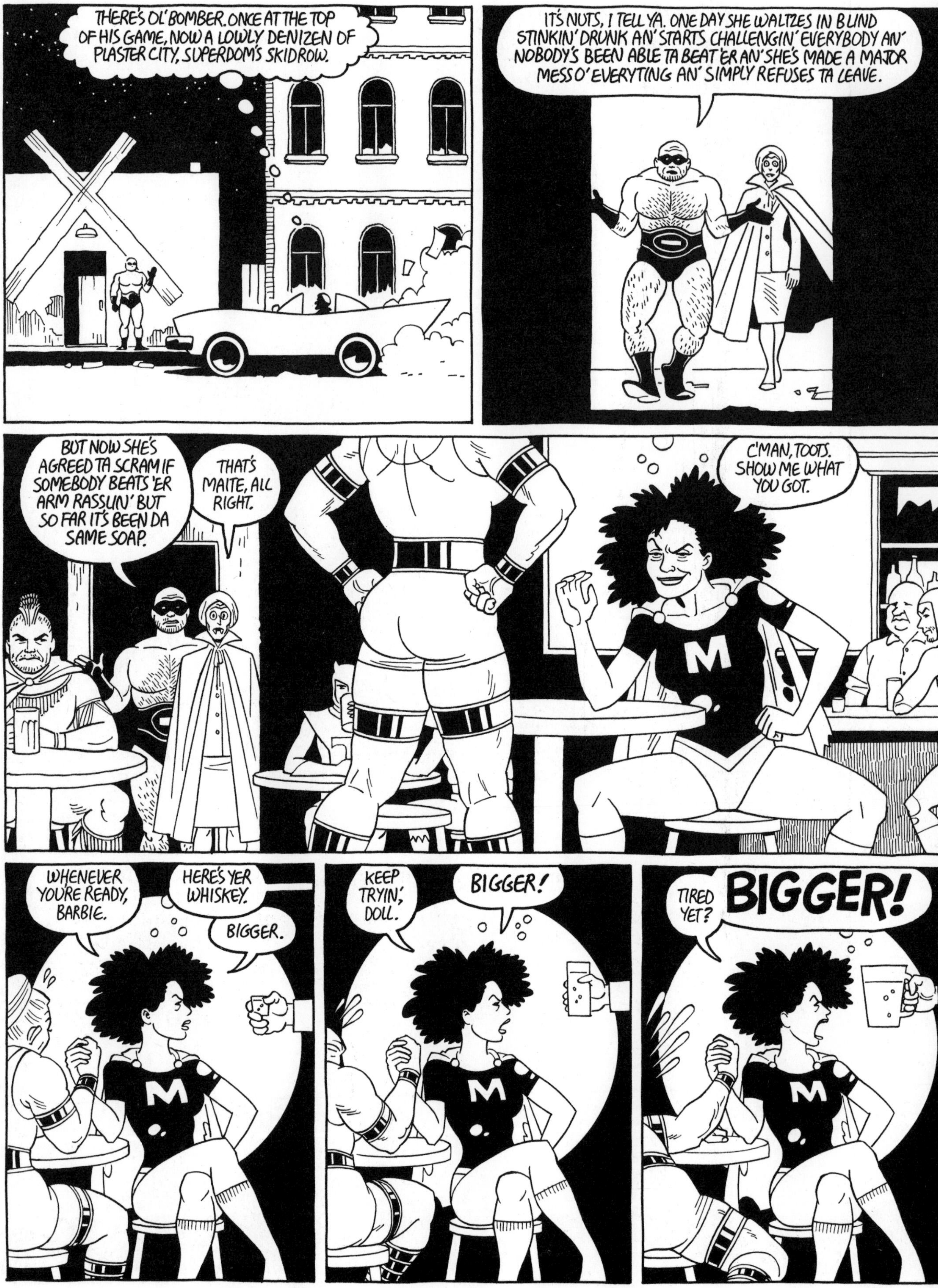
THERE'S OL' BOMBER. ONCE AT THE TOP OF HIS GAME, NOW A LOWLY DENIZEN OF PLASTER CITY, SUPERDOM'S SKIDROW.
IT'S NUTS, I TELL YA. ONE DAY SHE WALTZES IN BLIND STINKIN' DRUNK AN' STARTS CHALLENGIN' EVERYBODY AN' NOBODY'S BEEN ABLE TA BEAT 'ER AN' SHE'S MADE A MAJOR MESS O' EVERYTING AN' SIMPLY REFUSES TA LEAVE.
BUT NOW SHE'S AGREED TA SCRAM IF SOMEBODY BEATS 'ER ARM RASSLIN' BUT SO FAR IT'S BEEN DA SAME SOAP.
THAT'S MAITE, ALL RIGHT.
C'MAN, TOOTS. SHOW ME WHAT YOU GOT.
WHENEVER YOU'RE READY, BARBIE.
HERE'S YER WHISKEY.
BIGGER.
KEEP TRYIN', DOLL.
BIGGER!
TIRED YET?
BIGGER!

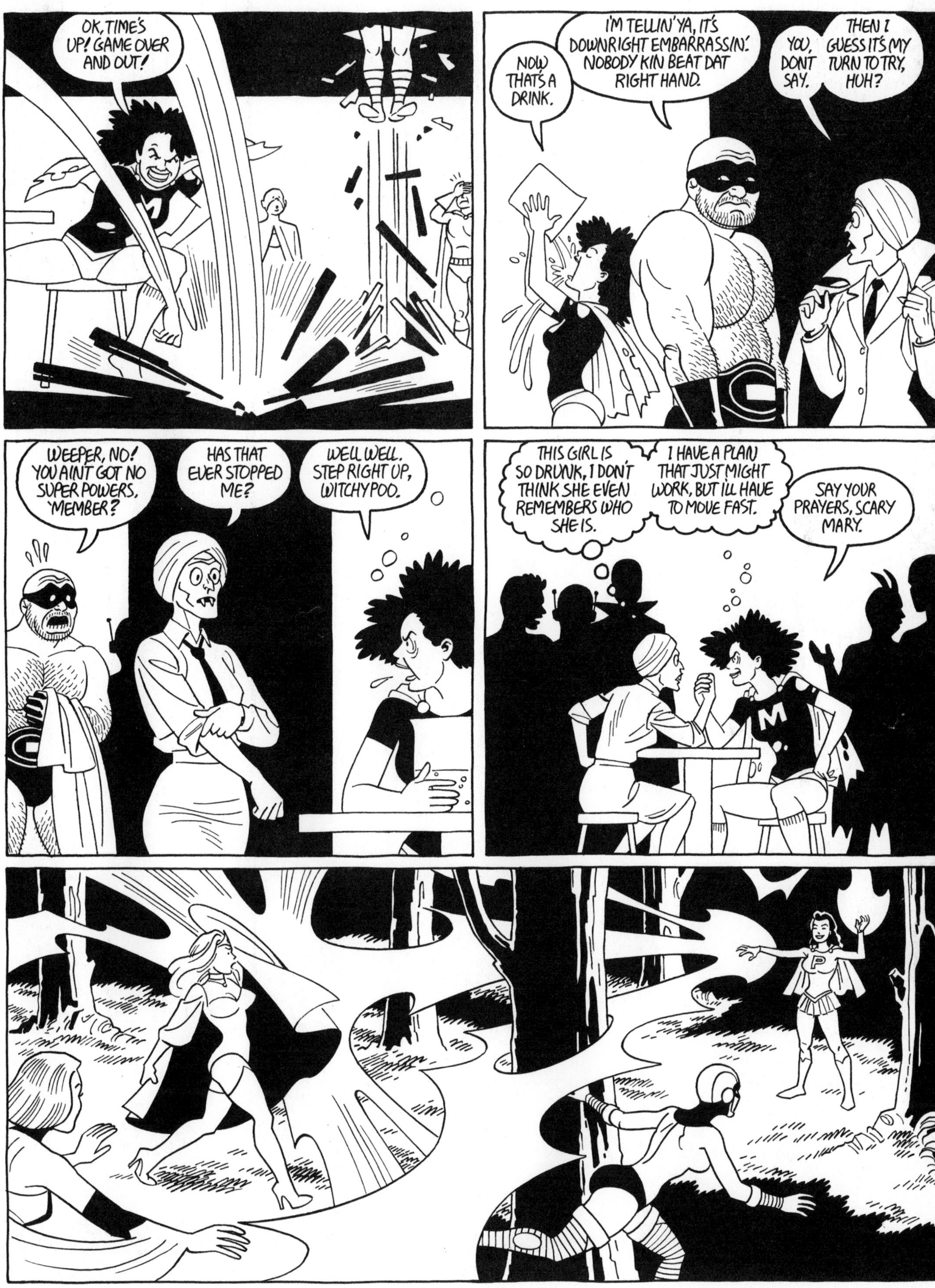
OK, TIME'S UP! GAME OVER AND OUT!
NOW THAT'S A DRINK.
I'M TELLIN' YA, IT'S DOWNRIGHT EMBARRASSIN'. NOBODY KIN BEAT DAT RIGHT HAND.
YOU, DONT SAY.
THEN I GUESS IT'S MY TURN TO TRY, HUH?
WEEPER, NO! YOU AINT GOT NO SUPER POWERS, 'MEMBER?
HAS THAT EVER STOPPED ME?
WELL WELL. STEP RIGHT UP, WITCHYPOO.
THIS GIRL IS SO DRUNK, I DON'T THINK SHE EVEN REMEMBERS WHO SHE IS.
I HAVE A PLAN THAT JUST MIGHT WORK, BUT I'LL HAVE TO MOVE FAST.
SAY YOUR PRAYERS, SCARY MARY.

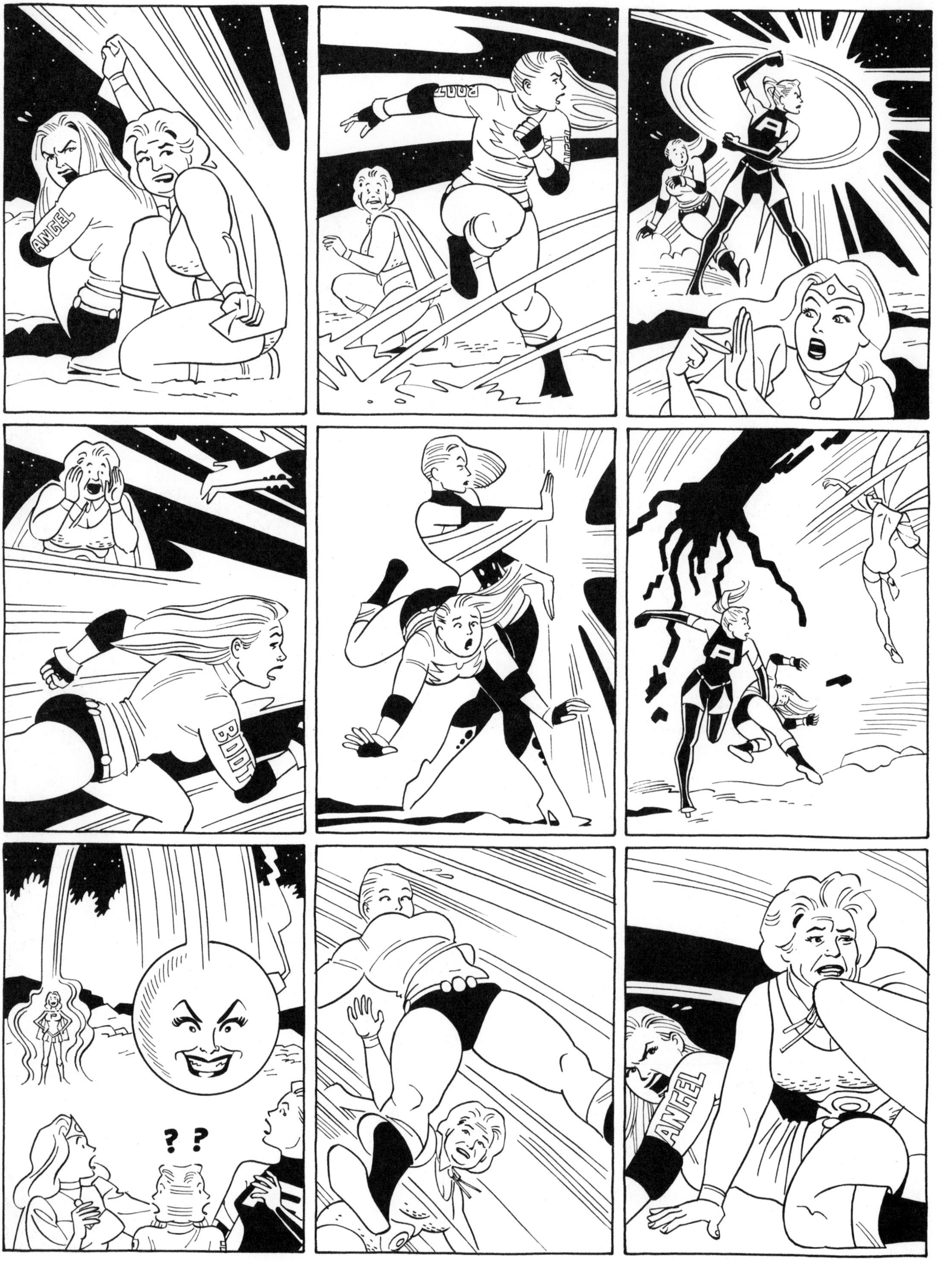
ANGEL
? ?
ANGEL

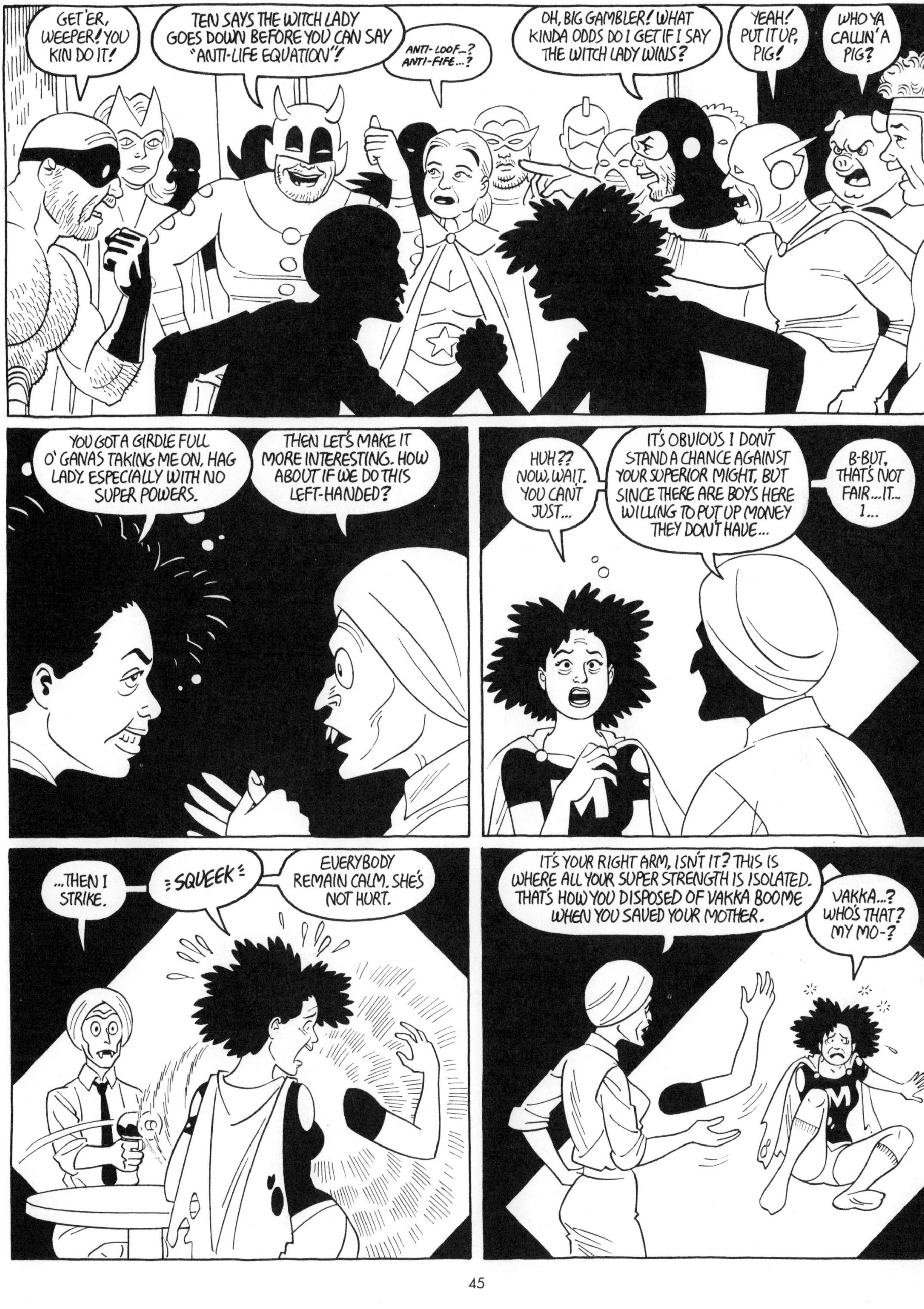

GET'ER, WEEPER! YOU KIN DO IT!
TEN SAYS THE WITCH LADY GOES DOWN BEFORE YOU CAN SAY "ANTI-LIFE EQUATION"!
ANTI-LOOF...? ANTI-FIFE...?
OH, BIG GAMBLER! WHAT KINDA ODDS DO I GET IF I SAY THE WITCH LADY WINS?
YEAH! PUT IT UP, PIG!
WHO YA CALLIN' A PIG?
YOU GOT A GIRDLE FULL O' GANAS TAKING ME ON, HAG LADY. ESPECIALLY WITH NO SUPER POWERS.
THEN LET'S MAKE IT MORE INTERESTING. HOW ABOUT IF WE DO THIS LEFT-HANDED?
HUH?? NOW, WAIT. YOU CAN'T JUST...
IT'S OBVIOUS I DON'T STAND A CHANCE AGAINST YOUR SUPERIOR MIGHT, BUT SINCE THERE ARE BOYS HERE WILLING TO PUT UP MONEY THEY DON'T HAVE...
B-BUT, THAT'S NOT FAIR... IT... I...
...THEN I STRIKE.
SQUEEK
EVERYBODY REMAIN CALM. SHE'S NOT HURT.
IT'S YOUR RIGHT ARM, ISN'T IT? THIS IS WHERE ALL YOUR SUPER STRENGTH IS ISOLATED. THAT'S HOW YOU DISPOSED OF VAKKA BOOME WHEN YOU SAVED YOUR MOTHER.
VAKKA...? WHO'S THAT? MY MO-?

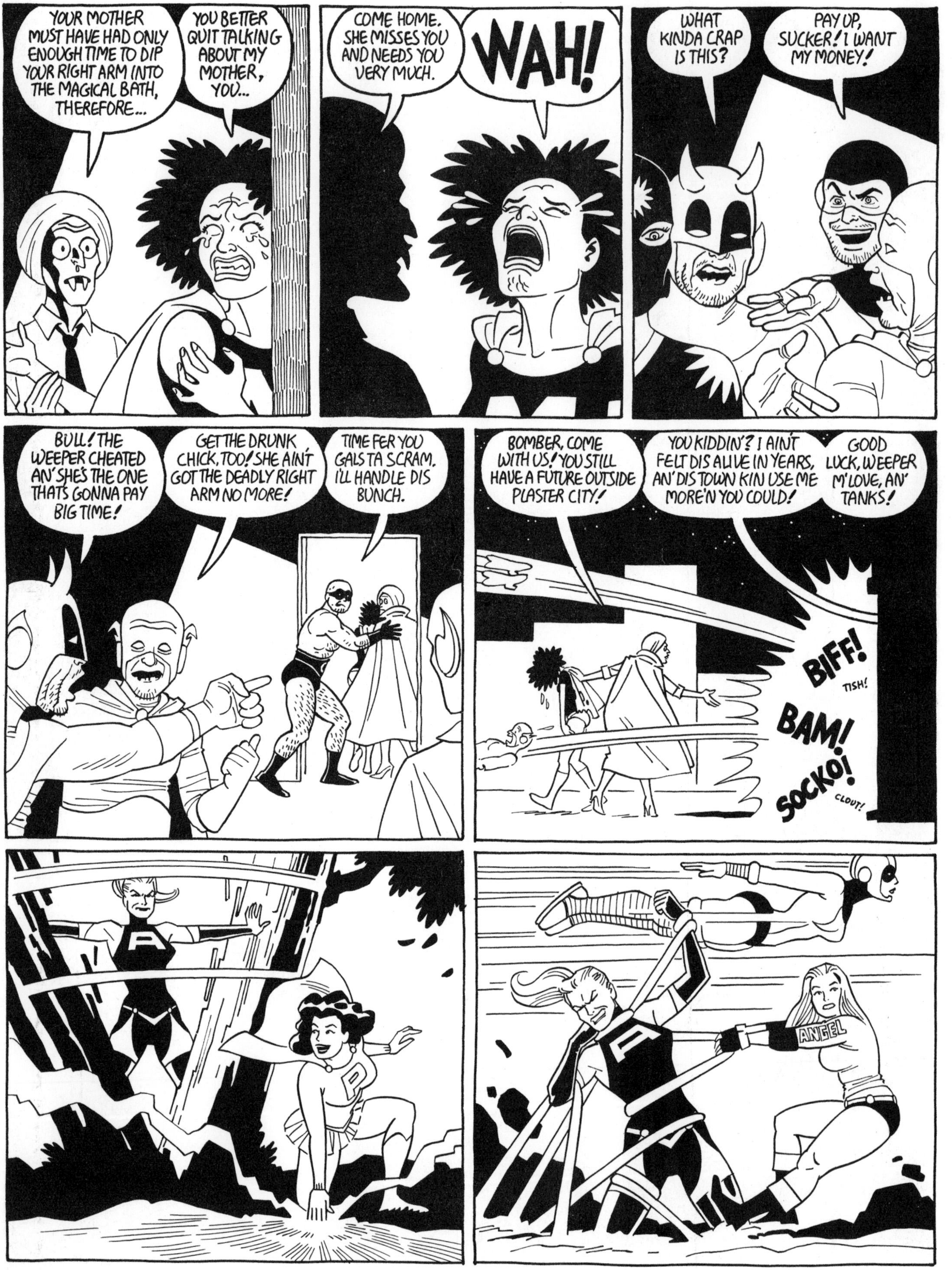
YOUR MOTHER MUST HAVE HAD ONLY ENOUGH TIME TO DIP YOUR RIGHT ARM INTO THE MAGICAL BATH, THEREFORE...
YOU BETTER QUIT TALKING ABOUT MY MOTHER, YOU...
COME HOME. SHE MISSES YOU AND NEEDS YOU VERY MUCH.
WAH!
WHAT KINDA CRAP IS THIS?
PAY UP, SUCKER! I WANT MY MONEY!
BULL! THE WEEPER CHEATED AN' SHE'S THE ONE THATS GONNA PAY BIG TIME!
GET THE DRUNK CHICK, TOO! SHE AIN'T GOT THE DEADLY RIGHT ARM NO MORE!
TIME FER YOU GALS TA SCRAM. I'LL HANDLE DIS BUNCH.
BOMBER, COME WITH US! YOU STILL HAVE A FUTURE OUTSIDE PLASTER CITY!
YOU KIDDIN'? I AIN'T FELT DIS ALIVE IN YEARS, AN' DIS TOWN KIN USE ME MORE'N YOU COULD!
GOOD LUCK, WEEPER M'LOVE, AN' TANKS!
BIFF!
TISH!
BAM!
SOCKO!
CLOUT!
ANGEL

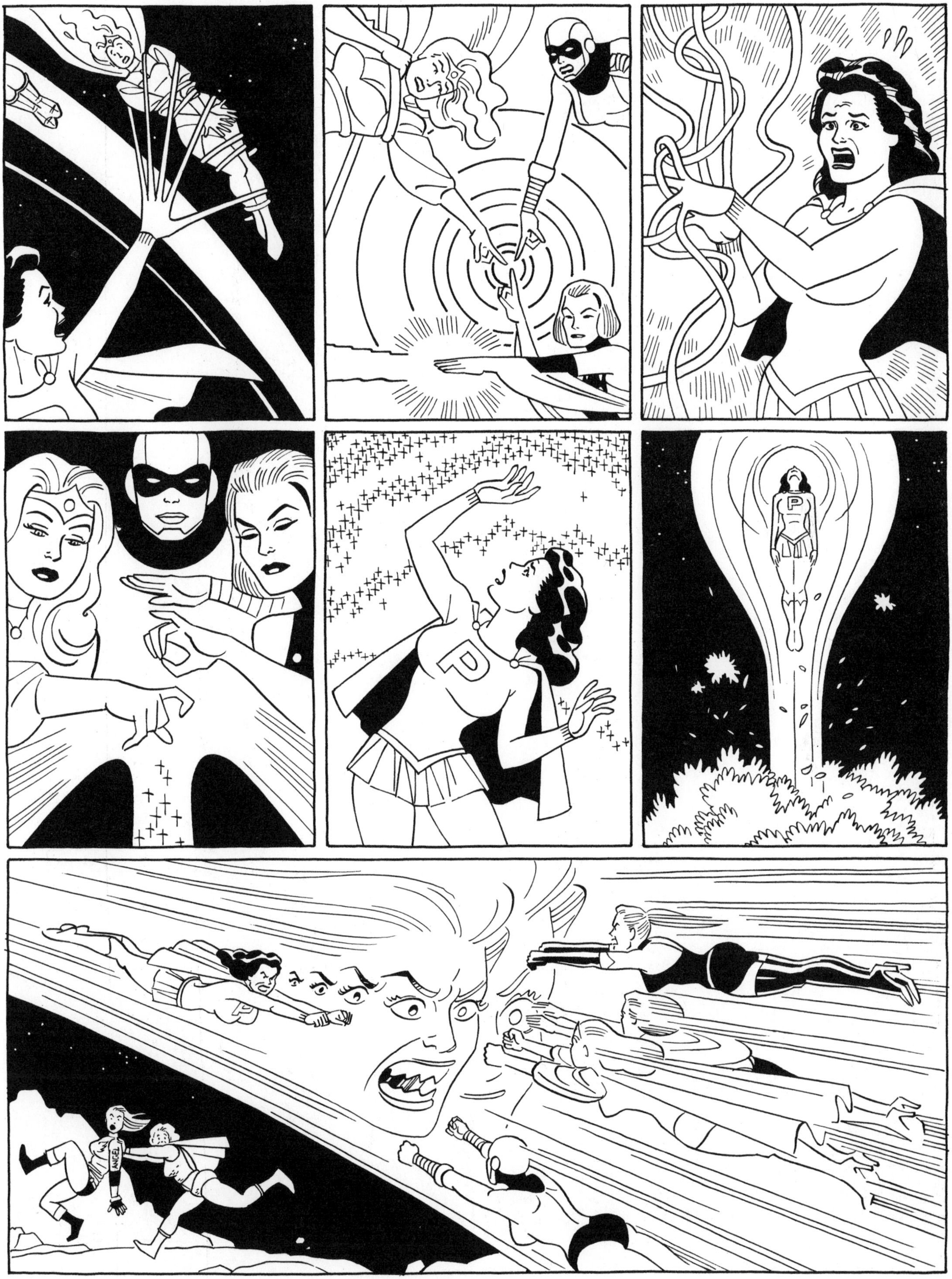
ANGEL

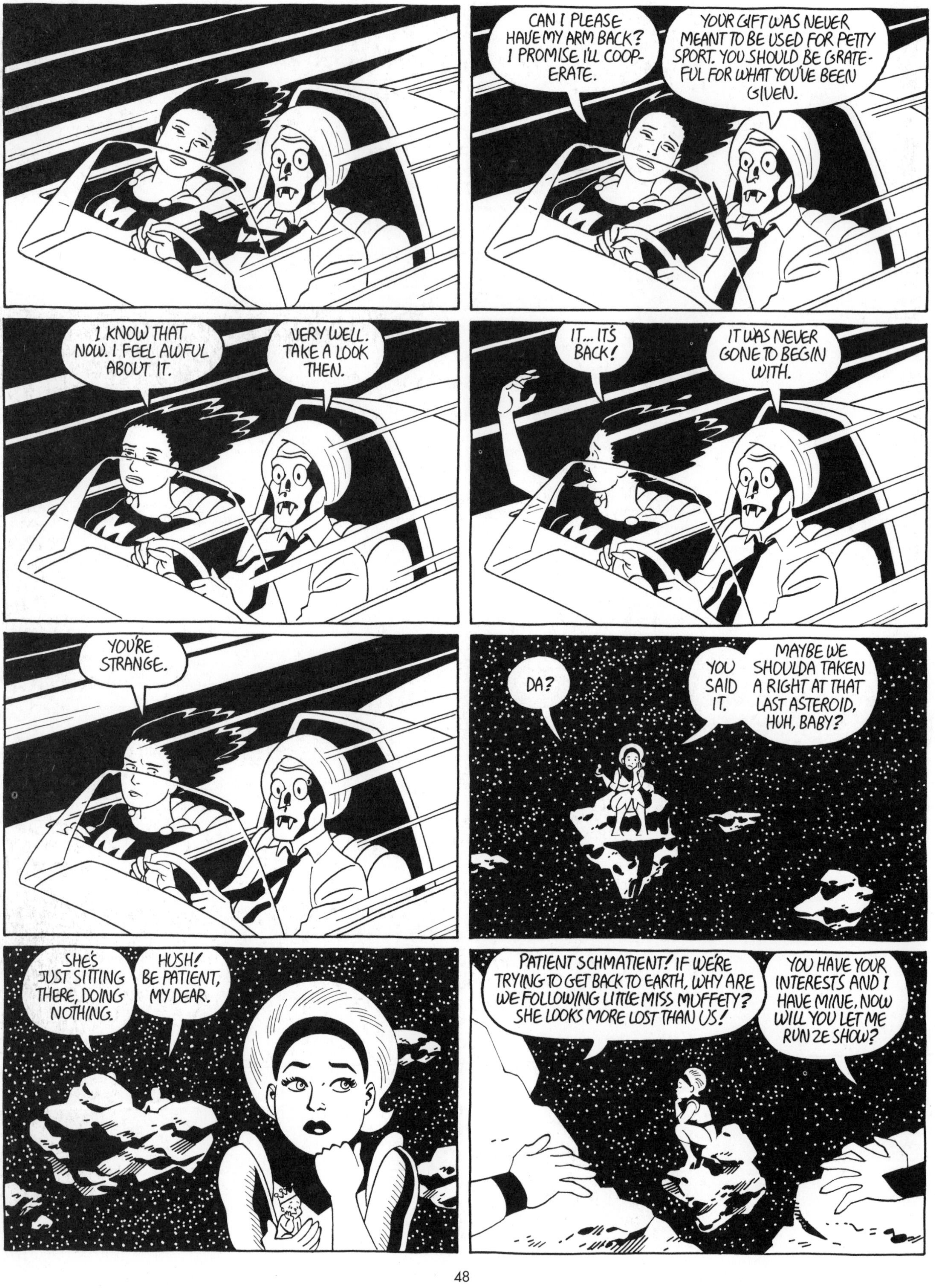
CAN I PLEASE HAVE MY ARM BACK? I PROMISE I'LL COOP-ERATE.
YOUR GIFT WAS NEVER MEANT TO BE USED FOR PETTY SPORT. YOU SHOULD BE GRATE-FUL FOR WHAT YOU'VE BEEN GIVEN.
I KNOW THAT NOW. I FEEL AWFUL ABOUT IT.
VERY WELL. TAKE A LOOK THEN.
IT... IT'S BACK!
IT WAS NEVER GONE TO BEGIN WITH.
YOU'RE STRANGE.
DA?
YOU SAID IT.
MAYBE WE SHOULDA TAKEN A RIGHT AT THAT LAST ASTEROID, HUH, BABY?
SHE'S JUST SITTING THERE, DOING NOTHING.
HUSH! BE PATIENT, MY DEAR.
PATIENT SCHMATIENT! IF WE'RE TRYING TO GET BACK TO EARTH, WHY ARE WE FOLLOWING LITTLE MISS MUFFETY? SHE LOOKS MORE LOST THAN US!
YOU HAVE YOUR INTERESTS AND I HAVE MINE. NOW WILL YOU LET ME RUN ZE SHOW?

WHA...? WHAT ARE YOU DOING?
DON'T YOU SEE IT'S HOPELESS? I'M GONNA DIE IN SIX OR SEVEN YEARS ANYWAY!
AND IT'S ALL BECAUSE OF MY MOTHER!
MY SICK...
SELFISH...
SCATTER-BRAINED...
EVIL...
MOTHER...
HONEY, THE ELECTRIC COMPANY SAYS IT'S NOT THEIR PROBLEM!
DIDN'T I TELL YOU? IT'S THOSE GOD DAMN CRIMEFIGHTERS AGAIN!
KA-DASH!
HONEY, DON'T GO NEAR IT! IT MAY BE A VILLAIN!
VILLAIN OR NOT, THEY CAN'T GO AROUND DISTURBING PRIVATE PROPERTY AS IF IT BELONGS TO THEM!

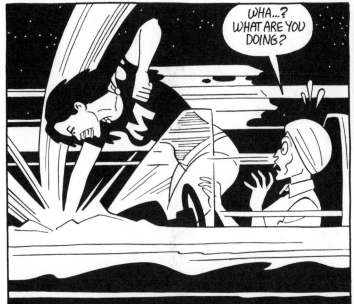

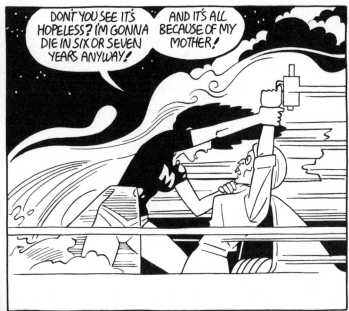

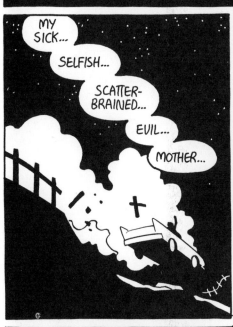

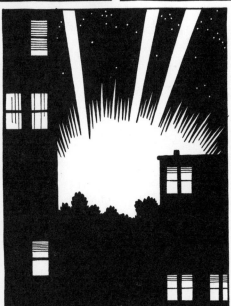

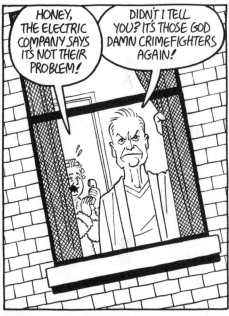

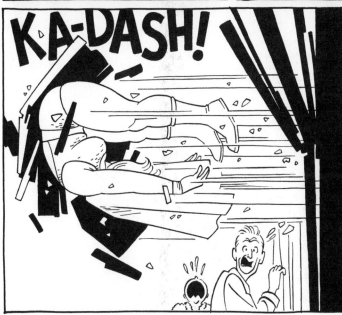

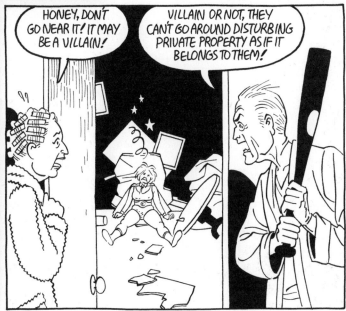

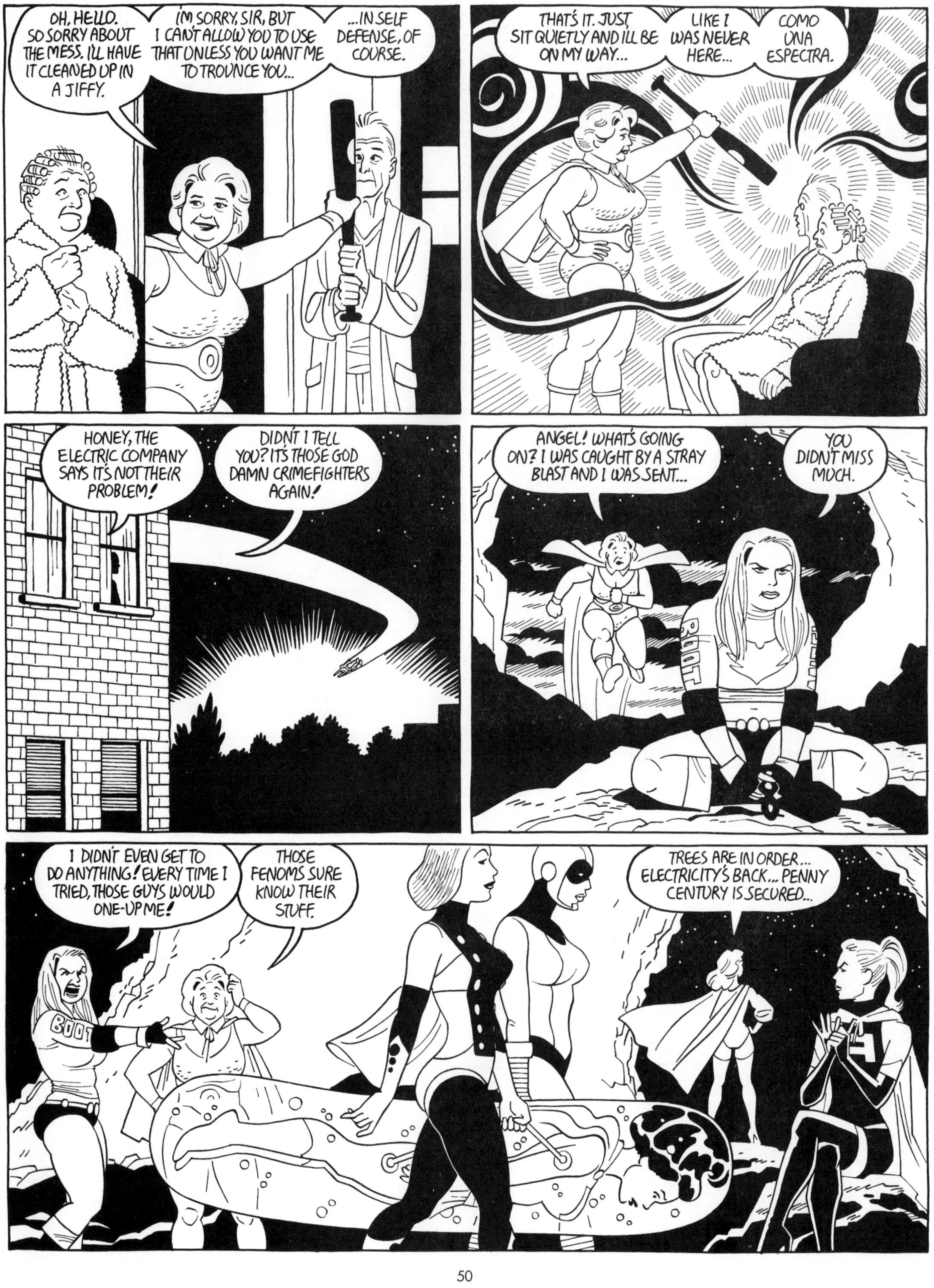
OH, HELLO. SO SORRY ABOUT THE MESS. I'LL HAVE IT CLEANED UP IN A JIFFY.
I'M SORRY, SIR, BUT I CAN'T ALLOW YOU TO USE THAT UNLESS YOU WANT ME TO TROUNCE YOU...
...IN SELF DEFENSE, OF COURSE.
THAT'S IT. JUST, SIT QUIETLY AND I'LL BE ON MY WAY...
LIKE I WAS NEVER HERE...
COMO UNA ESPECTRA.
HONEY, THE ELECTRIC COMPANY SAYS IT'S NOT THEIR PROBLEM!
DIDN'T I TELL YOU? IT'S THOSE GOD DAMN CRIMEFIGHTERS AGAIN!
ANGEL! WHAT'S GOING ON? I WAS CAUGHT BY A STRAY BLAST AND I WAS SENT...
YOU DIDN'T MISS MUCH.
BOOT
I DIDN'T EVEN GET TO DO ANYTHING! EVERY TIME I TRIED, THOSE GUYS WOULD ONE-UP ME!
THOSE FENOMS SURE KNOW THEIR STUFF.
TREES ARE IN ORDER... ELECTRICITY'S BACK... PENNY CENTURY IS SECURED...

WE CAN'T TAKE ANY CHANCES, SO I'M AFRAID WE'LL HAVE TO TAKE HER INTO CUSTODY. YOU'LL CONTACT US WHEN YOU'VE FOUND THE CHILDREN, WON'T YOU?

WE WILL. WE WILL??

YOU'RE NOT COMING.

NO.

I KNOW. THERE GO MY BENEFITS.

YOU ALWAYS SAID YOU FELT LIKE YOU NEVER REALLY FIT IN, 'LAR.

YEAH.

THANKS, SUNNY.

SO THAT'S IT, HUH? SISTER HUGS ALL AROUND AND THEN EVERYBODY GOES HOME?

WHAT DID YOU EXPECT, ANGEL? EVERYBODY KEEPS SOCKING EACH OTHER UNTIL SOMEONE DIES?

S'MATTER, KIDDO? NOT ENOUGH ACTION FOR YA?

I SHOULDA TOLD YA THAT'S THE WAY THE FENOMS WORK! FAST AND CLEAN! NO UNNECESSARY SPILLAGE, THAT'S THEM!

IT'S A GOOD SYSTEM.

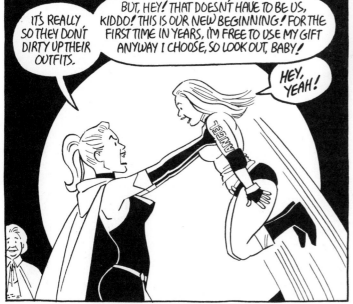

IT'S REALLY SO THEY DON'T DIRTY UP THEIR OUTFITS.

BUT, HEY! THAT DOESN'T HAVE TO BE US, KIDDO! THIS IS OUR NEW BEGINNING! FOR THE FIRST TIME IN YEARS, I'M FREE TO USE MY GIFT ANYWAY I CHOOSE, SO LOOK OUT, BABY!

HEY, YEAH!

ALARMA, TO THINK THAT ALL THIS WAS HAPPENING JUST A SHORT JOG ACROSS THE COURTYARD FROM MAGGIE'S APARTMENT.

THAT'S WHAT YOU GUYS GET FOR READING COMICS ALL DAY.

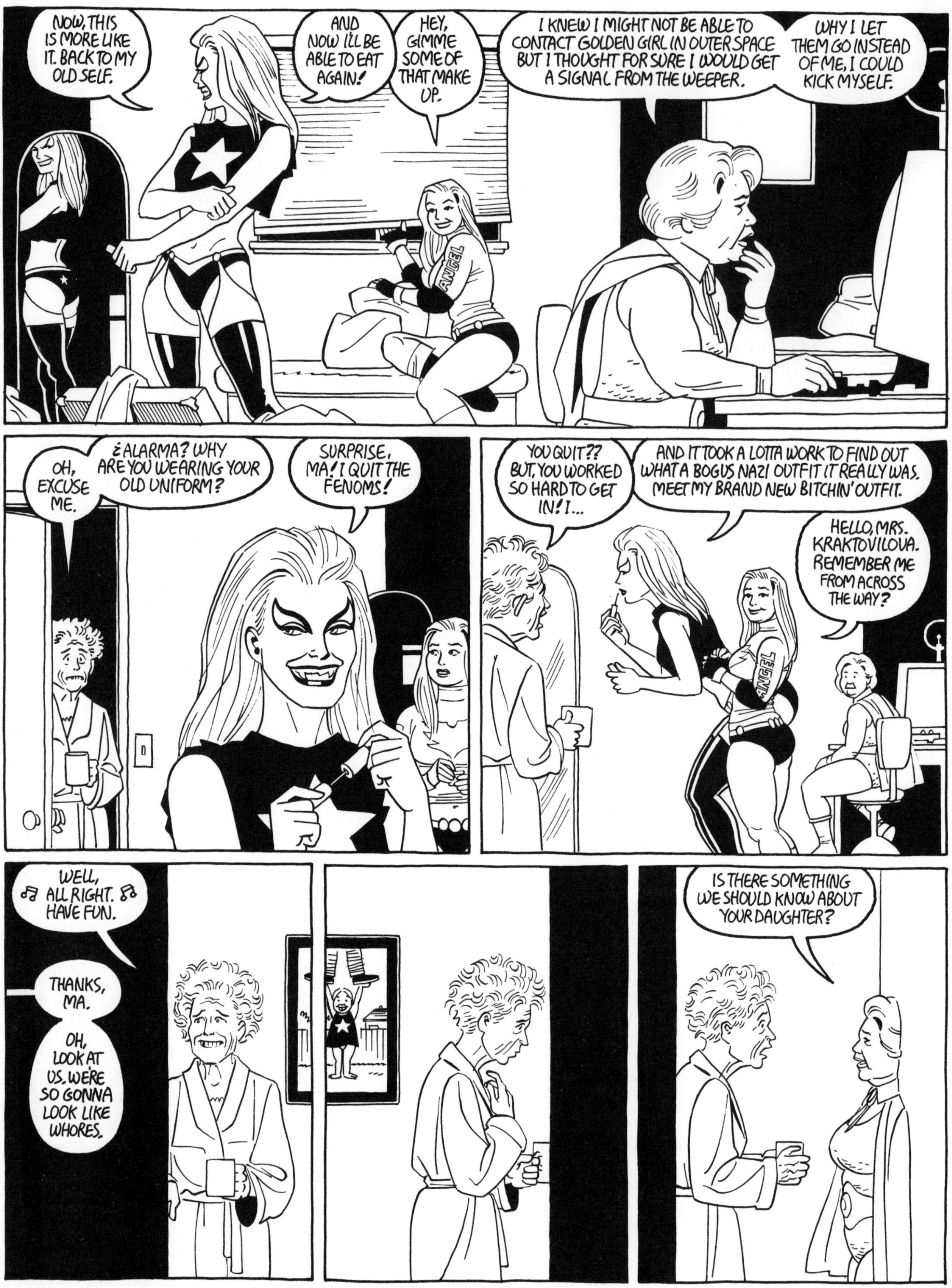
NOW, THIS IS MORE LIKE IT. BACK TO MY OLD SELF.
AND NOW I'LL BE ABLE TO EAT AGAIN!
HEY, GIMME SOME OF THAT MAKE UP.
I KNEW I MIGHT NOT BE ABLE TO CONTACT GOLDEN GIRL IN OUTER SPACE BUT I THOUGHT FOR SURE I WOULD GET A SIGNAL FROM THE WEEPER.
WHY I LET THEM GO INSTEAD OF ME, I COULD KICK MYSELF.
ANGEL
OH, EXCUSE ME.
¿ALARMA? WHY ARE YOU WEARING YOUR OLD UNIFORM?
SURPRISE, MA! I QUIT THE FENOMS!
YOU QUIT?? BUT, YOU WORKED SO HARD TO GET IN! I...
AND IT TOOK A LOTTA WORK TO FIND OUT WHAT A BOGUS NAZI OUTFIT IT REALLY WAS. MEET MY BRAND NEW BITCHIN' OUTFIT.
HELLO, MRS. KRAKTOVILOVA. REMEMBER ME FROM ACROSS THE WAY?
ANGEL
WELL, ALL RIGHT. HAVE FUN.
THANKS, MA.
OH, LOOK AT US. WE'RE SO GONNA LOOK LIKE WHORES.
IS THERE SOMETHING WE SHOULD KNOW ABOUT YOUR DAUGHTER?

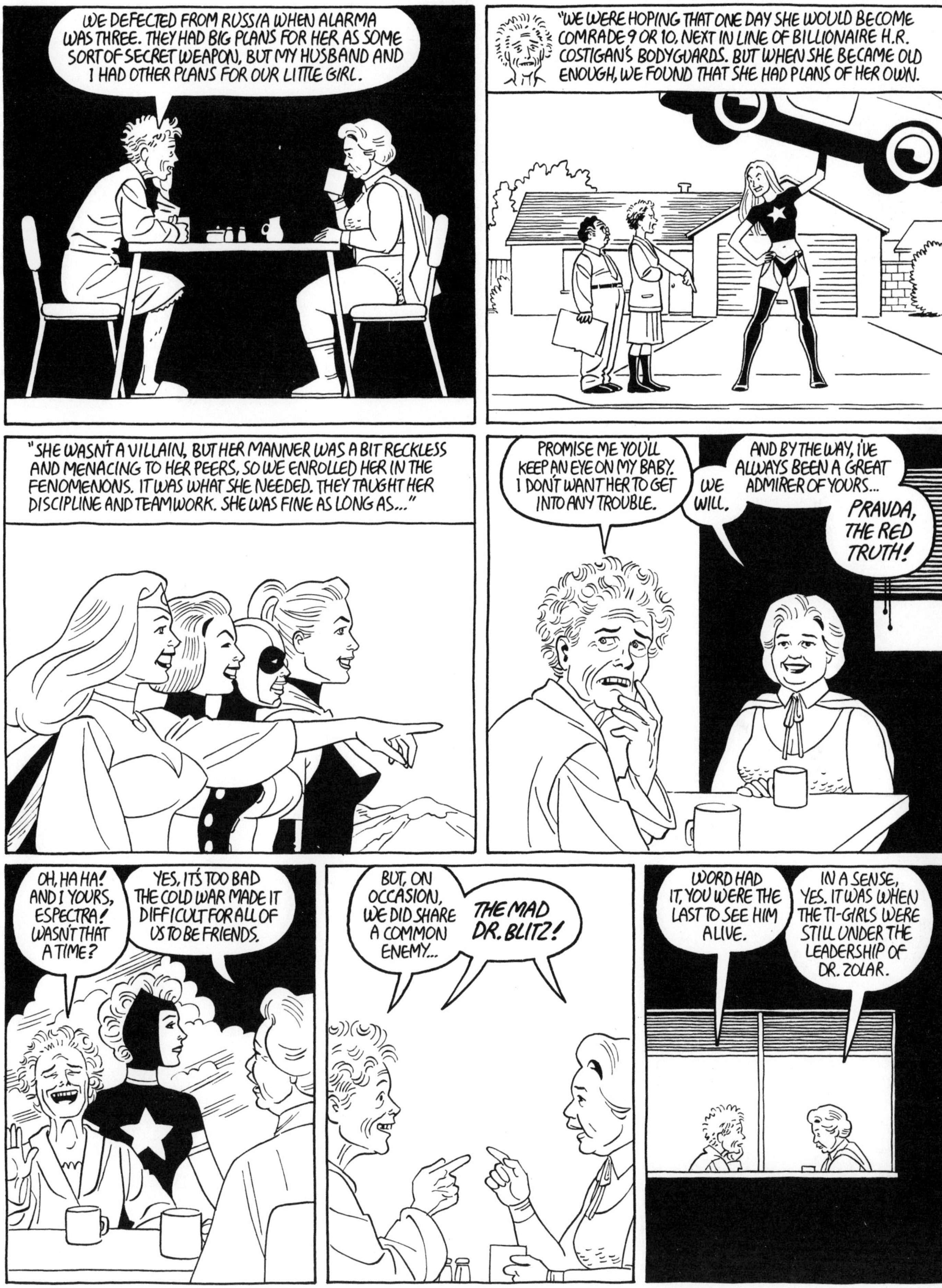
WE DEFECTED FROM RUSSIA WHEN ALARMA WAS THREE. THEY HAD BIG PLANS FOR HER AS SOME SORT OF SECRET WEAPON, BUT MY HUSBAND AND I HAD OTHER PLANS FOR OUR LITTLE GIRL.
"WE WERE HOPING THAT ONE DAY SHE WOULD BECOME COMRADE 9 OR 10, NEXT IN LINE OF BILLIONAIRE H.R. COSTIGAN'S BODYGUARDS. BUT WHEN SHE BECAME OLD ENOUGH, WE FOUND THAT SHE HAD PLANS OF HER OWN.
"SHE WASN'T A VILLAIN, BUT HER MANNER WAS A BIT RECKLESS AND MENACING TO HER PEERS, SO WE ENROLLED HER IN THE FENOMENONS. IT WAS WHAT SHE NEEDED. THEY TAUGHT HER DISCIPLINE AND TEAMWORK. SHE WAS FINE AS LONG AS..."
PROMISE ME YOU'LL KEEP AN EYE ON MY BABY. I DON'T WANT HER TO GET INTO ANY TROUBLE.
WE WILL.
AND BY THE WAY, I'VE ALWAYS BEEN A GREAT ADMIRER OF YOURS...
PRAVDA, THE RED TRUTH!
OH, HA HA! AND I YOURS, ESPECTRA! WASN'T THAT A TIME?
YES, IT'S TOO BAD THE COLD WAR MADE IT DIFFICULT FOR ALL OF US TO BE FRIENDS.
BUT, ON OCCASION, WE DID SHARE A COMMON ENEMY...
THE MAD DR. BLITZ!
WORD HAD IT, YOU WERE THE LAST TO SEE HIM ALIVE.
IN A SENSE, YES. IT WAS WHEN THE TI-GIRLS WERE STILL UNDER THE LEADERSHIP OF DR. ZOLAR.

"IN THOSE DAYS I WAS CALLED FUERZA. THE MAD DOCTOR HAD BOASTED THAT HE CREATED A TIME PORTAL THAT HE WAS GOING TO USE TO TELEPORT DINOSAURS AND NAZIS TO OUR TIME TO DO HIS EVIL BIDDING, BUT THE TI-GIRLS WERE CLOSING IN FAST.

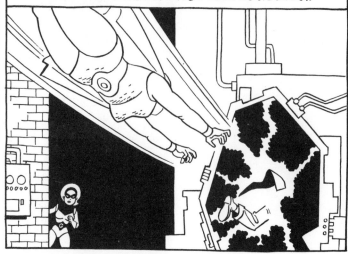

"WE INFILTRATED HIS LAIR AND I WAS RIGHT ON HIS TAIL. HE RAN THROUGH HIS TIME PORTAL AND I FOLLOWED HIM NOT KNOWING THAT HE HAD INSERTED AN EXPLOSIVE DEVICE IN THE MACHINE THAT HE WOULD DETONATE IF EVER THE JIG WAS UP.

"I WAS HALFWAY THROUGH THE PORTAL WHEN IT EXPLODED. I COULD FEEL HALF OF ME VENTURING INTO ANOTHER TIME PERIOD AND THE OTHER HALF REMAINING IN THE PRESENT, KNOWING THAT THE MAD DOCTOR HAD POSSIBLY ESCAPED FOREVER.

"FROM THEN ON, I POSSESS THE MAKE UP AND SPIRIT OF A GHOST, HENCE MY CURRENT NAME. WHILE I USE MY GIVEN GIFT TO AID THE CAUSE OF GOOD IN THE WORLD, I REMAIN FOREVER HALF A PERSON, NEITHER HERE NOR THERE... COMO UNA ESPECTRA."

BUT PERHAPS YOU CAN FEEL WHOLE KNOWING THAT SOMEWHERE ELSE IN TIME YOU ARE AIDING THE CAUSE OF GOOD IN THE WORLD AS YOU ARE HERE AND NOW.

THANK YOU, PRAVDA.

HEY MA!

THERE'S A WOMEN'S PRISON BREAK IN RANCHO CUCAMONGA.

RELAX AND ENJOY YOUR COFFEE, ESPECTRA. WE'LL HANDLE IT.

DON'T WAIT UP, MA!

54

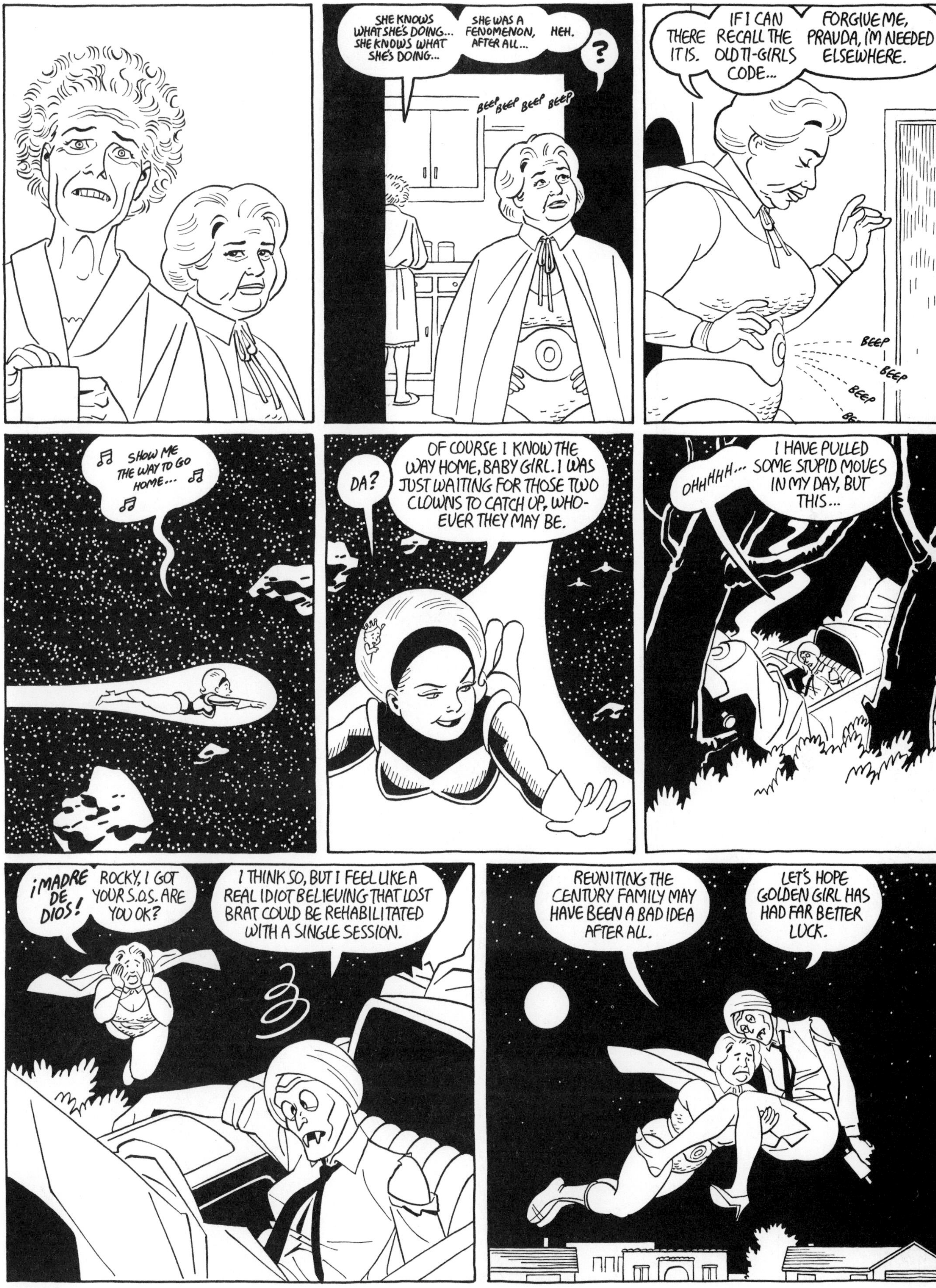
SHE KNOWS WHAT SHE'S DOING... SHE KNOWS WHAT SHE'S DOING...
SHE WAS A FENOMENON, AFTER ALL...
HEH.
?
BEEP BEEP BEEP BEEP
THERE IT IS.
IF I CAN RECALL THE OLD TI-GIRLS CODE...
FORGIVE ME, PRAVDA, I'M NEEDED ELSEWHERE.
BEEP
BEEP
BEEP
SHOW ME THE WAY TO GO HOME...
DA?
OF COURSE I KNOW THE WAY HOME, BABY GIRL. I WAS JUST WAITING FOR THOSE TWO CLOWNS TO CATCH UP, WHO-EVER THEY MAY BE.
OHHHHH... I HAVE PULLED SOME STUPID MOVES IN MY DAY, BUT THIS...
¡MADRE DE DIOS!
ROCKY, I GOT YOUR S.O.S. ARE YOU OK?
I THINK SO, BUT I FEEL LIKE A REAL IDIOT BELIEVING THAT LOST BRAT COULD BE REHABILITATED WITH A SINGLE SESSION.
REUNITING THE CENTURY FAMILY MAY HAVE BEEN A BAD IDEA AFTER ALL.
LET'S HOPE GOLDEN GIRL HAS HAD FAR BETTER LUCK.

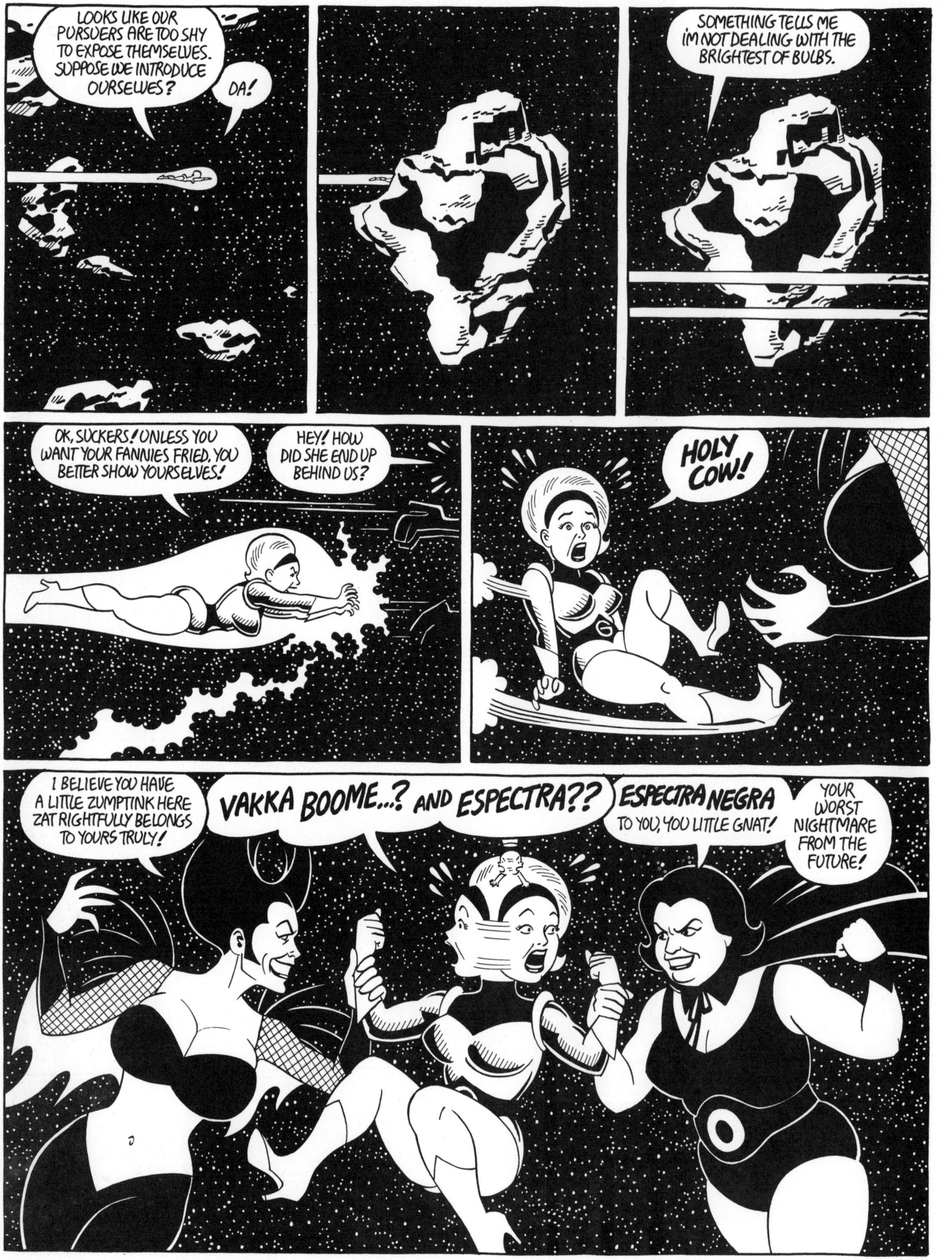

LOOKS LIKE OUR PURSUERS ARE TOO SHY TO EXPOSE THEMSELVES. SUPPOSE WE INTRODUCE OURSELVES?
DA!
SOMETHING TELLS ME I'M NOT DEALING WITH THE BRIGHTEST OF BULBS.
OK, SUCKERS! UNLESS YOU WANT YOUR FANNIES FRIED, YOU BETTER SHOW YOURSELVES!
HEY! HOW DID SHE END UP BEHIND US?
HOLY COW!
I BELIEVE YOU HAVE A LITTLE ZUMPTINK HERE ZAT RIGHTFULLY BELONGS TO YOURS TRULY!
VAKKA BOOME...? AND ESPECTRA??
ESPECTRA NEGRA TO YOU, YOU LITTLE GNAT!
YOUR WORST NIGHTMARE FROM THE FUTURE!

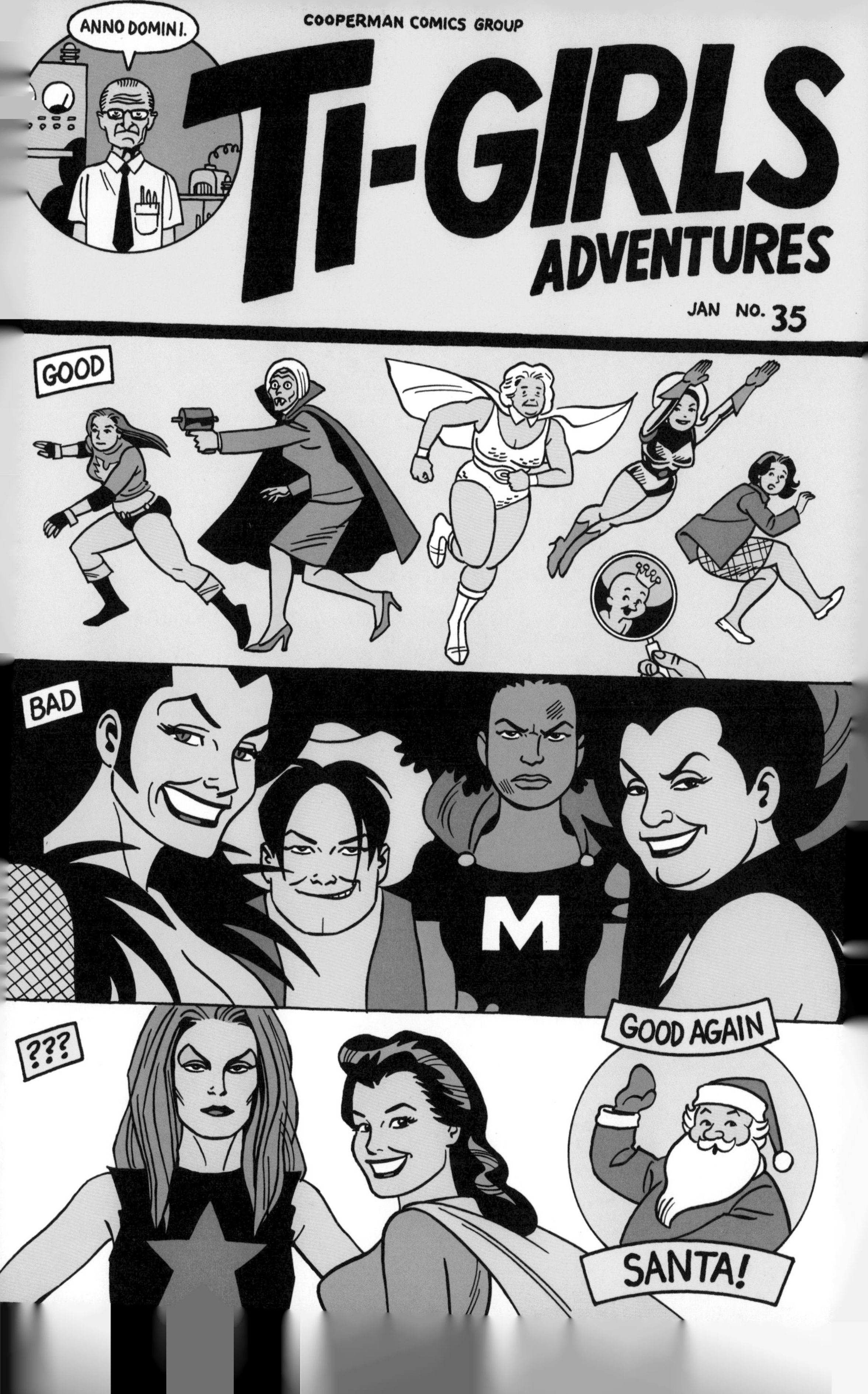
ANNO DOMINI.
COOPERMAN COMICS GROUP
TI-GIRLS
ADVENTURES
JAN NO. 35
GOOD
BAD
M
???
GOOD AGAIN
SANTA!

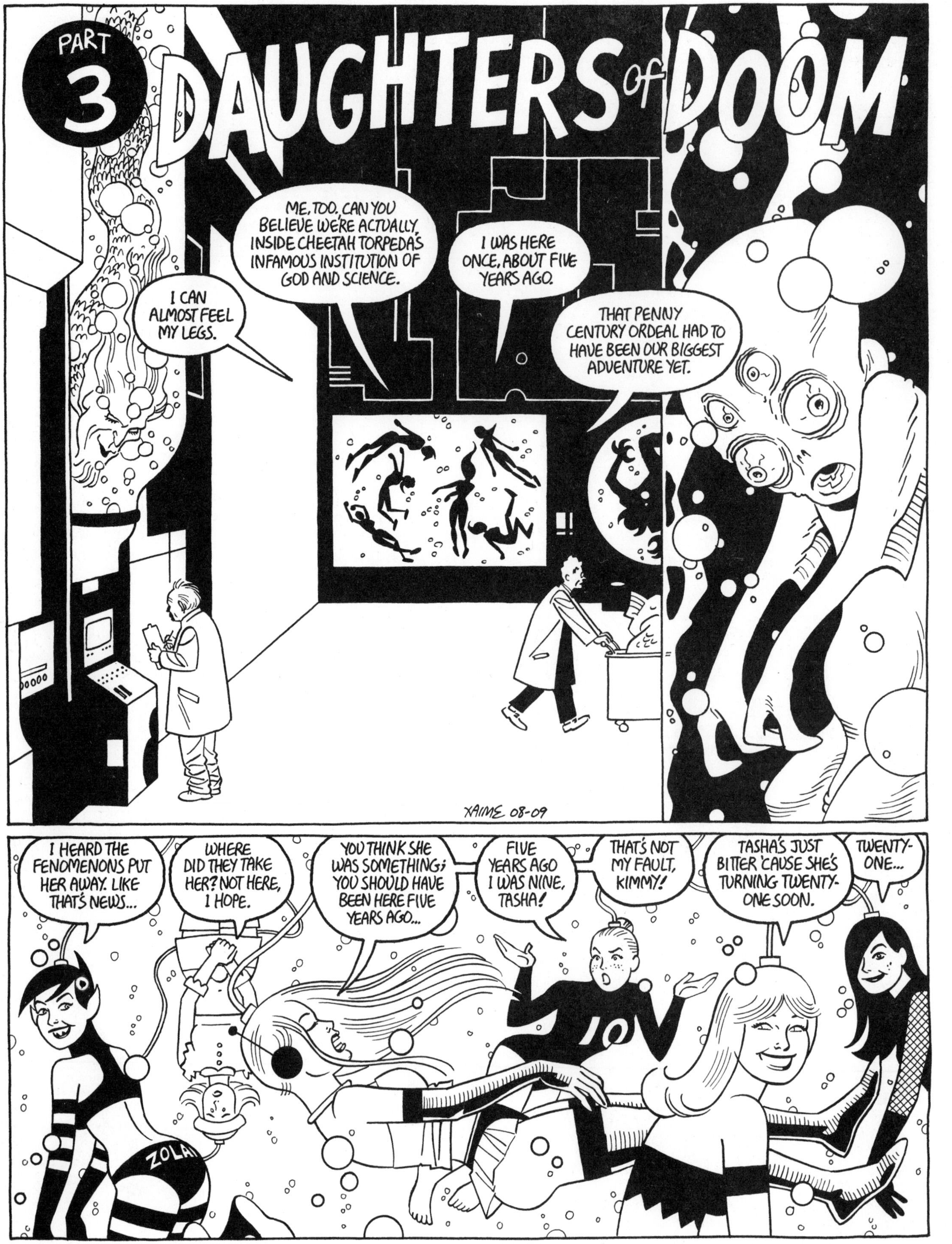
PART 3
DAUGHTERS of DOOM
I CAN ALMOST FEEL MY LEGS.
ME, TOO. CAN YOU BELIEVE WE'RE ACTUALLY INSIDE CHEETAH TORPEDA'S INFAMOUS INSTITUTION OF GOD AND SCIENCE.
I WAS HERE ONCE, ABOUT FIVE YEARS AGO.
THAT PENNY CENTURY ORDEAL HAD TO HAVE BEEN OUR BIGGEST ADVENTURE YET.
XAIME 08-09
I HEARD THE FENOMENONS PUT HER AWAY. LIKE THAT'S NEWS...
WHERE DID THEY TAKE HER? NOT HERE, I HOPE.
YOU THINK SHE WAS SOMETHING; YOU SHOULD HAVE BEEN HERE FIVE YEARS AGO...
FIVE YEARS AGO I WAS NINE, TASHA!
THAT'S NOT MY FAULT, KIMMY!
TASHA'S JUST BITTER 'CAUSE SHE'S TURNING TWENTY-ONE SOON.
TWENTY-ONE...
10
ZOLA

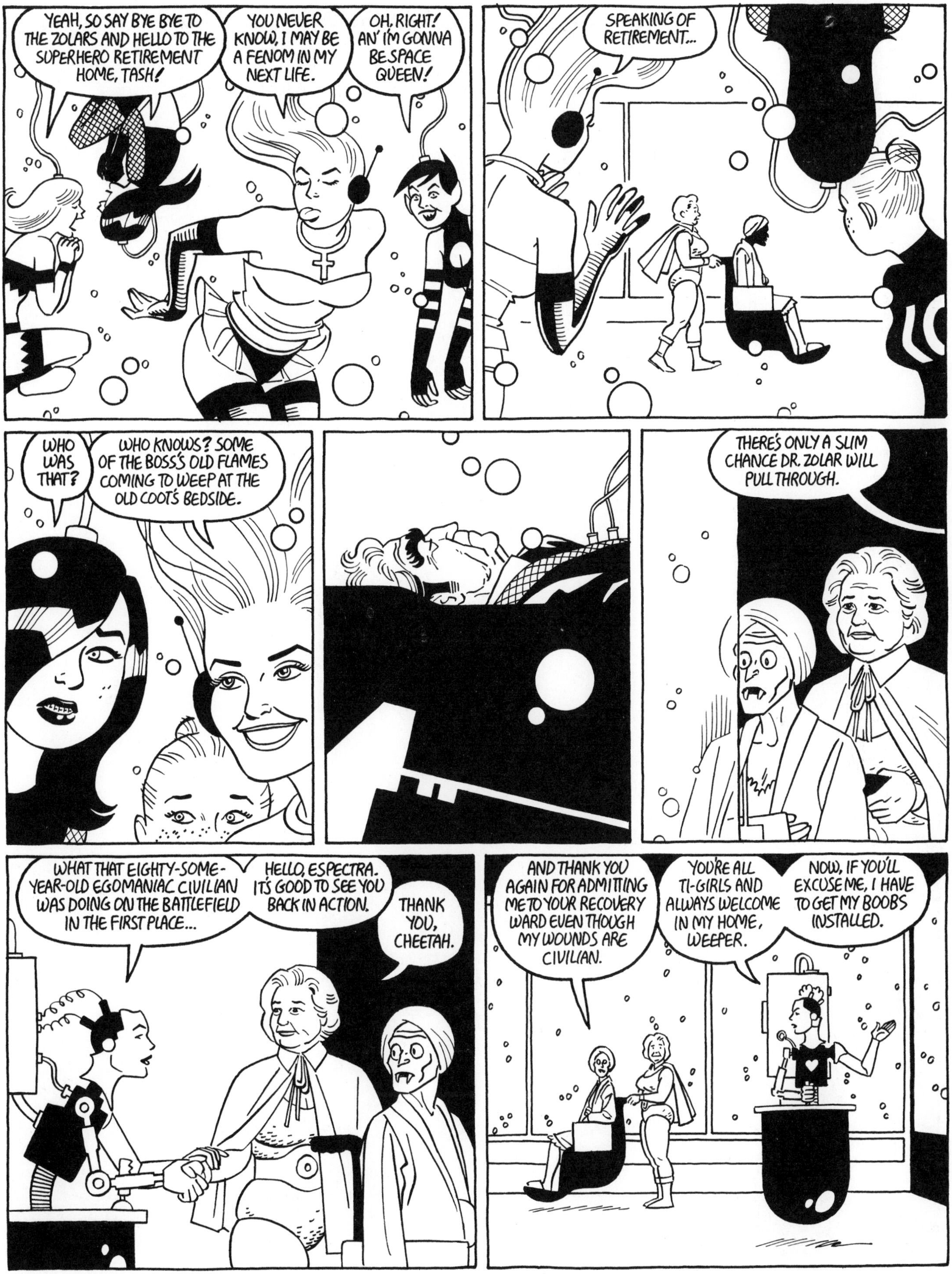
YEAH, SO SAY BYE BYE TO THE ZOLARS AND HELLO TO THE SUPERHERO RETIREMENT HOME, TASH!
YOU NEVER KNOW, I MAY BE A FENOM IN MY NEXT LIFE.
OH, RIGHT! AN' I'M GONNA BE SPACE QUEEN!
SPEAKING OF RETIREMENT...
WHO WAS THAT?
WHO KNOWS? SOME OF THE BOSS'S OLD FLAMES COMING TO WEEP AT THE OLD COOT'S BEDSIDE.
THERE'S ONLY A SLIM CHANCE DR. ZOLAR WILL PULL THROUGH.
WHAT THAT EIGHTY-SOME-YEAR-OLD EGOMANIAC CIVILIAN WAS DOING ON THE BATTLEFIELD IN THE FIRST PLACE...
HELLO, ESPECTRA. IT'S GOOD TO SEE YOU BACK IN ACTION.
THANK YOU, CHEETAH.
AND THANK YOU AGAIN FOR ADMITTING ME TO YOUR RECOVERY WARD EVEN THOUGH MY WOUNDS ARE CIVILIAN.
YOU'RE ALL TI-GIRLS AND ALWAYS WELCOME IN MY HOME, WEEPER.
NOW, IF YOU'LL EXCUSE ME, I HAVE TO GET MY BOOBS INSTALLED.

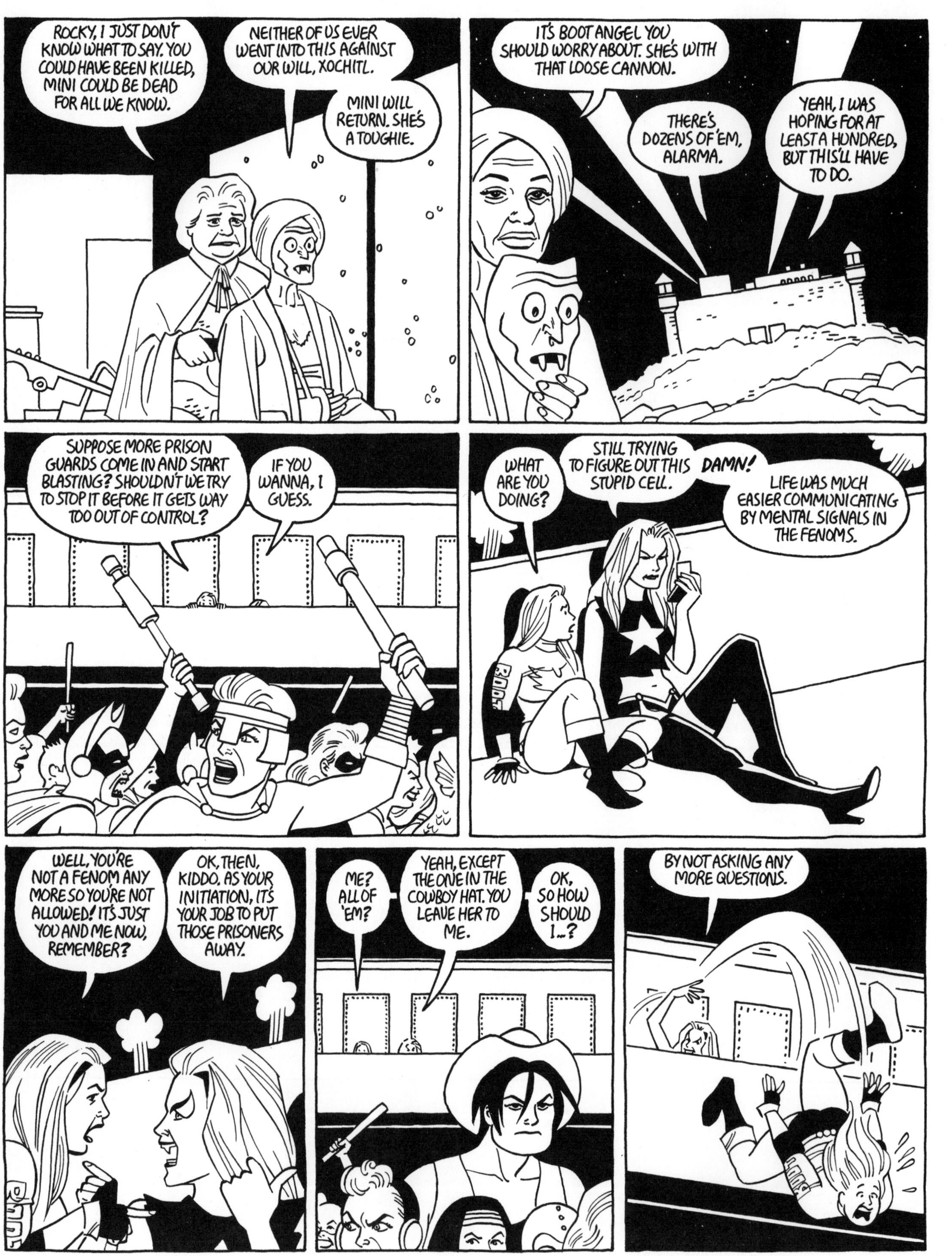
ROCKY, I JUST DON'T KNOW WHAT TO SAY. YOU COULD HAVE BEEN KILLED, MINI COULD BE DEAD FOR ALL WE KNOW.
NEITHER OF US EVER WENT INTO THIS AGAINST OUR WILL, XOCHITL.
MINI WILL RETURN. SHE'S A TOUGHIE.
IT'S BOOT ANGEL YOU SHOULD WORRY ABOUT. SHE'S WITH THAT LOOSE CANNON.
THERE'S DOZENS OF 'EM, ALARMA.
YEAH, I WAS HOPING FOR AT LEAST A HUNDRED, BUT THIS'LL HAVE TO DO.
SUPPOSE MORE PRISON GUARDS COME IN AND START BLASTING? SHOULDN'T WE TRY TO STOP IT BEFORE IT GETS WAY TOO OUT OF CONTROL?
IF YOU WANNA, I GUESS.
WHAT ARE YOU DOING?
STILL TRYING TO FIGURE OUT THIS STUPID CELL.
DAMN!
LIFE WAS MUCH EASIER COMMUNICATING BY MENTAL SIGNALS IN THE FENOMS.
WELL, YOU'RE NOT A FENOM ANY MORE SO YOU'RE NOT ALLOWED! IT'S JUST YOU AND ME NOW, REMEMBER?
OK, THEN, KIDDO. AS YOUR INITIATION, IT'S YOUR JOB TO PUT THOSE PRISONERS AWAY.
ME? ALL OF 'EM?
YEAH, EXCEPT THE ONE IN THE COWBOY HAT. YOU LEAVE HER TO ME.
OK, SO HOW SHOULD I...?
BY NOT ASKING ANY MORE QUESTIONS.

WHOOP!
SORRY.
SORRY.
OK, GIRLS! BACK TO YOUR CELLS!
SORRY.
R!
OW!
CLIP ME FROM BEHIND, WILL YA?
ANGEL.
ANGEL!
WHAT?
WHAT?
WHAT ABOUT THE REST OF'EM?
HUH?
OH, RIGHT! I'M ON IT!
OK, YOU GUYS AREN'T COOPERATING SO I'M JUST GONNA HAVE TO...
WHOA!
UCH!
SIGH...
HEY, ATCH T!
ET OFF Y HEAD!

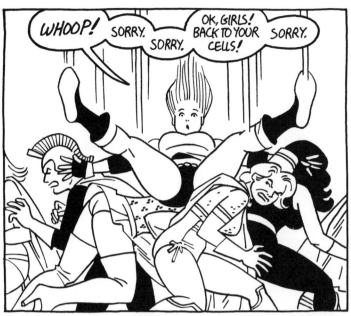

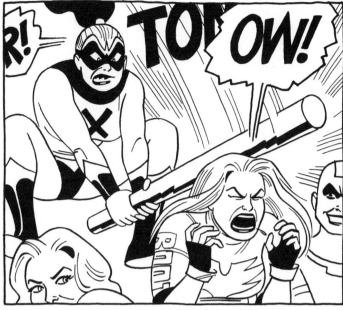

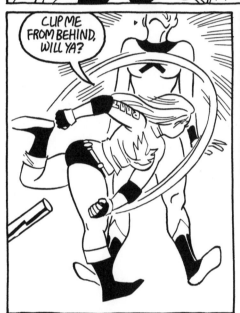

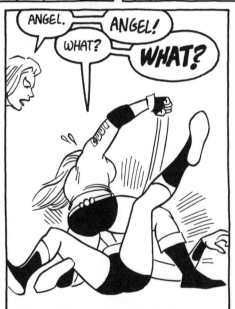

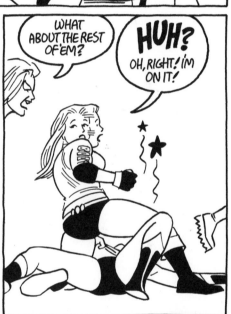

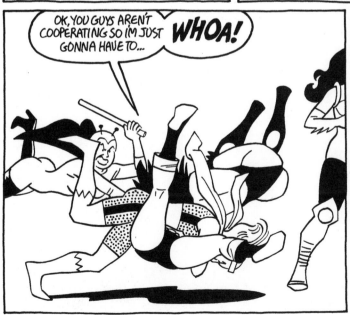

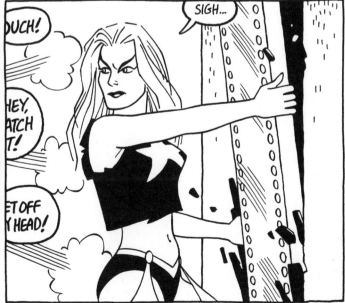

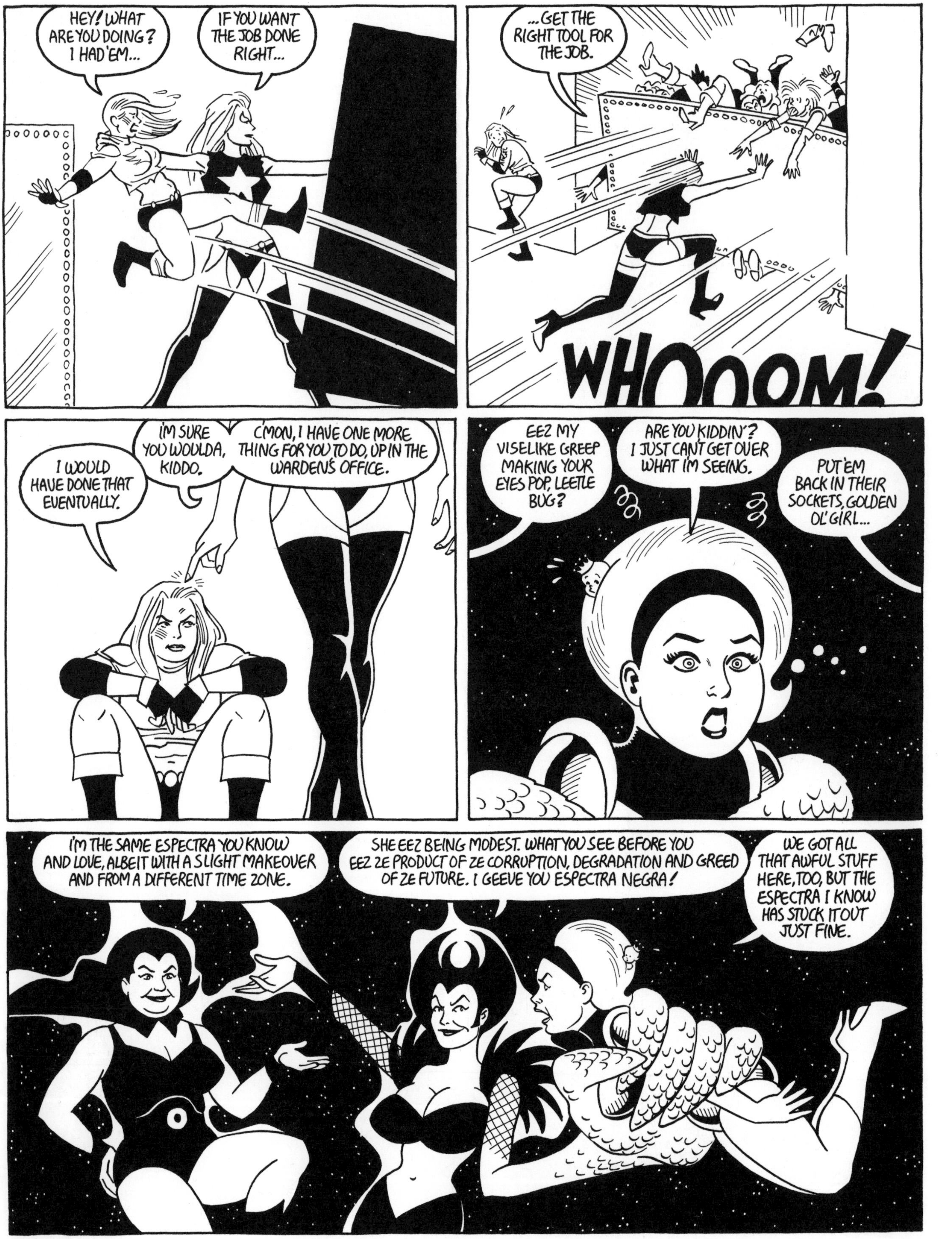
HEY! WHAT ARE YOU DOING? I HAD'EM...
IF YOU WANT THE JOB DONE RIGHT...
...GET THE RIGHT TOOL FOR THE JOB.
WHOOOM!
I WOULD HAVE DONE THAT EVENTUALLY.
I'M SURE YOU WOULDA, KIDDO.
C'MON, I HAVE ONE MORE THING FOR YOU TO DO, UP IN THE WARDEN'S OFFICE.
EEZ MY VISELIKE GREEP MAKING YOUR EYES POP, LEETLE BUG?
ARE YOU KIDDIN'? I JUST CAN'T GET OVER WHAT I'M SEEING.
PUT'EM BACK IN THEIR SOCKETS, GOLDEN OL'GIRL...
I'M THE SAME ESPECTRA YOU KNOW AND LOVE, ALBEIT WITH A SLIGHT MAKEOVER AND FROM A DIFFERENT TIME ZONE.
SHE EEZ BEING MODEST. WHAT YOU SEE BEFORE YOU EEZ ZE PRODUCT OF ZE CORRUPTION, DEGRADATION AND GREED OF ZE FUTURE. I GEEVE YOU ESPECTRA NEGRA!
WE GOT ALL THAT AWFUL STUFF HERE, TOO, BUT THE ESPECTRA I KNOW HAS STUCK IT OUT JUST FINE.

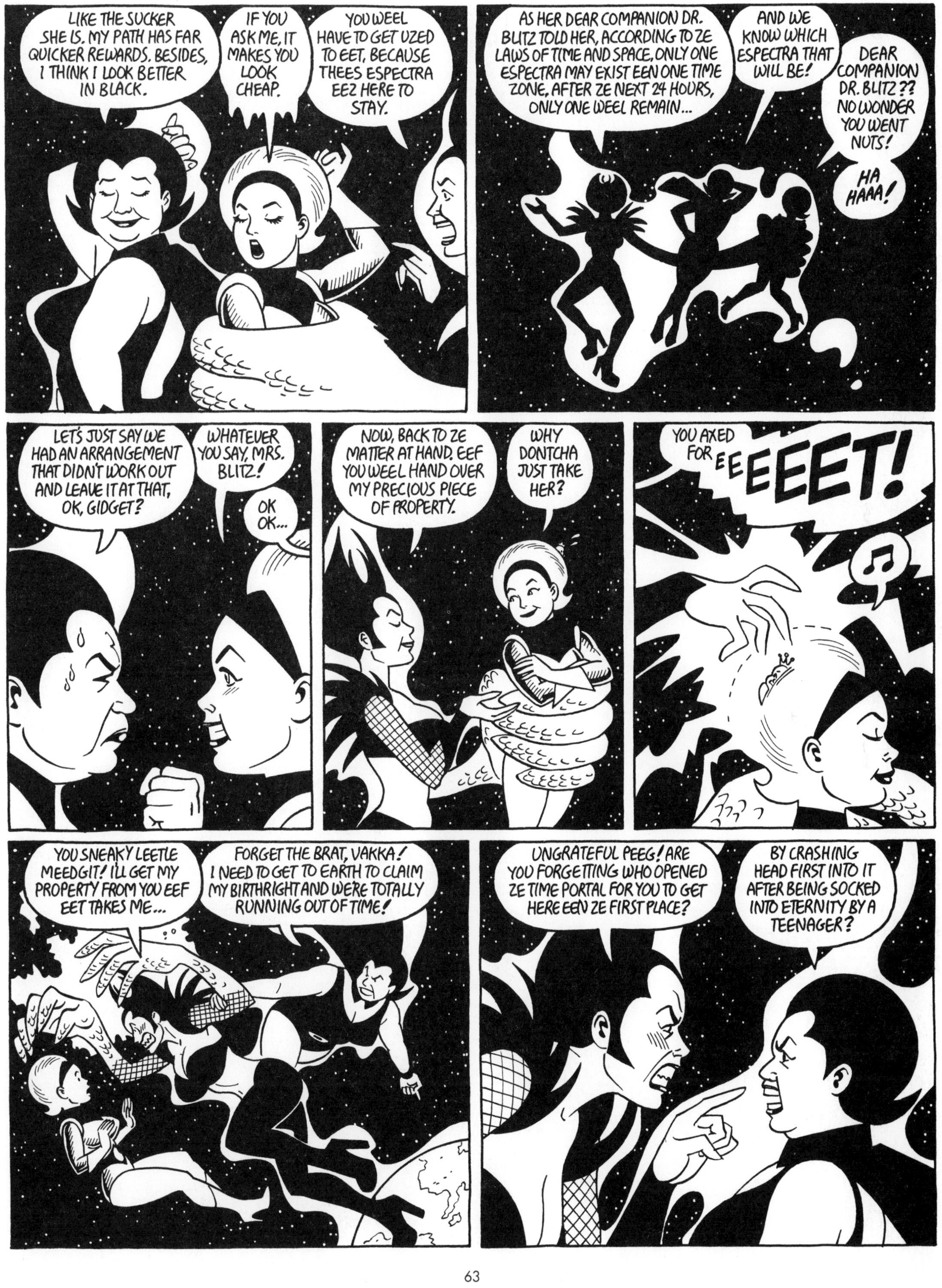
LIKE THE SUCKER SHE IS. MY PATH HAS FAR QUICKER REWARDS. BESIDES, I THINK I LOOK BETTER IN BLACK.
IF YOU ASK ME, IT MAKES YOU LOOK CHEAP.
YOU WEEL HAVE TO GET UZED TO EET, BECAUSE THEES ESPECTRA EEZ HERE TO STAY.
AS HER DEAR COMPANION DR. BLITZ TOLD HER, ACCORDING TO ZE LAWS OF TIME AND SPACE, ONLY ONE ESPECTRA MAY EXIST EEN ONE TIME ZONE. AFTER ZE NEXT 24 HOURS, ONLY ONE WEEL REMAIN...
AND WE KNOW WHICH ESPECTRA THAT WILL BE!
DEAR COMPANION DR. BLITZ?? NO WONDER YOU WENT NUTS!
HA HAAA!
LET'S JUST SAY WE HAD AN ARRANGEMENT THAT DIDN'T WORK OUT AND LEAVE IT AT THAT, OK, GIDGET?
WHATEVER YOU SAY, MRS. BLITZ!
OK OK...
NOW, BACK TO ZE MATTER AT HAND. EEF YOU WEEL HAND OVER MY PRECIOUS PIECE OF PROPERTY.
WHY DONTCHA JUST TAKE HER?
YOU AXED FOR
EEEEET!
YOU SNEAKY LEETLE MEEDGIT! I'LL GET MY PROPERTY FROM YOU EEF EET TAKES ME...
FORGET THE BRAT, VAKKA! I NEED TO GET TO EARTH TO CLAIM MY BIRTHRIGHT AND WE'RE TOTALLY RUNNING OUT OF TIME!
UNGRATEFUL PEEG! ARE YOU FORGETTING WHO OPENED ZE TIME PORTAL FOR YOU TO GET HERE EEN ZE FIRST PLACE?
BY CRASHING HEAD FIRST INTO IT AFTER BEING SOCKED INTO ETERNITY BY A TEENAGER?

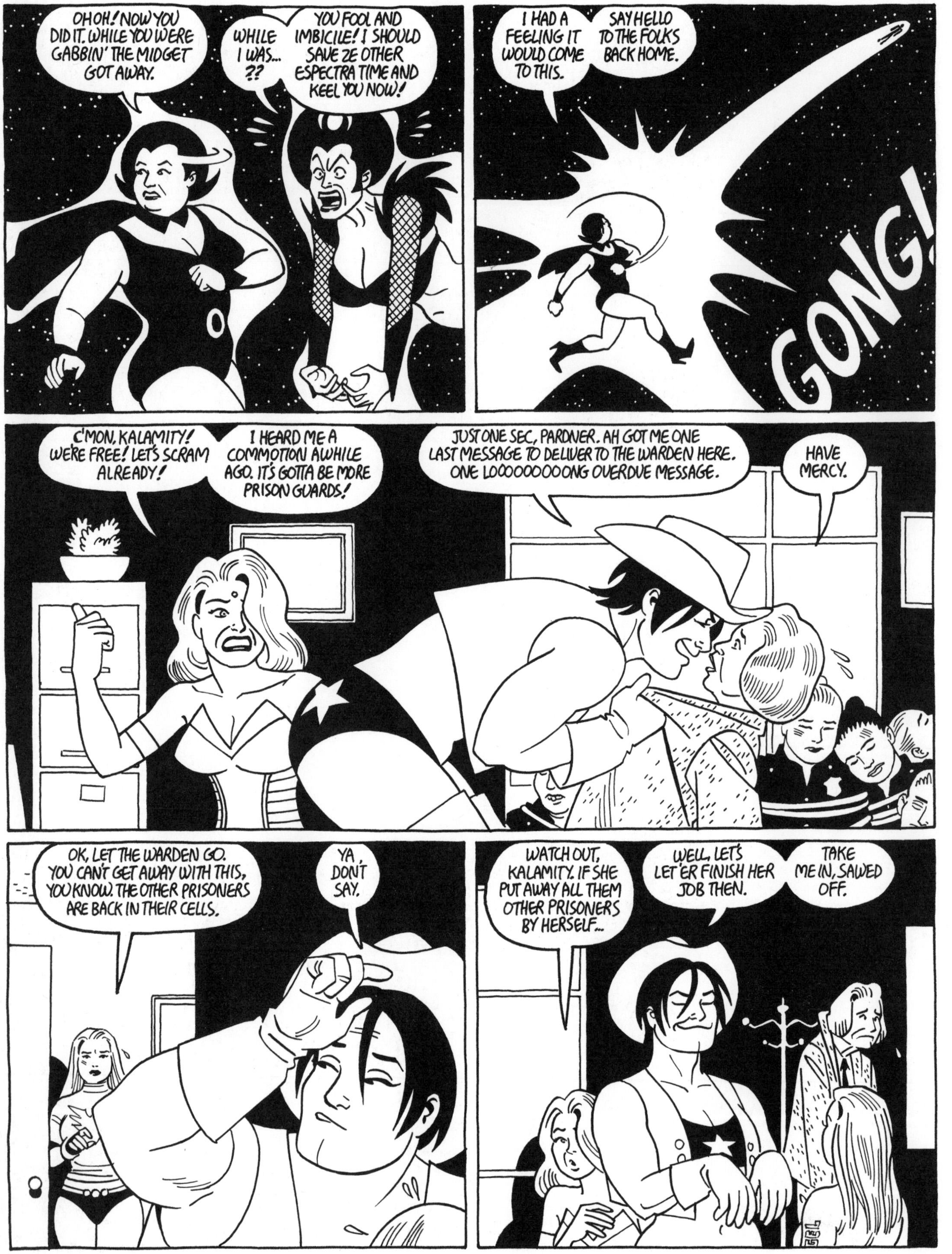
OH OH! NOW YOU DID IT. WHILE YOU WERE GABBIN' THE MIDGET GOT AWAY.
WHILE I WAS... ??
YOU FOOL AND IMBICILE! I SHOULD SAVE ZE OTHER ESPECTRA TIME AND KEEL YOU NOW!
I HAD A FEELING IT WOULD COME TO THIS.
SAY HELLO TO THE FOLKS BACK HOME.
GONG!
C'MON, KALAMITY! WE'RE FREE! LET'S SCRAM ALREADY!
I HEARD ME A COMMOTION AWHILE AGO. IT'S GOTTA BE MORE PRISON GUARDS!
JUST ONE SEC, PARDNER. AH GOT ME ONE LAST MESSAGE TO DELIVER TO THE WARDEN HERE. ONE LOOOOOOOOONG OVERDUE MESSAGE.
HAVE MERCY.
OK, LET THE WARDEN GO. YOU CAN'T GET AWAY WITH THIS, YOU KNOW. THE OTHER PRISONERS ARE BACK IN THEIR CELLS.
YA, DON'T SAY.
WATCH OUT, KALAMITY. IF SHE PUT AWAY ALL THEM OTHER PRISONERS BY HERSELF...
WELL, LET'S LET'ER FINISH HER JOB THEN.
TAKE ME IN, SAWED OFF.

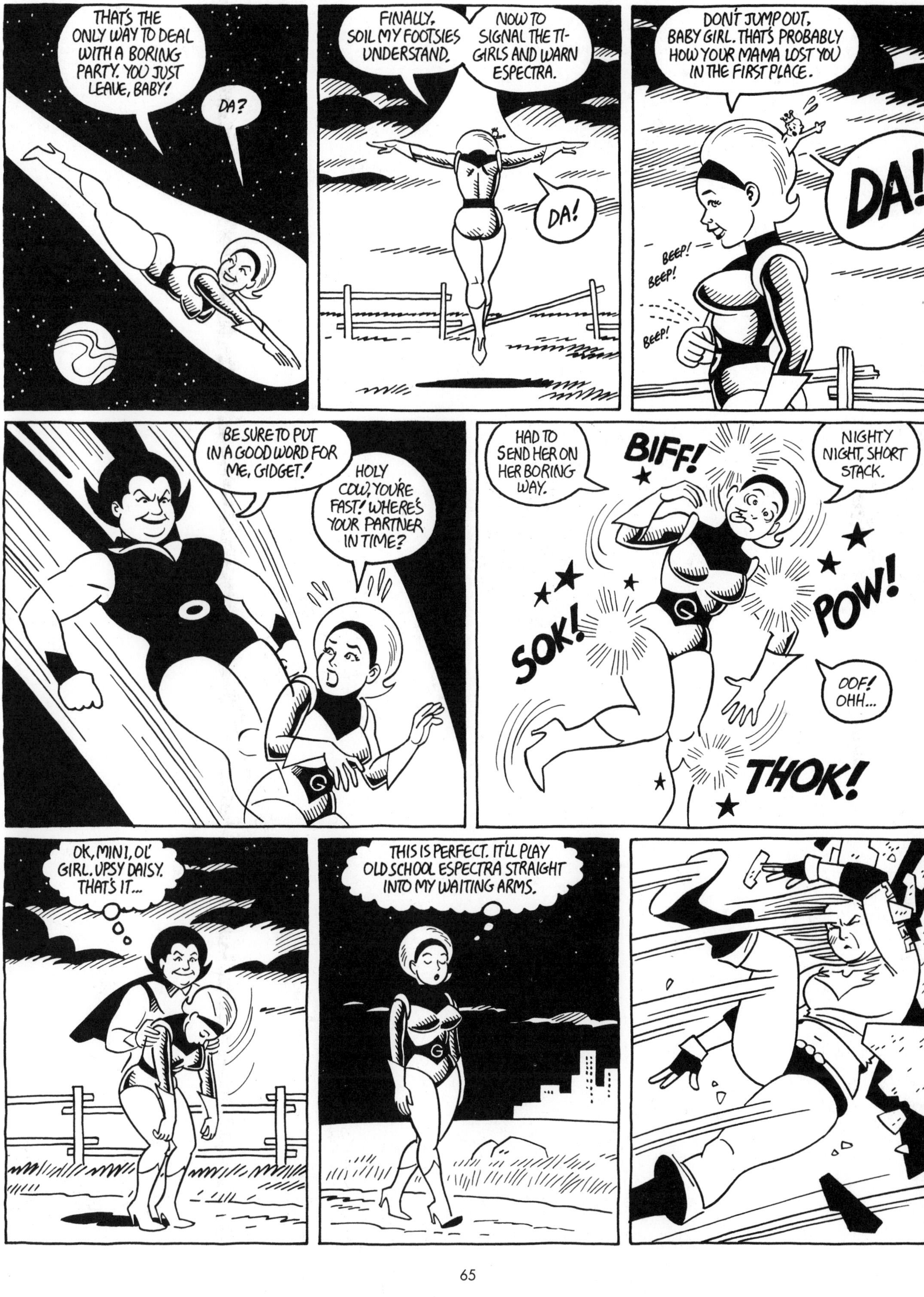
THAT'S THE ONLY WAY TO DEAL WITH A BORING PARTY. YOU JUST LEAVE, BABY!
DA?
FINALLY. SOIL MY FOOTSIES UNDERSTAND.
NOW TO SIGNAL THE TI-GIRLS AND WARN ESPECTRA.
DA!
DON'T JUMP OUT, BABY GIRL. THAT'S PROBABLY HOW YOUR MAMA LOST YOU IN THE FIRST PLACE.
DA!
BEEP!
BEEP!
BEEP!
BE SURE TO PUT IN A GOOD WORD FOR ME, GIDGET!
HOLY COW, YOU'RE FAST! WHERE'S YOUR PARTNER IN TIME?
HAD TO SEND HER ON HER BORING WAY.
BIFF!
NIGHTY NIGHT, SHORT STACK.
SOK!
POW!
OOF! OHH...
THOK!
OK, MINI, OL' GIRL. UPSY DAISY. THAT'S IT...
THIS IS PERFECT. IT'LL PLAY OLD SCHOOL ESPECTRA STRAIGHT INTO MY WAITING ARMS.

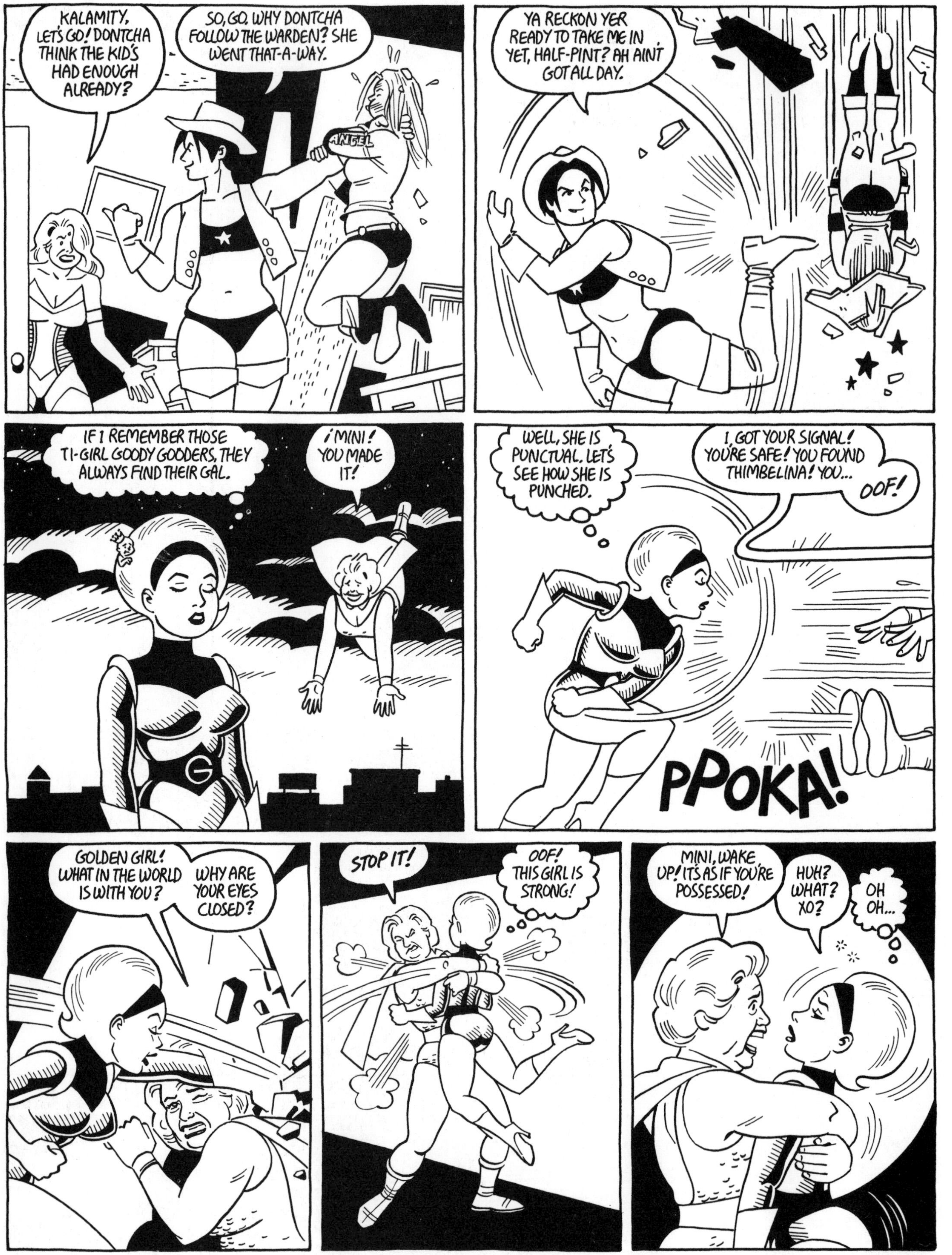
KALAMITY, LET'S GO! DONTCHA THINK THE KID'S HAD ENOUGH ALREADY?
SO, GO. WHY DONTCHA FOLLOW THE WARDEN? SHE WENT THAT-A-WAY.
ANGEL
YA RECKON YER READY TO TAKE ME IN YET, HALF-PINT? AH AIN'T GOT ALL DAY.
IF I REMEMBER THOSE TI-GIRL GOODY GOODERS, THEY ALWAYS FIND THEIR GAL.
¡MINI! YOU MADE IT!
WELL, SHE IS PUNCTUAL. LET'S SEE HOW SHE IS PUNCHED.
I, GOT YOUR SIGNAL! YOU'RE SAFE! YOU FOUND THIMBELINA! YOU...
OOF!
PPOKA!
GOLDEN GIRL! WHAT IN THE WORLD IS WITH YOU?
WHY ARE YOUR EYES CLOSED?
STOP IT!
OOF! THIS GIRL IS STRONG!
MINI, WAKE UP! IT'S AS IF YOU'RE POSSESSED!
HUH? WHAT? XO?
OH OH...

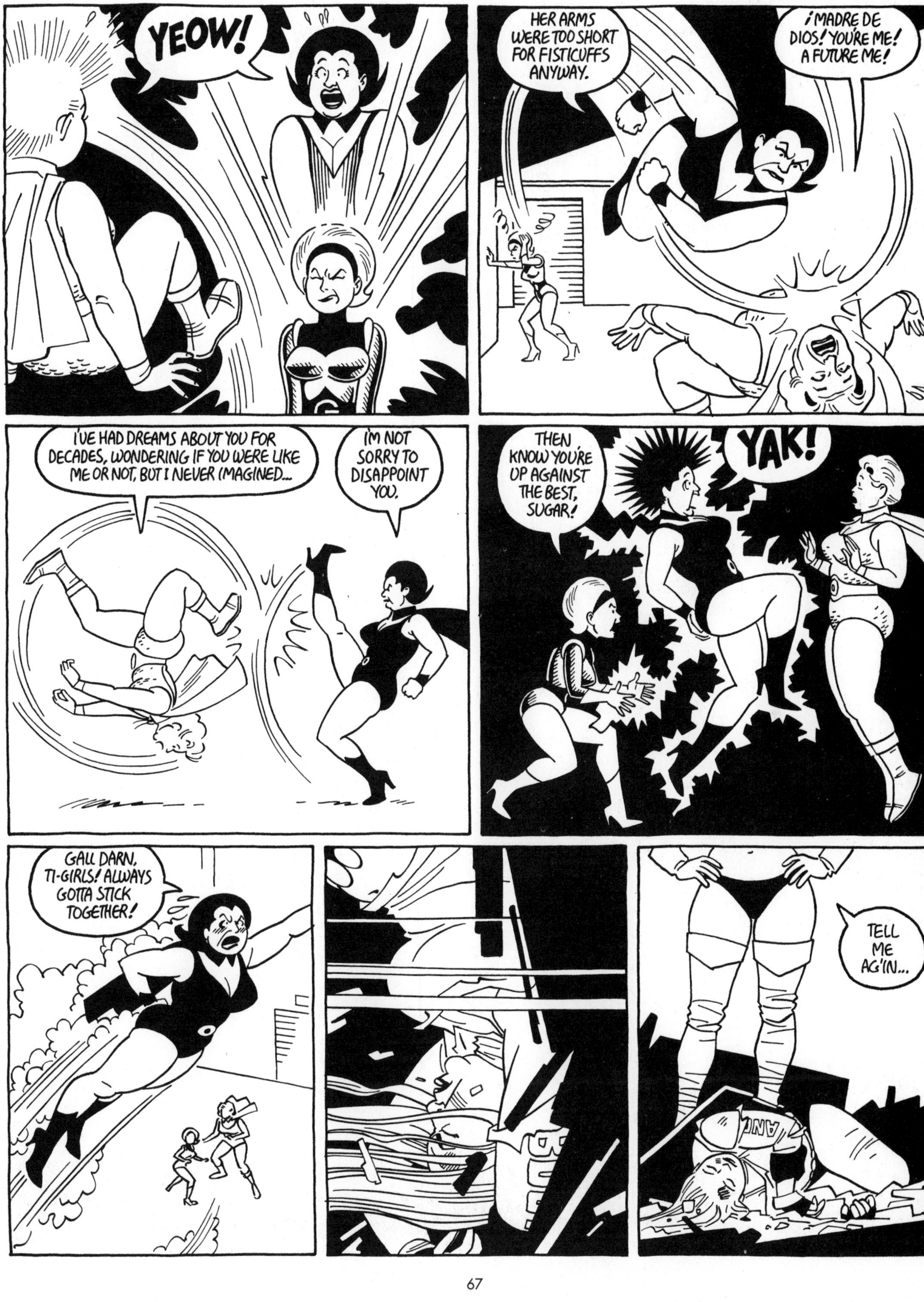
YEOW!
HER ARMS WERE TOO SHORT FOR FISTICUFFS ANYWAY.
¡MADRE DE DIOS! YOU'RE ME! A FUTURE ME!
I'VE HAD DREAMS ABOUT YOU FOR DECADES, WONDERING IF YOU WERE LIKE ME OR NOT, BUT I NEVER IMAGINED...
I'M NOT SORRY TO DISAPPOINT YOU.
THEN KNOW YOU'RE UP AGAINST THE BEST, SUGAR!
YAK!
GALL DARN, TI-GIRLS! ALWAYS GOTTA STICK TOGETHER!
TELL ME AG'IN...

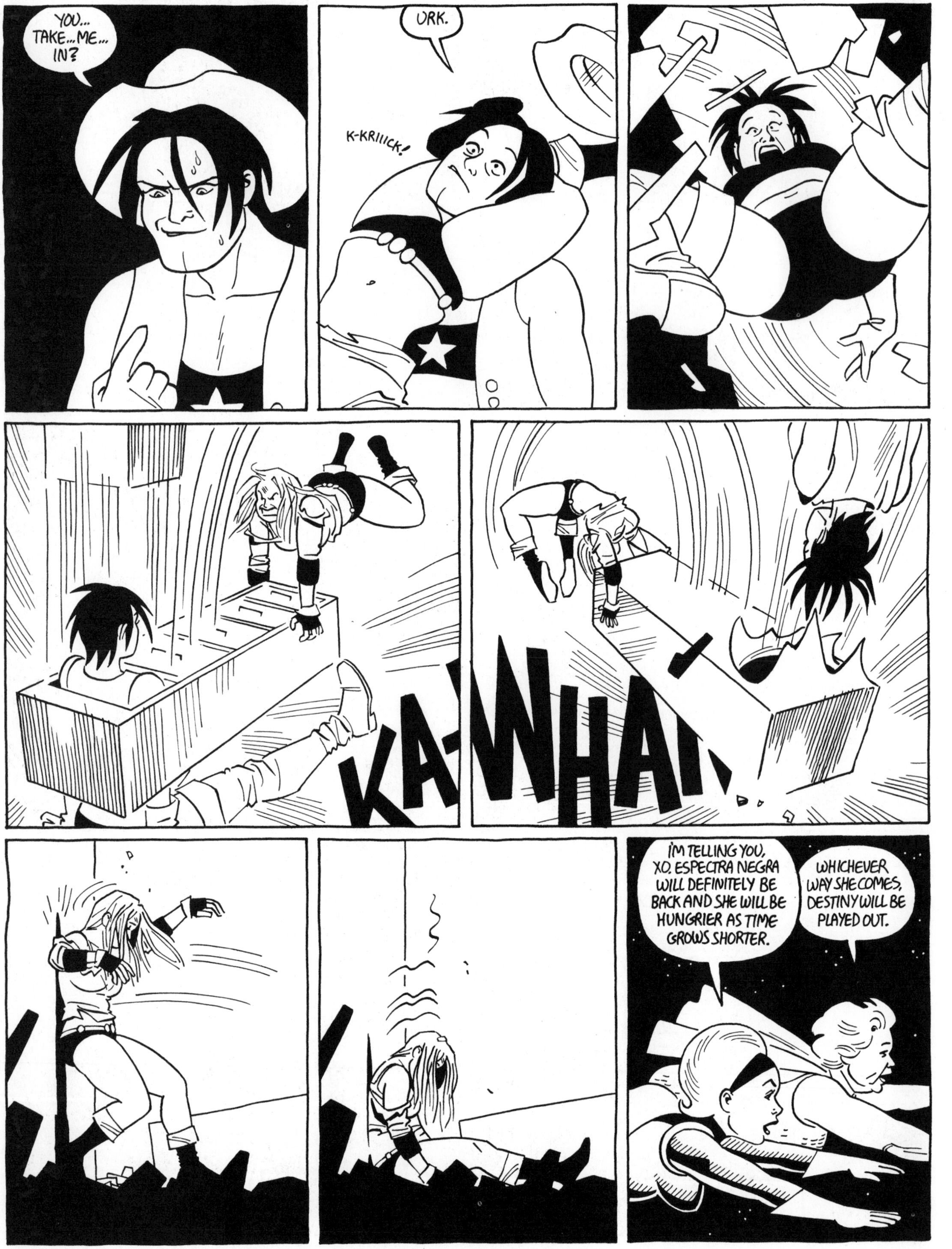

YOU... TAKE...ME... IN?
URK.
K-KRIIICK!
KA-WHA!
I'M TELLING YOU, XO, ESPECTRA NEGRA WILL DEFINITELY BE BACK AND SHE WILL BE HUNGRIER AS TIME GROWS SHORTER.
WHICHEVER WAY SHE COMES, DESTINY WILL BE PLAYED OUT.

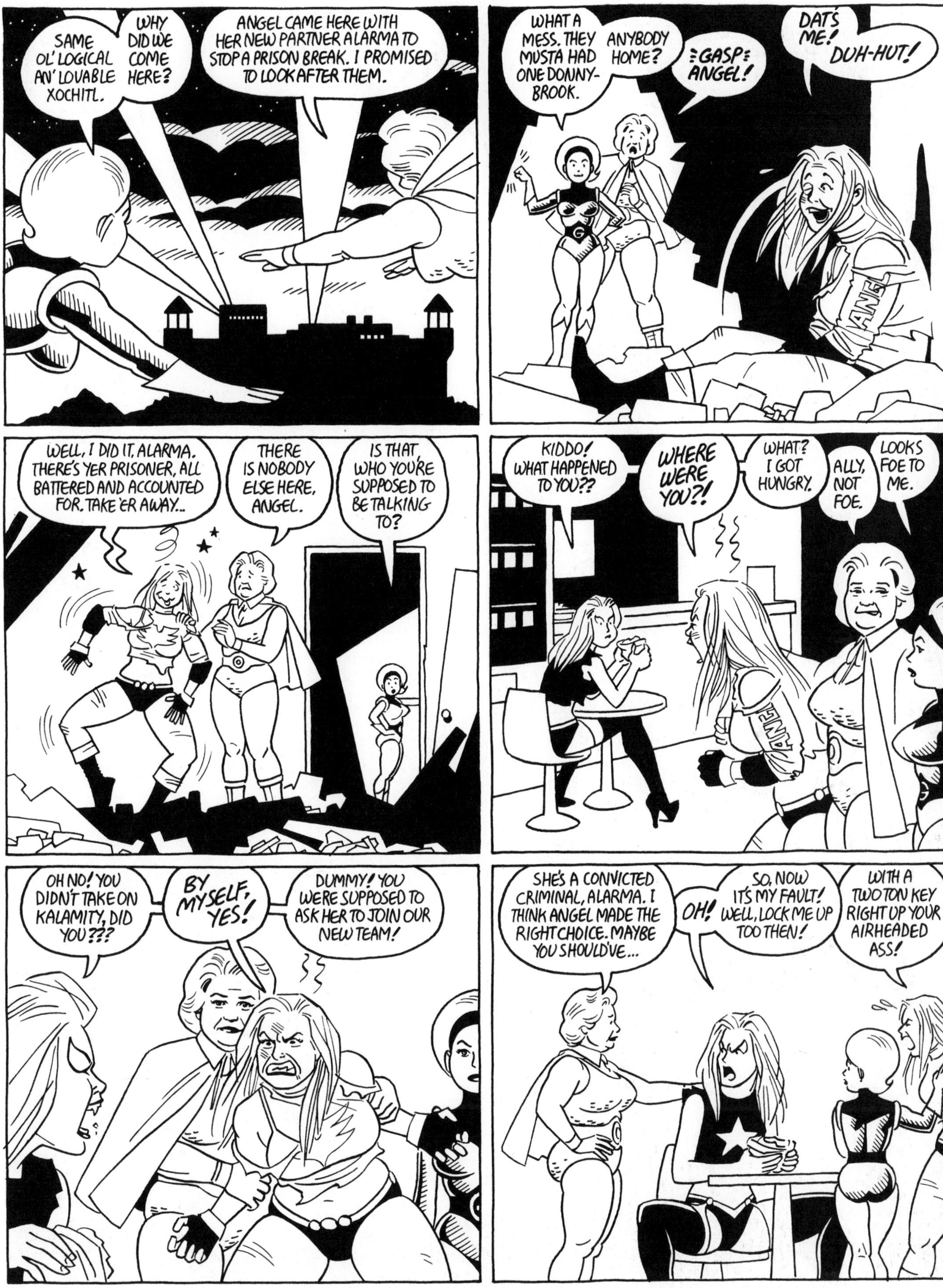
SAME OL' LOGICAL AN' LOVABLE XOCHITL.
WHY DID WE COME HERE?
ANGEL CAME HERE WITH HER NEW PARTNER ALARMA TO STOP A PRISON BREAK. I PROMISED TO LOOK AFTER THEM.
WHAT A MESS. THEY MUSTA HAD ONE DONNY-BROOK.
ANYBODY HOME?
GASP ANGEL!
DAT'S ME! DUH-HUT!
WELL, I DID IT, ALARMA. THERE'S YER PRISONER, ALL BATTERED AND ACCOUNTED FOR. TAKE 'ER AWAY...
THERE IS NOBODY ELSE HERE, ANGEL.
IS THAT WHO YOU'RE SUPPOSED TO BE TALKING TO?
KIDDO! WHAT HAPPENED TO YOU??
WHERE WERE YOU?!
WHAT? I GOT HUNGRY.
ALLY, NOT FOE.
LOOKS FOE TO ME.
OH NO! YOU DIDN'T TAKE ON KALAMITY, DID YOU???
BY MYSELF, YES!
DUMMY! YOU WERE SUPPOSED TO ASK HER TO JOIN OUR NEW TEAM!
SHE'S A CONVICTED CRIMINAL, ALARMA. I THINK ANGEL MADE THE RIGHT CHOICE. MAYBE YOU SHOULD'VE...
OH!
SO, NOW IT'S MY FAULT! WELL, LOCK ME UP TOO THEN!
WITH A TWO TON KEY RIGHT UP YOUR AIRHEADED ASS!

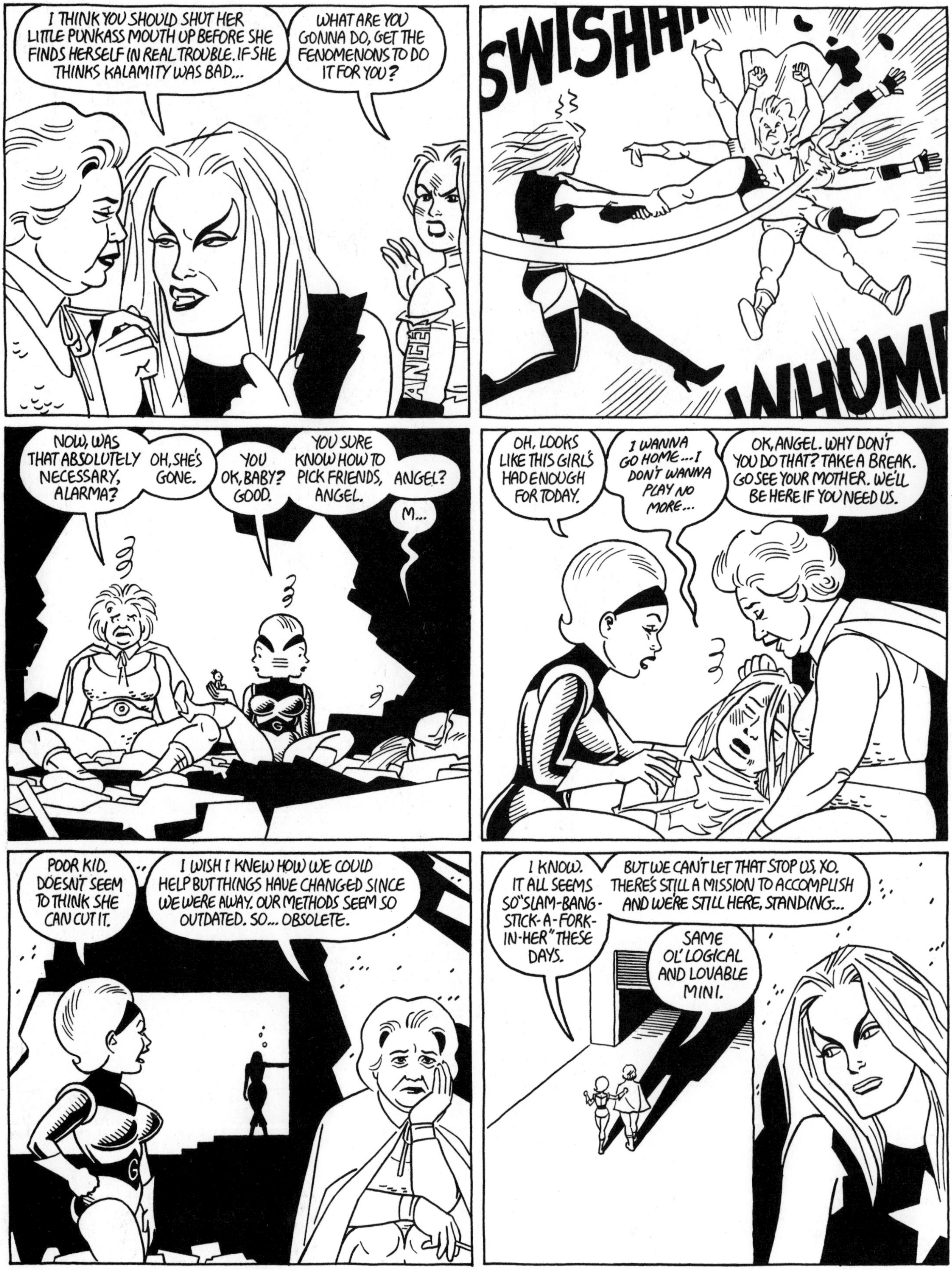
I THINK YOU SHOULD SHUT HER LITTLE PUNKASS MOUTH UP BEFORE SHE FINDS HERSELF IN REAL TROUBLE. IF SHE THINKS KALAMITY WAS BAD...
WHAT ARE YOU GONNA DO, GET THE FENOMENONS TO DO IT FOR YOU?
ANGEL
SWISHHH
WHUMP
NOW, WAS THAT ABSOLUTELY NECESSARY, ALARMA?
OH, SHE'S GONE.
YOU OK, BABY? GOOD.
YOU SURE KNOW HOW TO PICK FRIENDS, ANGEL.
ANGEL?
M...
OH, LOOKS LIKE THIS GIRL'S HAD ENOUGH FOR TODAY.
I WANNA GO HOME... I DON'T WANNA PLAY NO MORE...
OK, ANGEL. WHY DON'T YOU DO THAT? TAKE A BREAK. GO SEE YOUR MOTHER. WE'LL BE HERE IF YOU NEED US.
POOR KID. DOESN'T SEEM TO THINK SHE CAN CUT IT.
I WISH I KNEW HOW WE COULD HELP BUT THINGS HAVE CHANGED SINCE WE WERE AWAY. OUR METHODS SEEM SO OUTDATED. SO... OBSOLETE.
I KNOW. IT ALL SEEMS SO "SLAM-BANG-STICK-A-FORK-IN-HER" THESE DAYS.
BUT WE CAN'T LET THAT STOP US, XO. THERE'S STILL A MISSION TO ACCOMPLISH AND WE'RE STILL HERE, STANDING...
SAME OL' LOGICAL AND LOVABLE MINI.

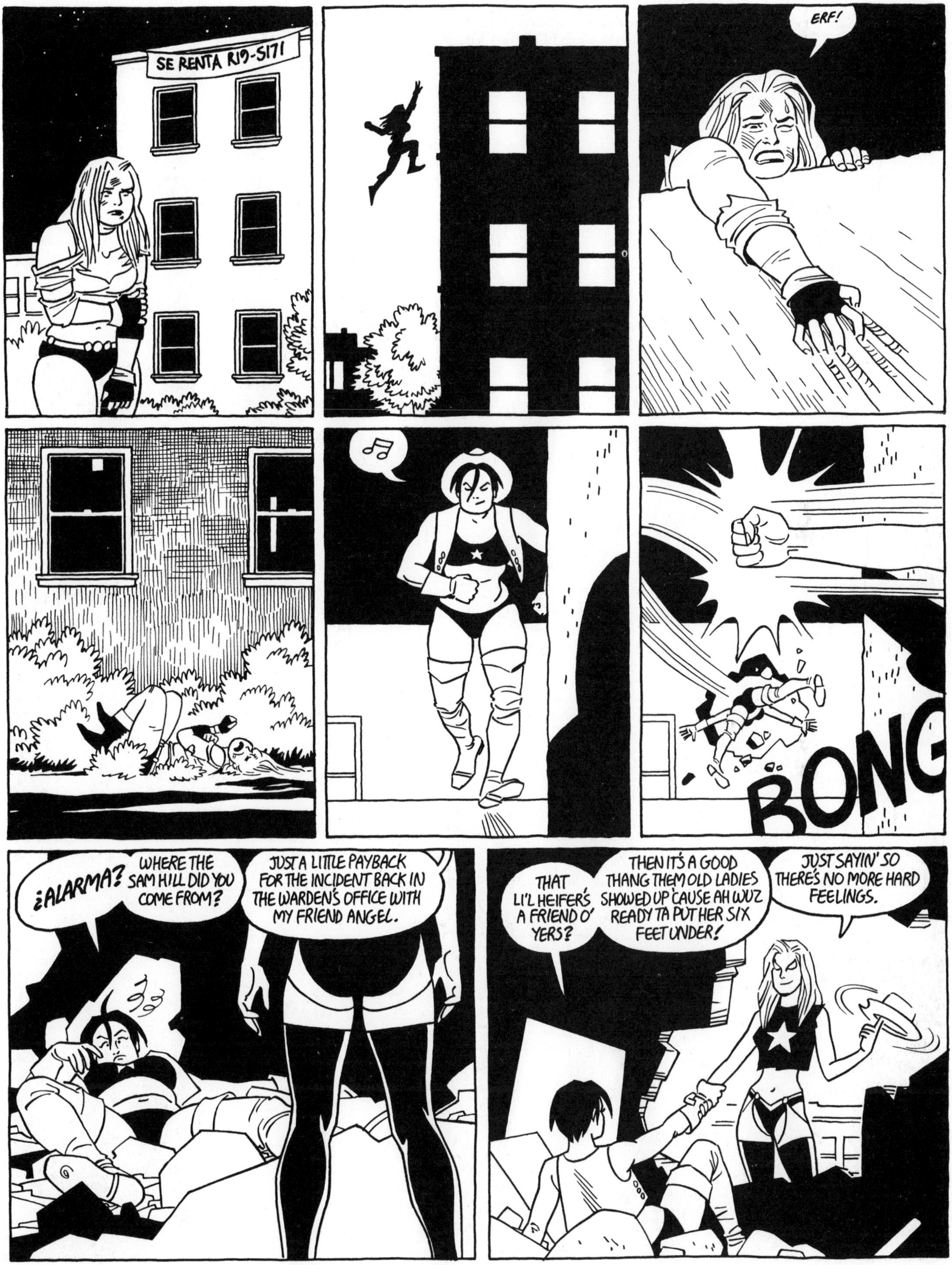
SE RENTA R19-5171
ERF!
BONG
¿ALARMA?
WHERE THE SAM HILL DID YOU COME FROM?
JUST A LITTLE PAYBACK FOR THE INCIDENT BACK IN THE WARDEN'S OFFICE WITH MY FRIEND ANGEL.
THAT LI'L HEIFER'S A FRIEND O' YERS?
THEN IT'S A GOOD THANG THEM OLD LADIES SHOWED UP 'CAUSE AH WUZ READY TA PUT HER SIX FEET UNDER!
JUST SAYIN' SO THERE'S NO MORE HARD FEELINGS.

THAT'S FER SENDIN' ME TO TH' HOOSEGOW IN TH' FIRST PLACE! WE WUZ PARDNERS ONCE, 'MEMBER?

OH, MAGGIE! HI, I HOPE I DIDN'T WAKE YOU.

NO, I'VE BEEN UP.

WHAT ARE YOU DOING?

OH, JUST... YOU KNOW...

I'M GONNA GO HOME FOR A BIT AND SEE MY PARENTS...

...SO, NATURALLY I'M TAKING MY LAUNDRY.

HA HA!

BUT, ARE YOU OK? WHAT HAPPENED?

OH!

WELL, THEY GOT YOUR FRIEND PENNY, BUT IT'S COOL BECAUSE THE FENOMENONS WERE REAL GENTLE WITH HER AND....

HEE HEE!

ANGEL, THERE'S SOMEONE HERE I THINK YOU SHOULD TALK TO...

BWAA HAA HA

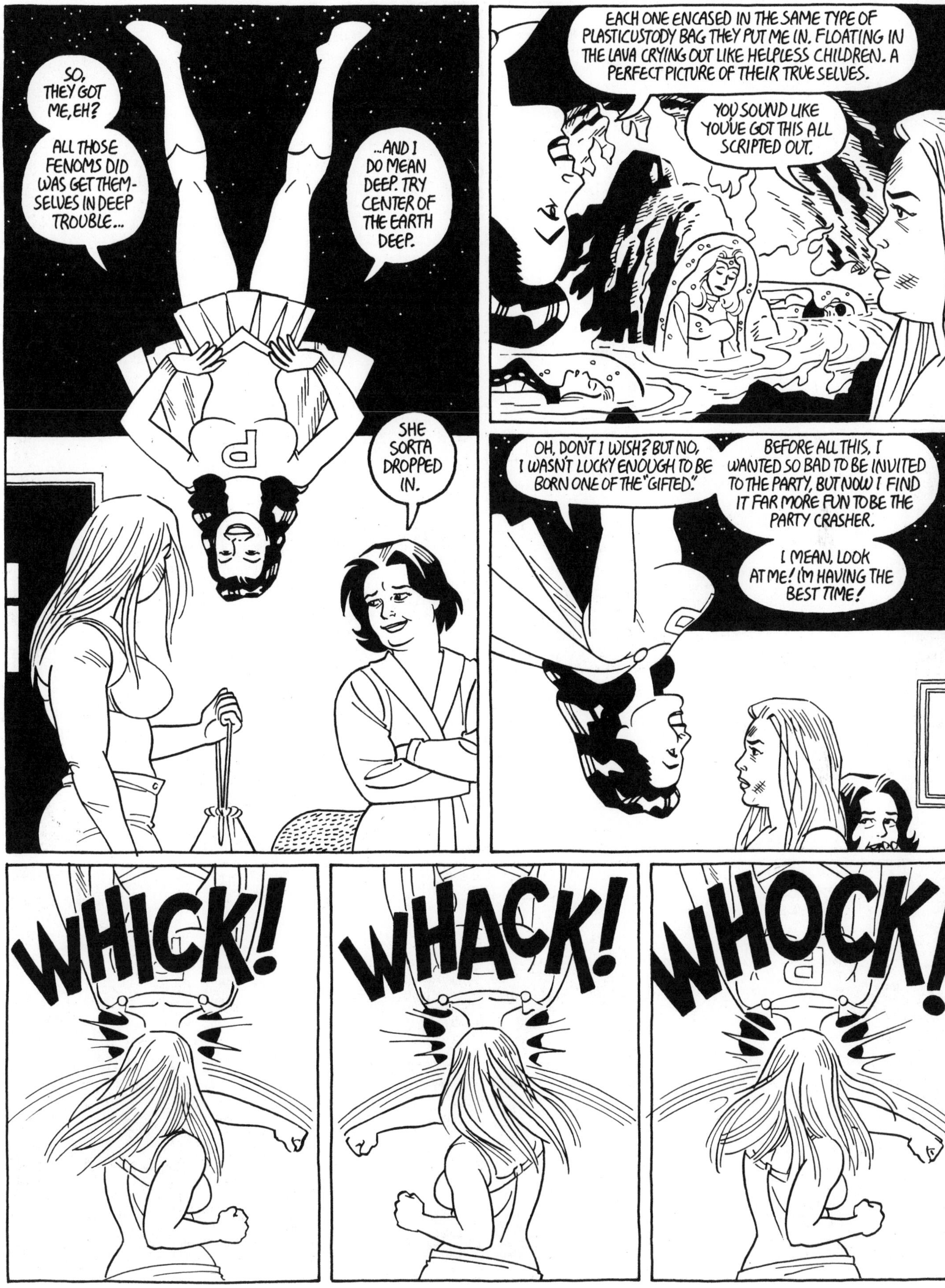
SO, THEY GOT ME, EH?
ALL THOSE FENOMS DID WAS GET THEMSELVES IN DEEP TROUBLE...
...AND I DO MEAN DEEP. TRY CENTER OF THE EARTH DEEP.
EACH ONE ENCASED IN THE SAME TYPE OF PLASTICUSTODY BAG THEY PUT ME IN. FLOATING IN THE LAVA CRYING OUT LIKE HELPLESS CHILDREN. A PERFECT PICTURE OF THEIR TRUE SELVES.
YOU SOUND LIKE YOU'VE GOT THIS ALL SCRIPTED OUT.
SHE SORTA DROPPED IN.
OH, DON'T I WISH? BUT NO, I WASN'T LUCKY ENOUGH TO BE BORN ONE OF THE "GIFTED."
BEFORE ALL THIS, I WANTED SO BAD TO BE INVITED TO THE PARTY, BUT NOW I FIND IT FAR MORE FUN TO BE THE PARTY CRASHER.
I MEAN, LOOK AT ME! I'M HAVING THE BEST TIME!
WHICK!
WHACK!
WHOCK!

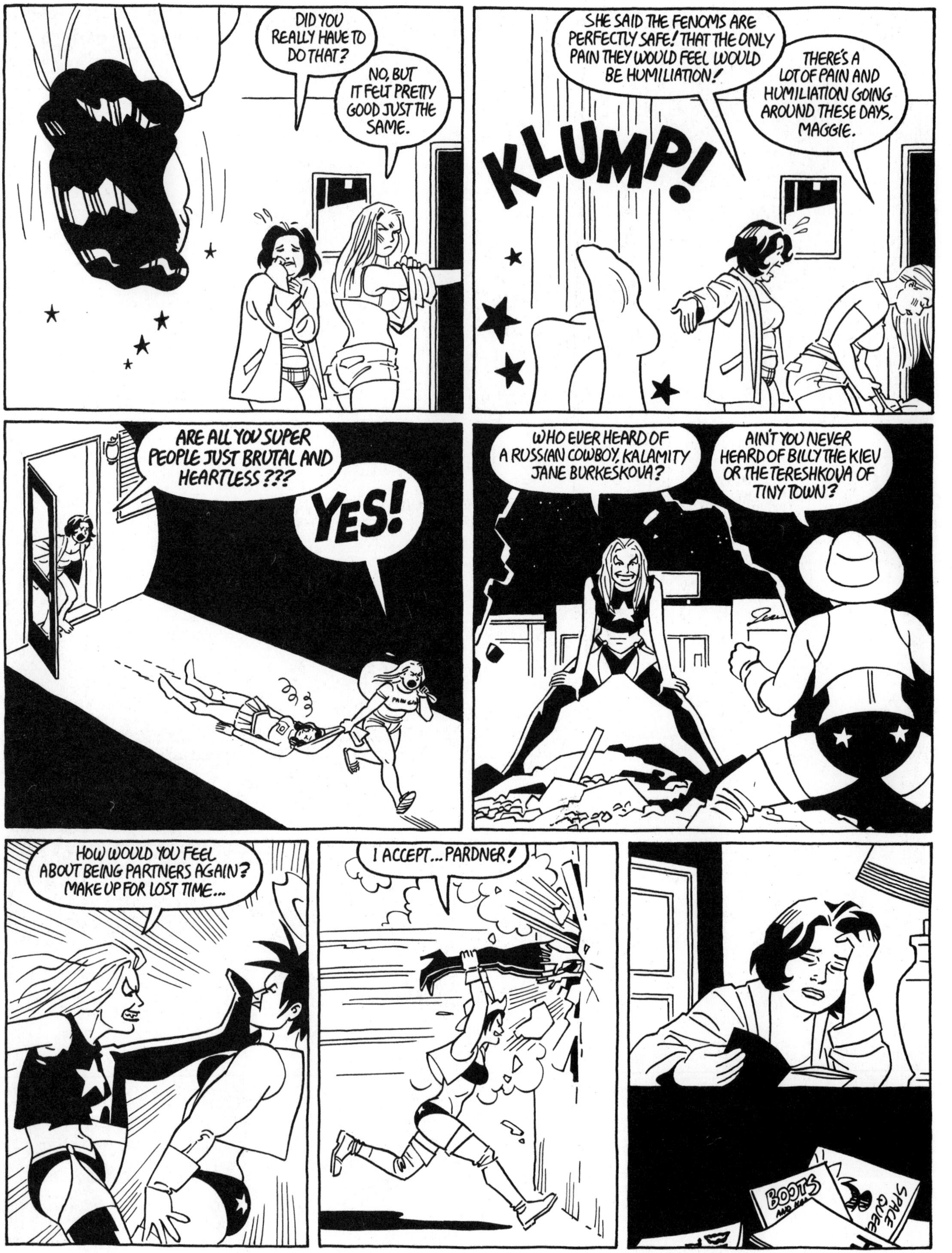
DID YOU REALLY HAVE TO DO THAT?
NO, BUT IT FELT PRETTY GOOD JUST THE SAME.
SHE SAID THE FENOMS ARE PERFECTLY SAFE! THAT THE ONLY PAIN THEY WOULD FEEL WOULD BE HUMILIATION!
THERE'S A LOT OF PAIN AND HUMILIATION GOING AROUND THESE DAYS, MAGGIE.
KLUMP!
ARE ALL YOU SUPER PEOPLE JUST BRUTAL AND HEARTLESS???
YES!
WHO EVER HEARD OF A RUSSIAN COWBOY, KALAMITY JANE BURKESKOVA?
AIN'T YOU NEVER HEARD OF BILLY THE KIEV OR THE TERESHKOVA OF TINY TOWN?
HOW WOULD YOU FEEL ABOUT BEING PARTNERS AGAIN? MAKE UP FOR LOST TIME...
I ACCEPT... PARDNER!
BOOTS
SPACE QUEEN

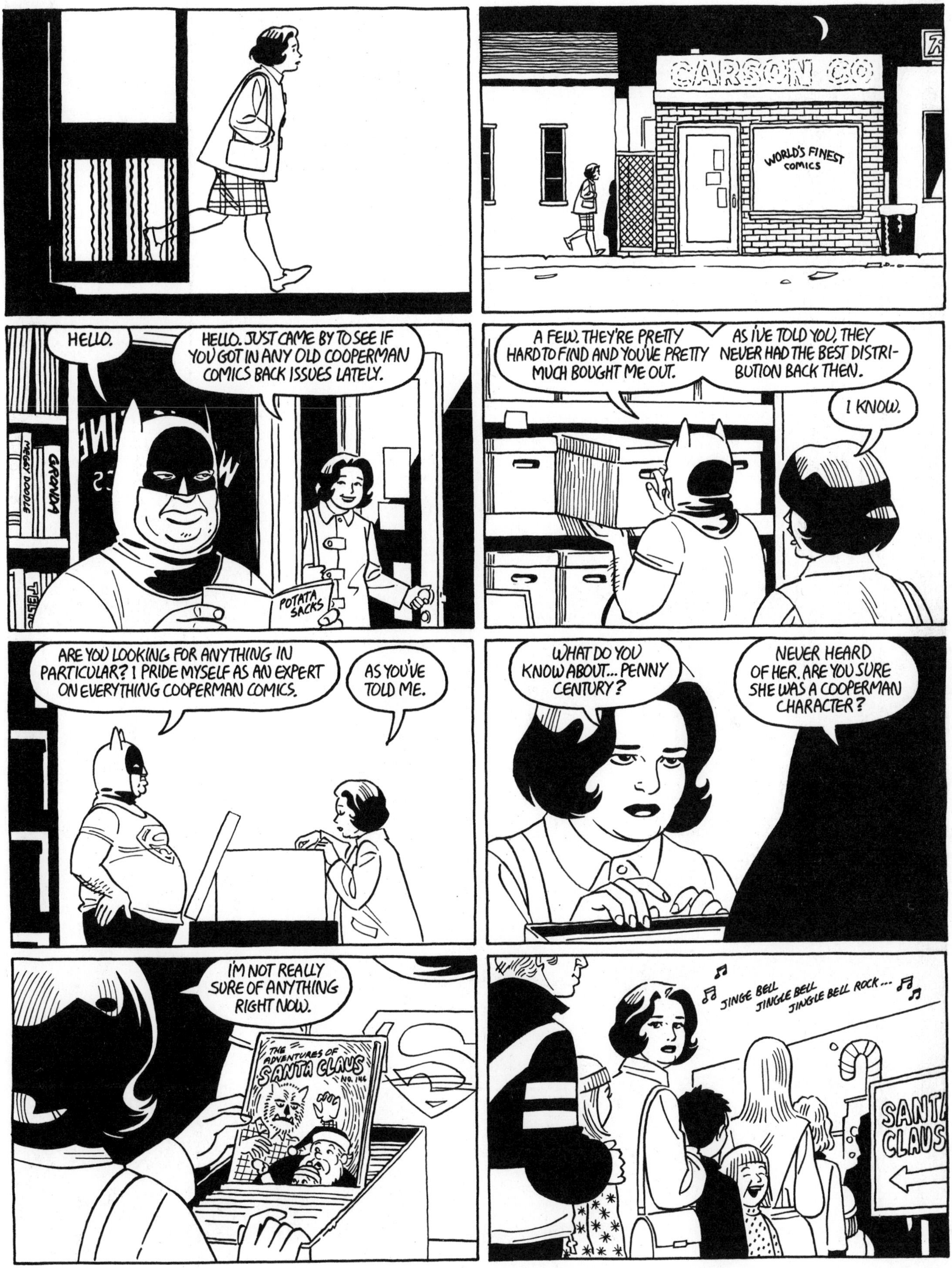
CARSON CO
WORLD'S FINEST COMICS
HELLO.
HELLO. JUST CAME BY TO SEE IF YOU GOT IN ANY OLD COOPERMAN COMICS BACK ISSUES LATELY.
POTATA SACKS
A FEW. THEY'RE PRETTY HARD TO FIND AND YOU'VE PRETTY MUCH BOUGHT ME OUT.
AS I'VE TOLD YOU, THEY NEVER HAD THE BEST DISTRIBUTION BACK THEN.
I KNOW.
ARE YOU LOOKING FOR ANYTHING IN PARTICULAR? I PRIDE MYSELF AS AN EXPERT ON EVERYTHING COOPERMAN COMICS.
AS YOU'VE TOLD ME.
WHAT DO YOU KNOW ABOUT... PENNY CENTURY?
NEVER HEARD OF HER. ARE YOU SURE SHE WAS A COOPERMAN CHARACTER?
I'M NOT REALLY SURE OF ANYTHING RIGHT NOW.
THE ADVENTURES OF SANTA CLAUS NO. 146
JINGLE BELL JINGLE BELL JINGLE BELL ROCK...
SANTA CLAUS

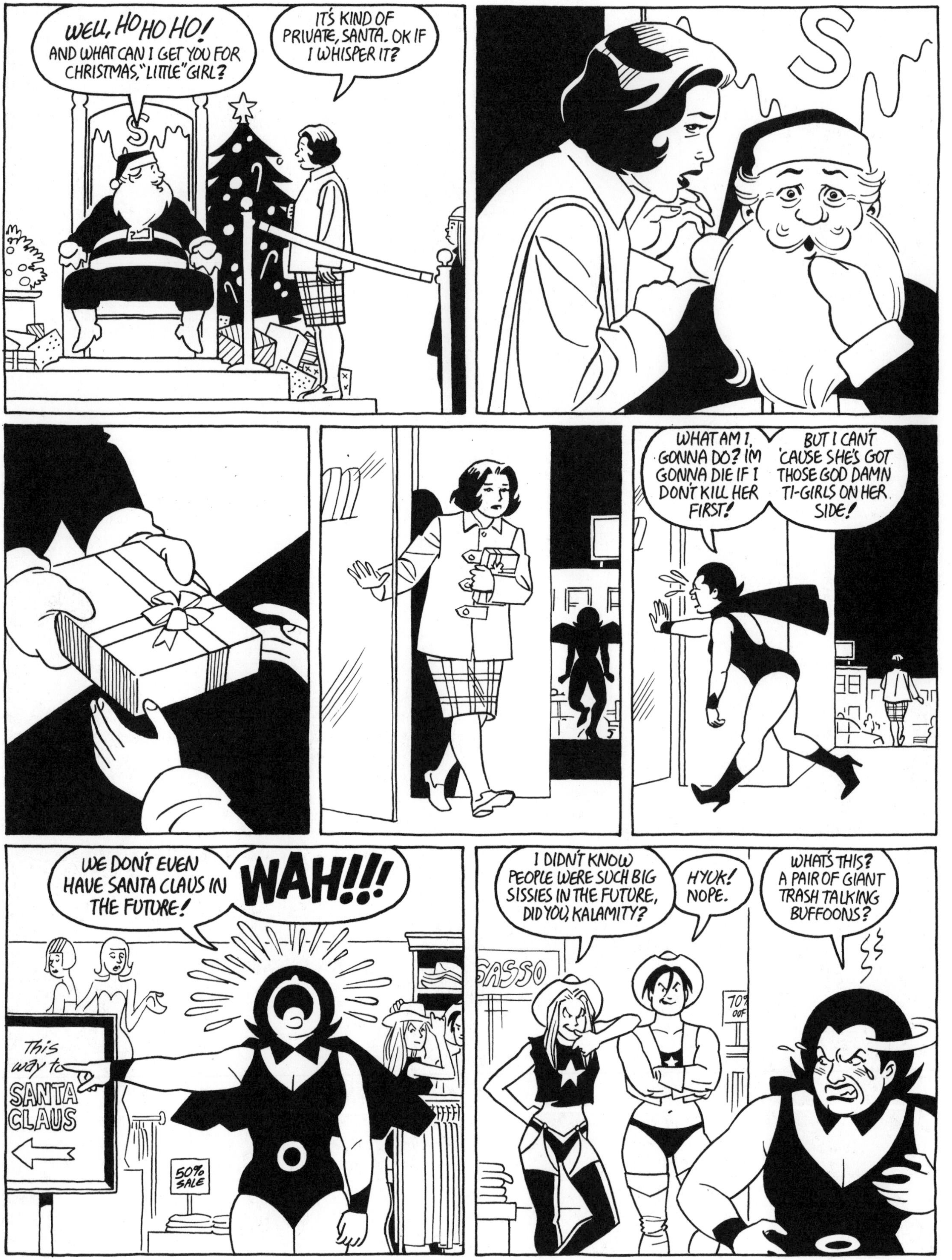
WELL, HO HO HO! AND WHAT CAN I GET YOU FOR CHRISTMAS, "LITTLE" GIRL?
IT'S KIND OF PRIVATE, SANTA. OK IF I WHISPER IT?
S
S
WHAT AM I GONNA DO? I'M GONNA DIE IF I DON'T KILL HER FIRST!
BUT I CAN'T 'CAUSE SHE'S GOT THOSE GOD DAMN TI-GIRLS ON HER SIDE!
WE DON'T EVEN HAVE SANTA CLAUS IN THE FUTURE!
WAH!!!
This way to SANTA CLAUS
50% SALE
I DIDN'T KNOW PEOPLE WERE SUCH BIG SISSIES IN THE FUTURE, DID YOU, KALAMITY?
HYUK! NOPE.
WHAT'S THIS? A PAIR OF GIANT TRASH TALKING BUFFOONS?
SASSO
70% OFF

YOU'RE GOING ABOUT THIS ALL WRONG. YOU GOTTA HIT 'EM WHERE THEY LIVE. FIND OUT HOW THEY TICK. FIND THEIR WEAK SPOTS AND *BAM!*

MAYBE IF YA HAD MIND READIN' POWERS.

WELL, I DON'T AND I'LL BET YOU BIG BRAINS DON'T EITHER!

WELL NO, BUT I THINK I KNOW SOMEONE WHO MIGHT BE HELPFUL TO YOU, AND BELIEVE IT OR NOT, SHE'S A CIVILIAN WHO ALSO HAPPENS TO BE MY APARTMENT MANAGER.

CIVILIAN?? EW, AH THINK AH'M GONNA HURL!

OK, SO WE AGREED NOT TO LAY A FINGER ON HER, JUST TO SCARE THE INFO OUT OF HER. BUT I DON'T HOLD THAT PROMISE TO ANY TI-GIRL!

?!

S'MATTER, 'LAR? YA GOT A HEADACHE?

I JUST THOUGHT I HEARD...

NOTHING. LET'S GO.

GOODNESS GRACIOUS. I BELIEVE IT'S TIME I NOTIFIED SOME OLD FRIENDS.

BEEP BEEP

BEEP

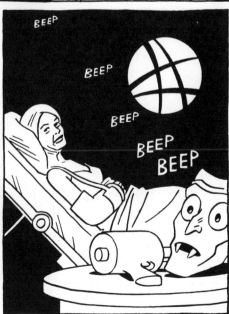

BEEP

BEEP

BEEP

BEEP BEEP

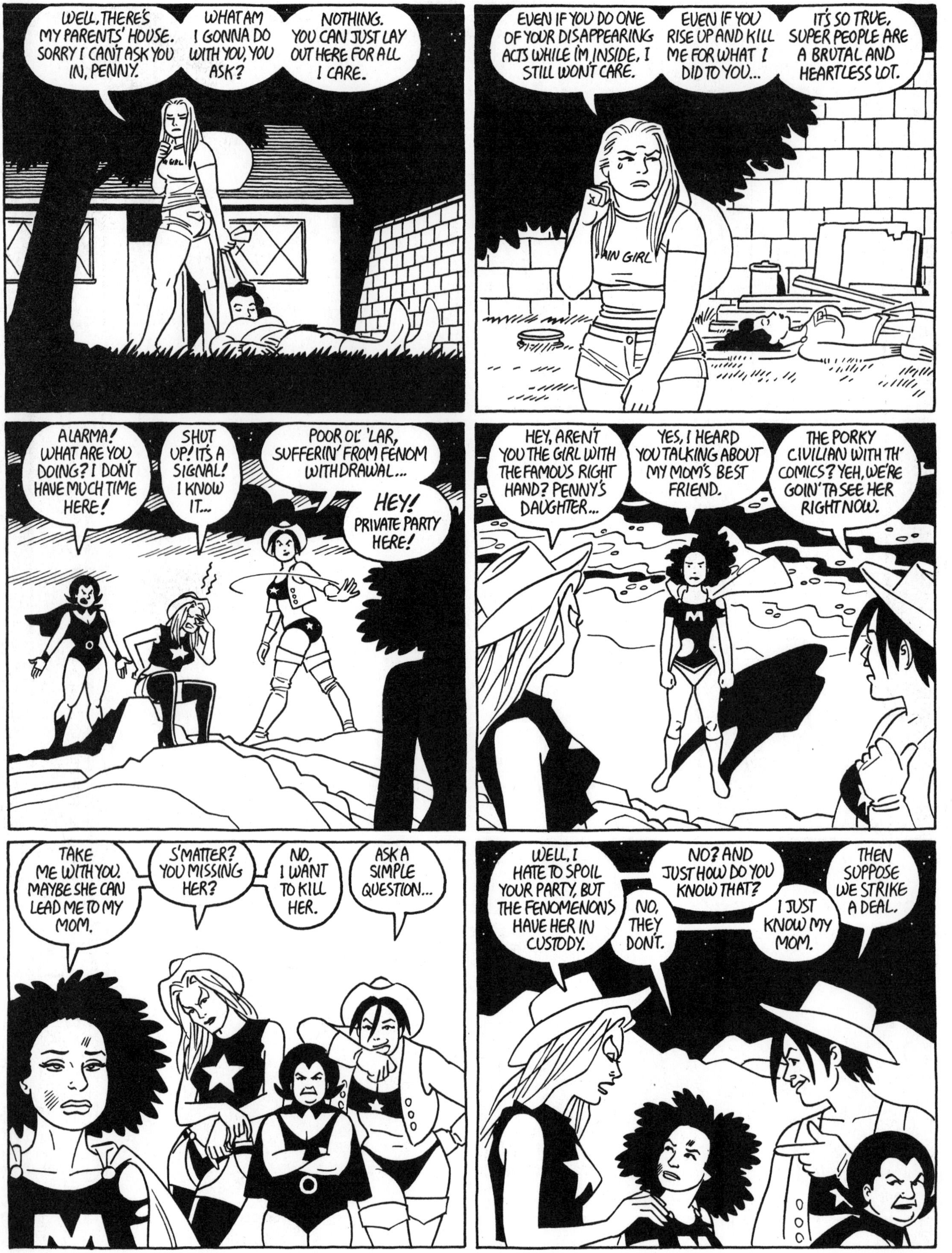
WELL, THERE'S MY PARENTS' HOUSE. SORRY I CAN'T ASK YOU IN, PENNY.
WHAT AM I GONNA DO WITH YOU, YOU ASK?
NOTHING. YOU CAN JUST LAY OUT HERE FOR ALL I CARE.
EVEN IF YOU DO ONE OF YOUR DISAPPEARING ACTS WHILE I'M INSIDE, I STILL WON'T CARE.
EVEN IF YOU RISE UP AND KILL ME FOR WHAT I DID TO YOU...
IT'S SO TRUE, SUPER PEOPLE ARE A BRUTAL AND HEARTLESS LOT.
ALARMA! WHAT ARE YOU DOING? I DON'T HAVE MUCH TIME HERE!
SHUT UP! IT'S A SIGNAL! I KNOW IT...
POOR OL' 'LAR, SUFFERIN' FROM FENOM WITHDRAWAL...
HEY! PRIVATE PARTY HERE!
HEY, AREN'T YOU THE GIRL WITH THE FAMOUS RIGHT HAND? PENNY'S DAUGHTER...
YES, I HEARD YOU TALKING ABOUT MY MOM'S BEST FRIEND.
THE PORKY CIVILIAN WITH TH' COMICS? YEH, WE'RE GOIN' TA SEE HER RIGHT NOW.
TAKE ME WITH YOU. MAYBE SHE CAN LEAD ME TO MY MOM.
S'MATTER? YOU MISSING HER?
NO, I WANT TO KILL HER.
ASK A SIMPLE QUESTION...
WELL, I HATE TO SPOIL YOUR PARTY, BUT THE FENOMENONS HAVE HER IN CUSTODY.
NO, THEY DON'T.
NO? AND JUST HOW DO YOU KNOW THAT?
I JUST KNOW MY MOM.
THEN SUPPOSE WE STRIKE A DEAL.

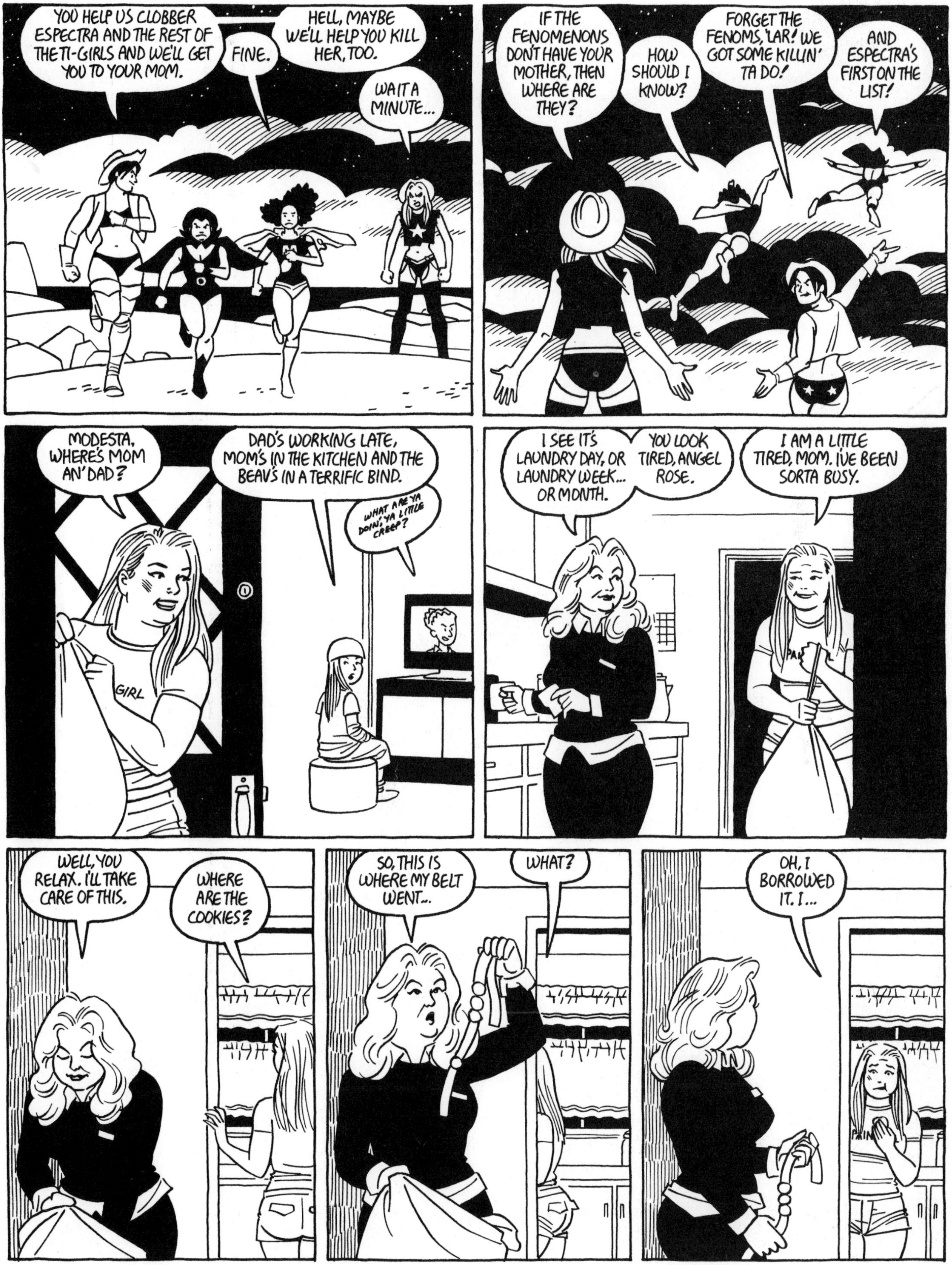
YOU HELP US CLOBBER ESPECTRA AND THE REST OF THE TI-GIRLS AND WE'LL GET YOU TO YOUR MOM.
FINE.
HELL, MAYBE WE'LL HELP YOU KILL HER, TOO.
WAIT A MINUTE...
IF THE FENOMENONS DON'T HAVE YOUR MOTHER, THEN WHERE ARE THEY?
HOW SHOULD I KNOW?
FORGET THE FENOMS, 'LAR! WE GOT SOME KILLIN' TA DO!
AND ESPECTRA'S FIRST ON THE LIST!
MODESTA, WHERE'S MOM AN' DAD?
DAD'S WORKING LATE, MOM'S IN THE KITCHEN AND THE BEAV'S IN A TERRIFIC BIND.
WHAT ARE YA DOIN', YA LITTLE CREEP?
GIRL
I SEE IT'S LAUNDRY DAY, OR LAUNDRY WEEK... OR MONTH.
YOU LOOK TIRED, ANGEL ROSE.
I AM A LITTLE TIRED, MOM. I'VE BEEN SORTA BUSY.
WELL, YOU RELAX. I'LL TAKE CARE OF THIS.
WHERE ARE THE COOKIES?
SO, THIS IS WHERE MY BELT WENT...
WHAT?
OH, I BORROWED IT. I...

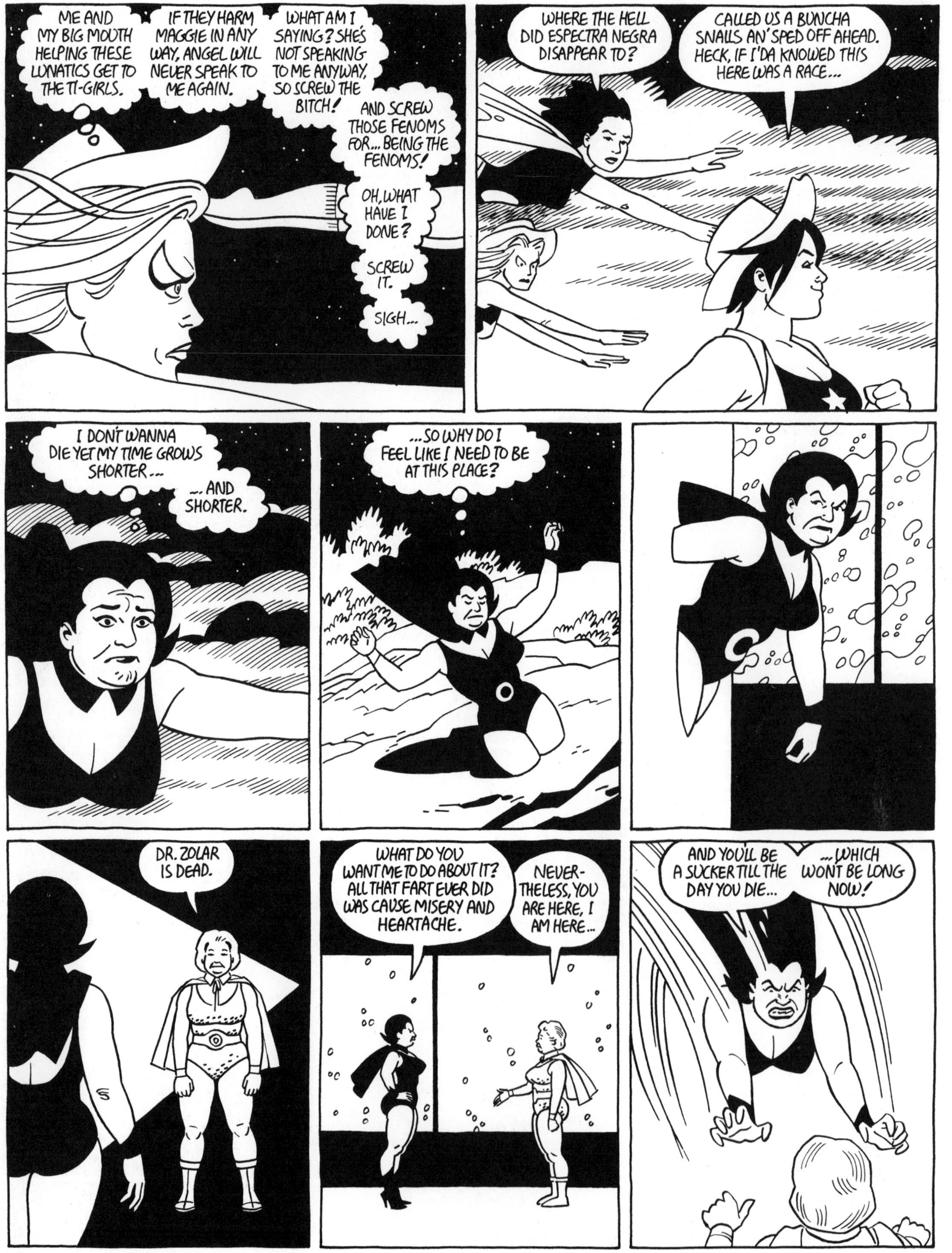
ME AND MY BIG MOUTH HELPING THESE LUNATICS GET TO THE TI-GIRLS.
IF THEY HARM MAGGIE IN ANY WAY, ANGEL WILL NEVER SPEAK TO ME AGAIN.
WHAT AM I SAYING? SHE'S NOT SPEAKING TO ME ANYWAY, SO SCREW THE BITCH!
AND SCREW THOSE FENOMS FOR... BEING THE FENOMS!
OH, WHAT HAVE I DONE?
SCREW IT.
SIGH...
WHERE THE HELL DID ESPECTRA NEGRA DISAPPEAR TO?
CALLED US A BUNCHA SNAILS AN' SPED OFF AHEAD. HECK, IF I'DA KNOWED THIS HERE WAS A RACE...
I DON'T WANNA DIE YET MY TIME GROWS SHORTER...
...AND SHORTER.
...SO WHY DO I FEEL LIKE I NEED TO BE AT THIS PLACE?
DR. ZOLAR IS DEAD.
WHAT DO YOU WANT ME TO DO ABOUT IT? ALL THAT FART EVER DID WAS CAUSE MISERY AND HEARTACHE.
NEVER-THELESS, YOU ARE HERE, I AM HERE...
AND YOU'LL BE A SUCKER TILL THE DAY YOU DIE...
...WHICH WON'T BE LONG NOW!

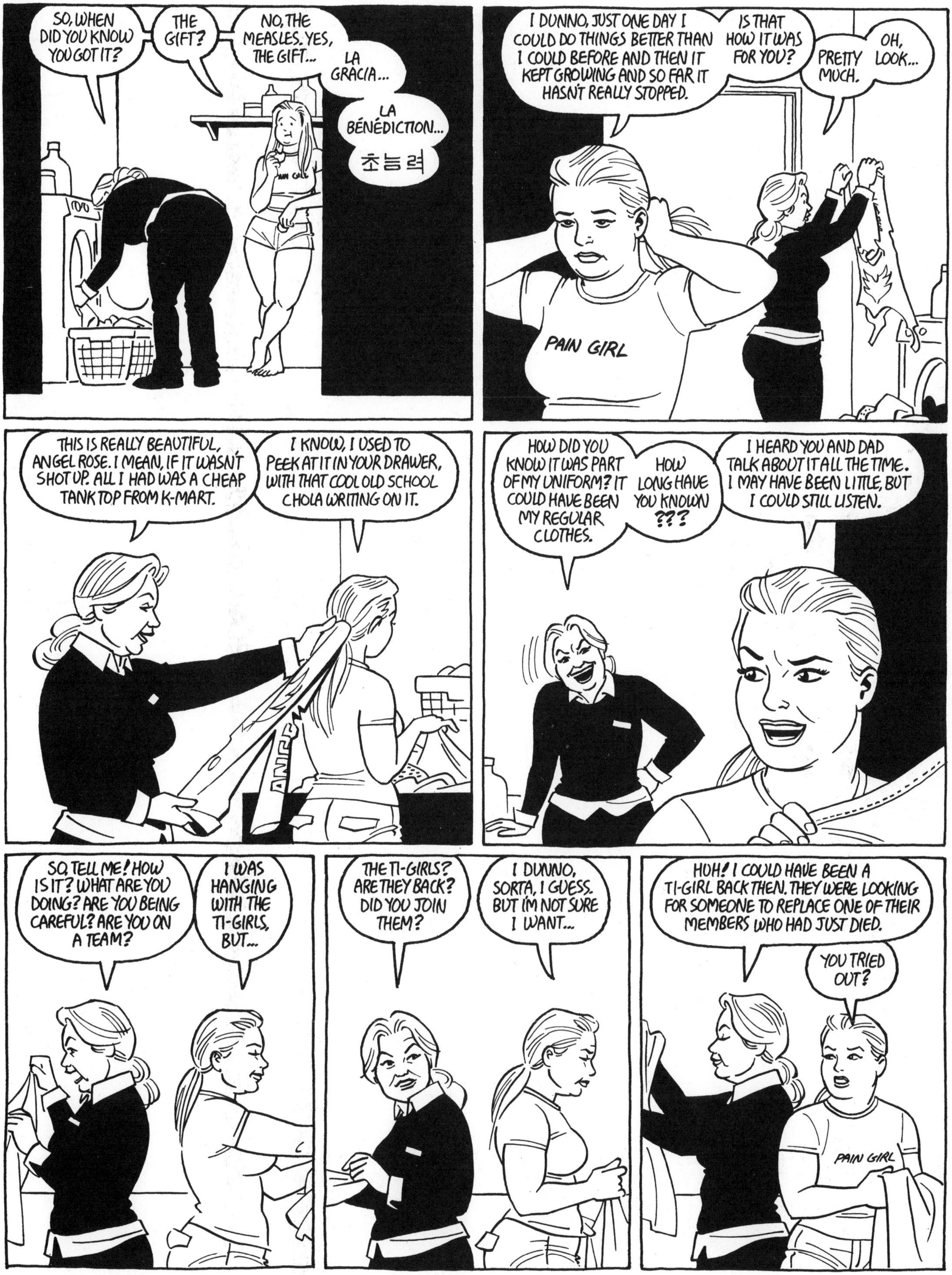
SO, WHEN DID YOU KNOW YOU GOT IT?
THE GIFT?
NO, THE MEASLES. YES, THE GIFT...
LA GRACIA...
LA BÉNÉDICTION...
초능력
PAIN GIRL
I DUNNO, JUST ONE DAY I COULD DO THINGS BETTER THAN I COULD BEFORE AND THEN IT KEPT GROWING AND SO FAR IT HASN'T REALLY STOPPED.
IS THAT HOW IT WAS FOR YOU?
PRETTY MUCH.
OH, LOOK...
PAIN GIRL
THIS IS REALLY BEAUTIFUL, ANGEL ROSE. I MEAN, IF IT WASN'T SHOT UP. ALL I HAD WAS A CHEAP TANK TOP FROM K-MART.
I KNOW, I USED TO PEEK AT IT IN YOUR DRAWER, WITH THAT COOL OLD SCHOOL CHOLA WRITING ON IT.
HOW DID YOU KNOW IT WAS PART OF MY UNIFORM? IT COULD HAVE BEEN MY REGULAR CLOTHES.
HOW LONG HAVE YOU KNOWN ???
I HEARD YOU AND DAD TALK ABOUT IT ALL THE TIME. I MAY HAVE BEEN LITTLE, BUT I COULD STILL LISTEN.
SO, TELL ME! HOW IS IT? WHAT ARE YOU DOING? ARE YOU BEING CAREFUL? ARE YOU ON A TEAM?
I WAS HANGING WITH THE TI-GIRLS, BUT...
THE TI-GIRLS? ARE THEY BACK? DID YOU JOIN THEM?
I DUNNO, SORTA, I GUESS. BUT I'M NOT SURE I WANT...
HUH! I COULD HAVE BEEN A TI-GIRL BACK THEN. THEY WERE LOOKING FOR SOMEONE TO REPLACE ONE OF THEIR MEMBERS WHO HAD JUST DIED.
YOU TRIED OUT?
PAIN GIRL

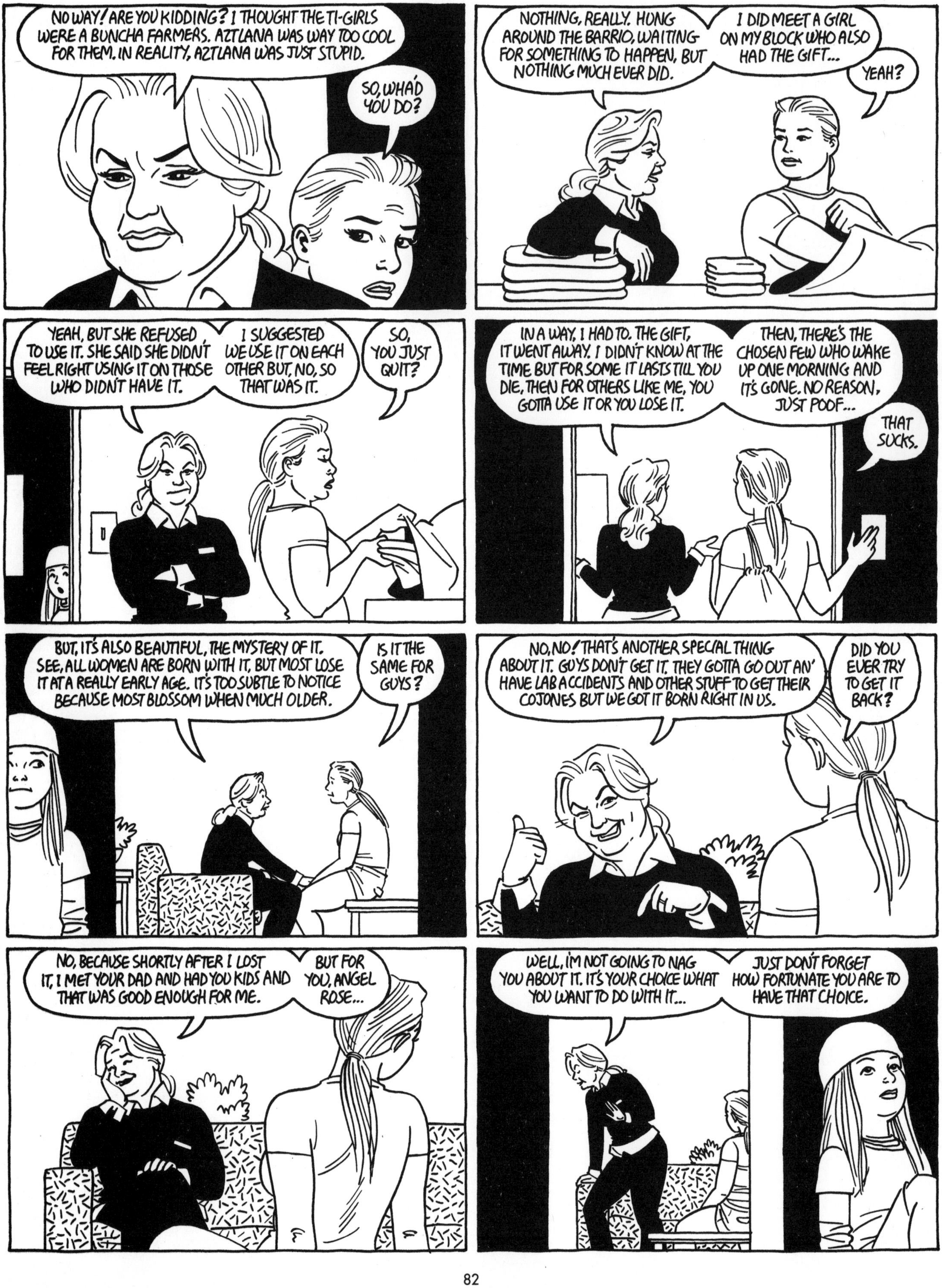
NO WAY! ARE YOU KIDDING? I THOUGHT THE TI-GIRLS WERE A BUNCHA FARMERS. AZTLANA WAS WAY TOO COOL FOR THEM. IN REALITY, AZTLANA WAS JUST STUPID.
SO, WHA'D YOU DO?
NOTHING, REALLY. HUNG AROUND THE BARRIO, WAITING FOR SOMETHING TO HAPPEN, BUT NOTHING MUCH EVER DID.
I DID MEET A GIRL ON MY BLOCK WHO ALSO HAD THE GIFT...
YEAH?
YEAH, BUT SHE REFUSED TO USE IT. SHE SAID SHE DIDN'T FEEL RIGHT USING IT ON THOSE WHO DIDN'T HAVE IT.
I SUGGESTED WE USE IT ON EACH OTHER BUT, NO, SO THAT WAS IT.
SO, YOU JUST QUIT?
IN A WAY, I HAD TO. THE GIFT, IT WENT AWAY. I DIDN'T KNOW AT THE TIME BUT FOR SOME IT LASTS TILL YOU DIE, THEN FOR OTHERS LIKE ME, YOU GOTTA USE IT OR YOU LOSE IT.
THEN, THERE'S THE CHOSEN FEW WHO WAKE UP ONE MORNING AND IT'S GONE. NO REASON, JUST POOF...
THAT SUCKS.
BUT, IT'S ALSO BEAUTIFUL, THE MYSTERY OF IT. SEE, ALL WOMEN ARE BORN WITH IT, BUT MOST LOSE IT AT A REALLY EARLY AGE. IT'S TOO SUBTLE TO NOTICE BECAUSE MOST BLOSSOM WHEN MUCH OLDER.
IS IT THE SAME FOR GUYS?
NO, NO! THAT'S ANOTHER SPECIAL THING ABOUT IT. GUYS DON'T GET IT. THEY GOTTA GO OUT AN' HAVE LAB ACCIDENTS AND OTHER STUFF TO GET THEIR COJONES BUT WE GOT IT BORN RIGHT IN US.
DID YOU EVER TRY TO GET IT BACK?
NO, BECAUSE SHORTLY AFTER I LOST IT, I MET YOUR DAD AND HAD YOU KIDS AND THAT WAS GOOD ENOUGH FOR ME.
BUT FOR YOU, ANGEL ROSE...
WELL, I'M NOT GOING TO NAG YOU ABOUT IT. IT'S YOUR CHOICE WHAT YOU WANT TO DO WITH IT...
JUST DON'T FORGET HOW FORTUNATE YOU ARE TO HAVE THAT CHOICE.

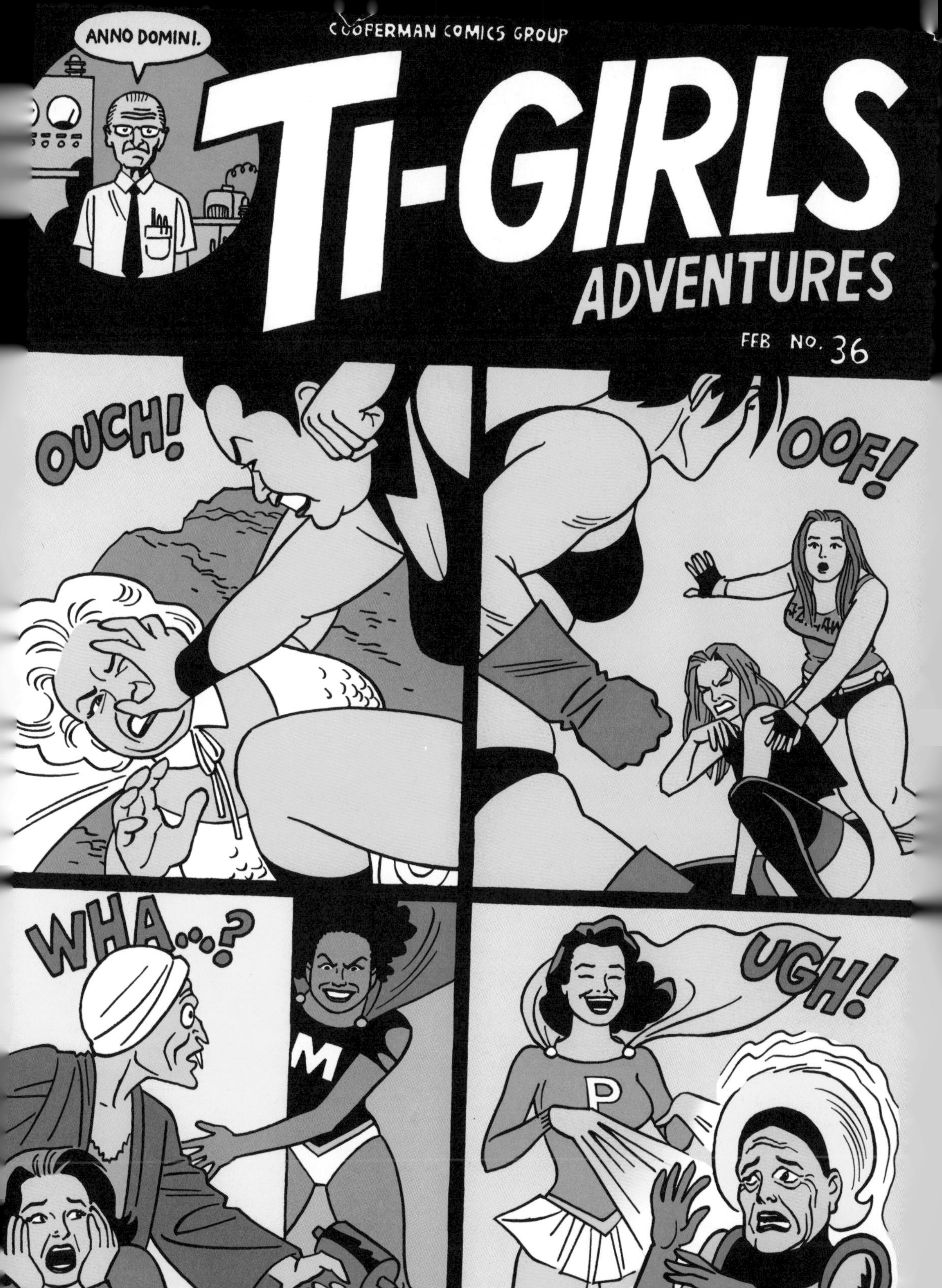

COOPERMAN COMICS GROUP
ANNO DOMINI.
TI-GIRLS
ADVENTURES
FEB NO. 36
OUCH!
OOF!
WHA...?
UGH!
M
P
G

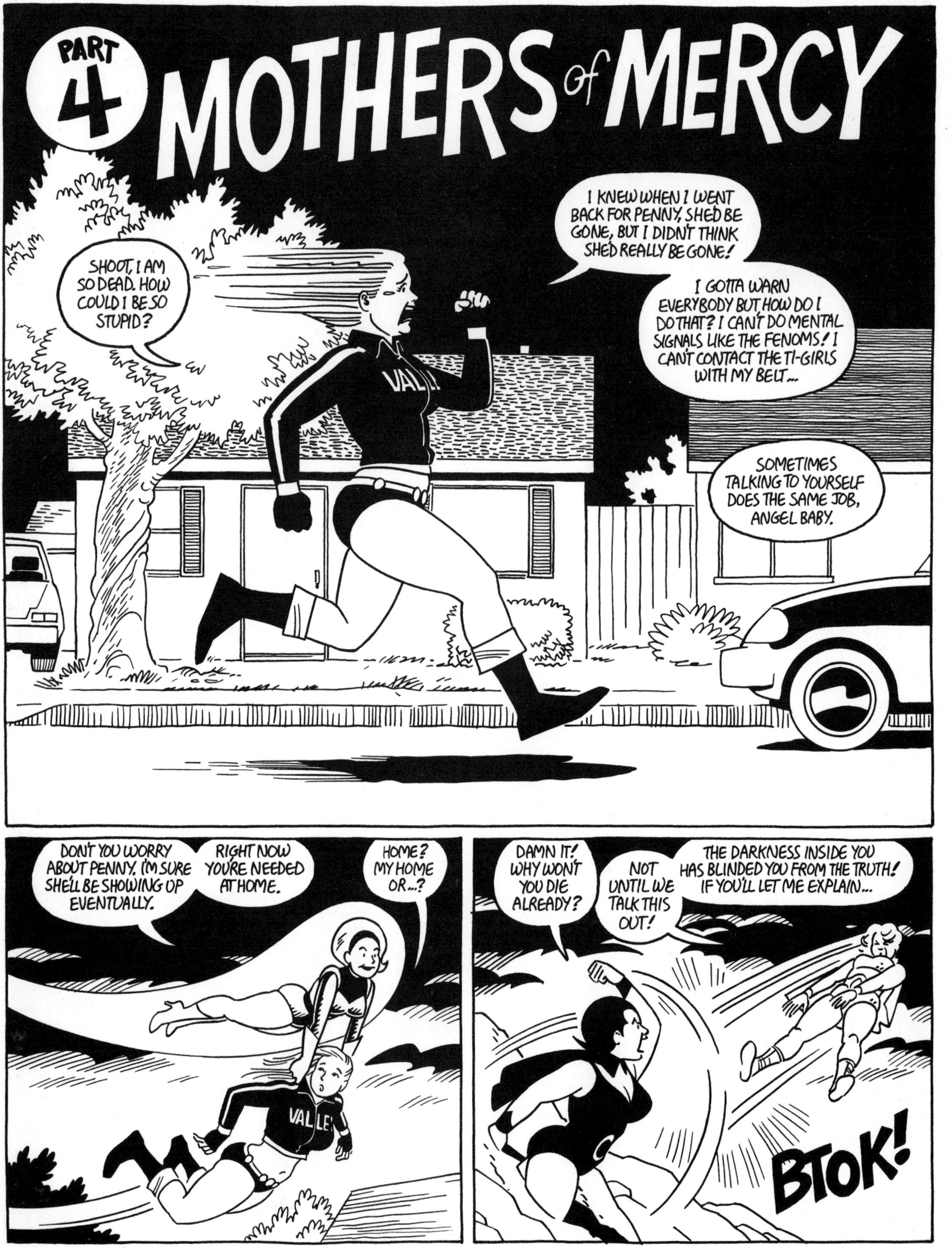
PART 4 MOTHERS of MERCY
SHOOT, I AM SO DEAD. HOW COULD I BE SO STUPID?
I KNEW WHEN I WENT BACK FOR PENNY, SHE'D BE GONE, BUT I DIDN'T THINK SHE'D REALLY BE GONE!
I GOTTA WARN EVERYBODY BUT HOW DO I DO THAT? I CAN'T DO MENTAL SIGNALS LIKE THE FENOMS! I CAN'T CONTACT THE TI-GIRLS WITH MY BELT...
SOMETIMES TALKING TO YOURSELF DOES THE SAME JOB, ANGEL BABY.
DON'T YOU WORRY ABOUT PENNY. I'M SURE SHE'LL BE SHOWING UP EVENTUALLY.
RIGHT NOW YOU'RE NEEDED AT HOME.
HOME? MY HOME OR...?
DAMN IT! WHY WON'T YOU DIE ALREADY?
NOT UNTIL WE TALK THIS OUT!
THE DARKNESS INSIDE YOU HAS BLINDED YOU FROM THE TRUTH! IF YOU'LL LET ME EXPLAIN...
BTOK!

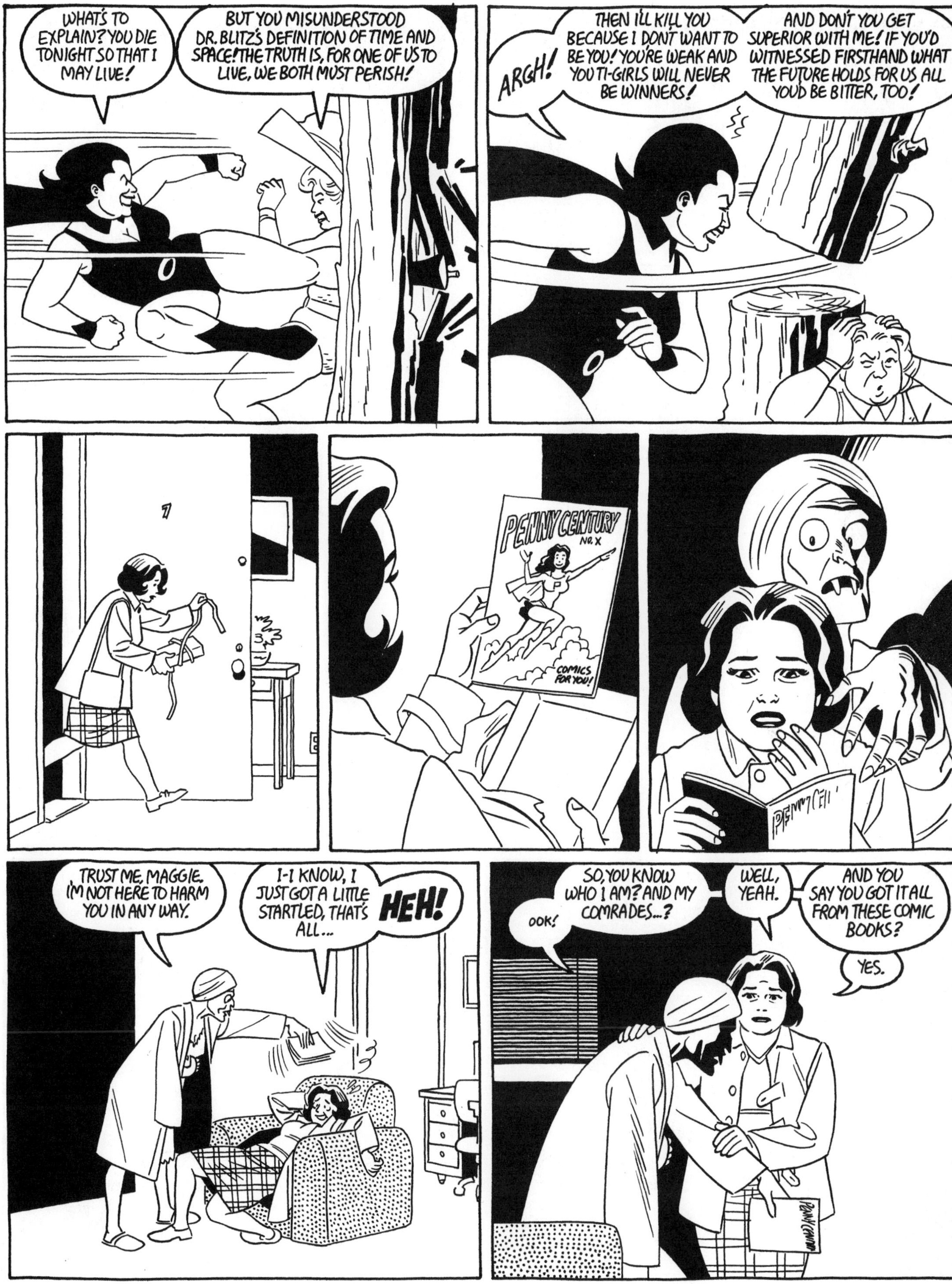
WHAT'S TO EXPLAIN? YOU DIE TONIGHT SO THAT I MAY LIVE!
BUT YOU MISUNDERSTOOD DR. BLITZ'S DEFINITION OF TIME AND SPACE! THE TRUTH IS, FOR ONE OF US TO LIVE, WE BOTH MUST PERISH!
ARGH!
THEN I'LL KILL YOU BECAUSE I DON'T WANT TO BE YOU! YOU'RE WEAK AND YOU TI-GIRLS WILL NEVER BE WINNERS!
AND DON'T YOU GET SUPERIOR WITH ME! IF YOU'D WITNESSED FIRSTHAND WHAT THE FUTURE HOLDS FOR US ALL YOU'D BE BITTER, TOO!
PENNY CENTURY
NO. X
COMICS FOR YOU!
TRUST ME, MAGGIE. I'M NOT HERE TO HARM YOU IN ANY WAY.
I-I KNOW, I JUST GOT A LITTLE STARTLED, THAT'S ALL...
HEH!
OOK!
SO, YOU KNOW WHO I AM? AND MY COMRADES...?
WELL, YEAH.
AND YOU SAY YOU GOT IT ALL FROM THESE COMIC BOOKS?
YES.

YOU KNOW, THE INFORMATION CONTAINED IN THESE COMIC BOOKS COULD BE DANGEROUS IN THE WRONG HANDS. THAT'S WHY I'M HERE. I... I...

HM.

COME. WE WILL BE EXPECTING VISITORS TONIGHT SO WE MUST BE READY.

V-VISITORS?

MAGGIE! WAKE UP! THE TI-GIRLS ARE HERE TO HELP YOU, NOT TO...

SHE KNOWS.

AND ESPECTRA? CAN WE BE EXPECTING HER SHORTLY?

IN ONE FORM OR ANOTHER.

LIES AND LIARS! ALL LIARS! DR. ZOLAR, DEAD LIAR! DR. BLITZ, DEADER LIAR!

YES, I KILLED HIM! KILLED HIM AND FLED THE DREADED FUTURE TO ESCAPE HIS LIES, AND YET THEY STILL LINGER, EVEN IN THE PAST!

THEN WHY DON'T WE STOP THIS SENSELESS VIOLENCE AND ACCEPT OUR FATE TOGETHER AS ONE SO WE CAN TRY TO CHANGE THINGS NOW FOR THE FUTURE?

BECAUSE YOU'RE GONNA DIE! HOW MANY TIMES DO I HAVE TO TELL YOU?

VERY WELL, THEN. THE CAPES ARE OFF.

NOW YOU'RE TALKING...

UH, REALLY?

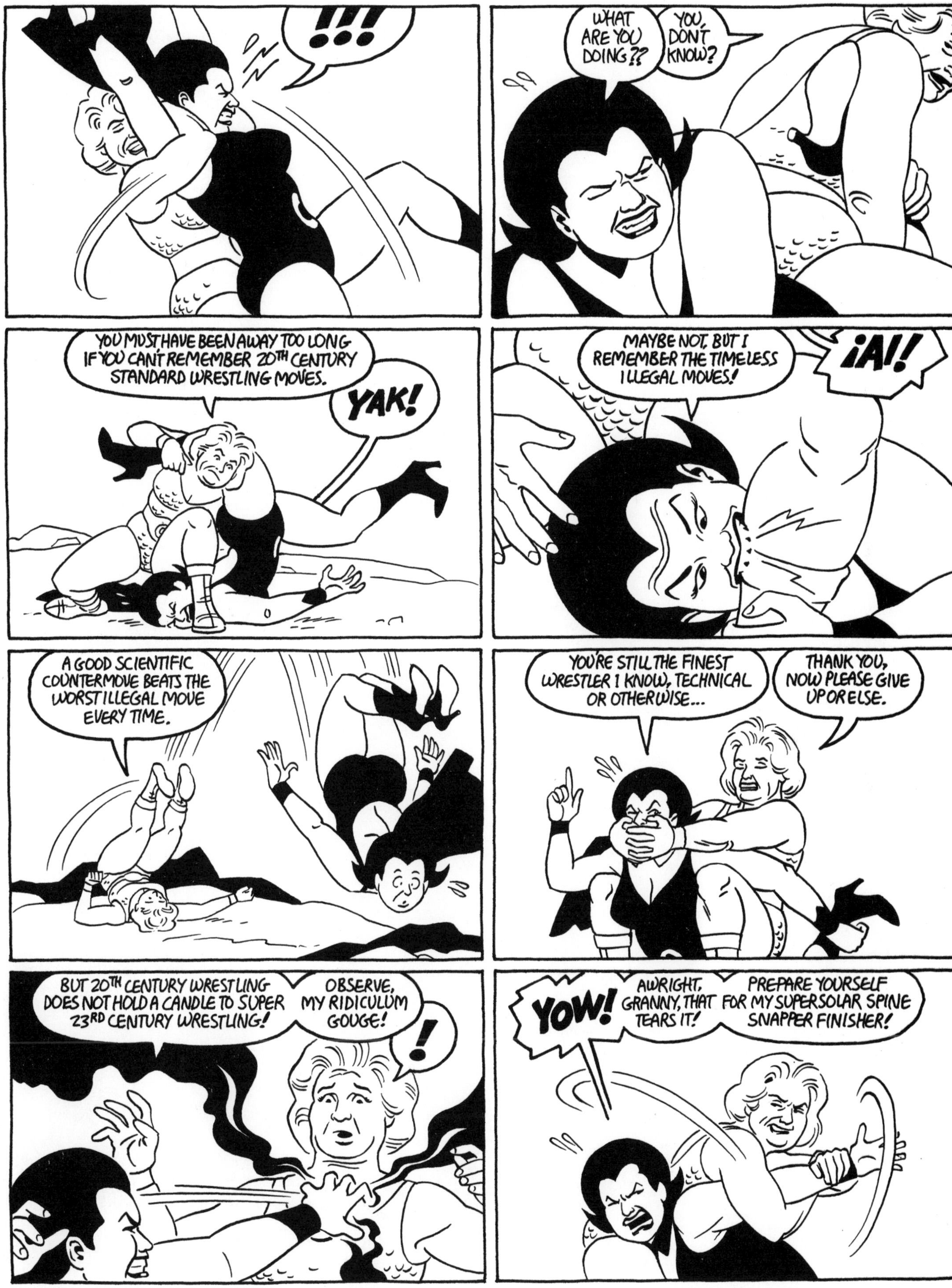
!!!
WHAT ARE YOU DOING??
YOU, DON'T KNOW?
YOU MUST HAVE BEEN AWAY TOO LONG IF YOU CAN'T REMEMBER 20TH CENTURY STANDARD WRESTLING MOVES.
YAK!
MAYBE NOT, BUT I REMEMBER THE TIMELESS ILLEGAL MOVES!
¡AI!
A GOOD SCIENTIFIC COUNTERMOVE BEATS THE WORST ILLEGAL MOVE EVERY TIME.
YOU'RE STILL THE FINEST WRESTLER I KNOW, TECHNICAL OR OTHERWISE...
THANK YOU, NOW PLEASE GIVE UP OR ELSE.
BUT 20TH CENTURY WRESTLING DOES NOT HOLD A CANDLE TO SUPER 23RD CENTURY WRESTLING!
OBSERVE, MY RIDICULUM GOUGE!
!
YOW!
AWRIGHT, GRANNY, THAT TEARS IT!
PREPARE YOURSELF FOR MY SUPERSOLAR SPINE SNAPPER FINISHER!

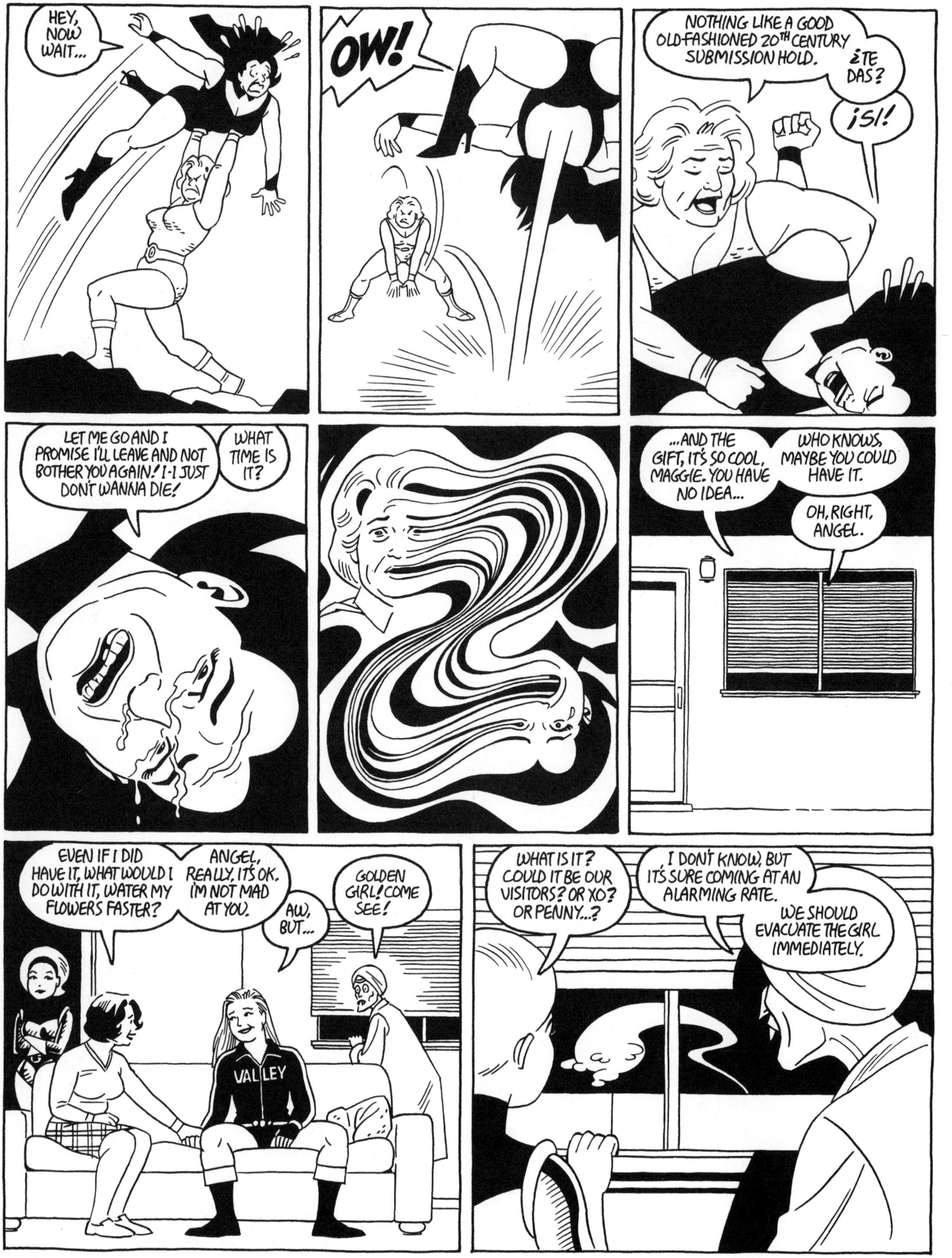
HEY, NOW WAIT...
OW!
NOTHING LIKE A GOOD OLD-FASHIONED 20TH CENTURY SUBMISSION HOLD.
¿TE DAS?
¡SI!
LET ME GO AND I PROMISE I'LL LEAVE AND NOT BOTHER YOU AGAIN! I-I JUST DON'T WANNA DIE!
WHAT TIME IS IT?
...AND THE GIFT, IT'S SO COOL, MAGGIE. YOU HAVE NO IDEA...
WHO KNOWS, MAYBE YOU COULD HAVE IT.
OH, RIGHT, ANGEL.
EVEN IF I DID HAVE IT, WHAT WOULD I DO WITH IT, WATER MY FLOWERS FASTER?
ANGEL, REALLY, IT'S OK. I'M NOT MAD AT YOU.
AW, BUT...
GOLDEN GIRL! COME SEE!
VALLEY
WHAT IS IT? COULD IT BE OUR VISITORS? OR XO? OR PENNY...?
I DON'T KNOW, BUT IT'S SURE COMING AT AN ALARMING RATE.
WE SHOULD EVACUATE THE GIRL IMMEDIATELY.

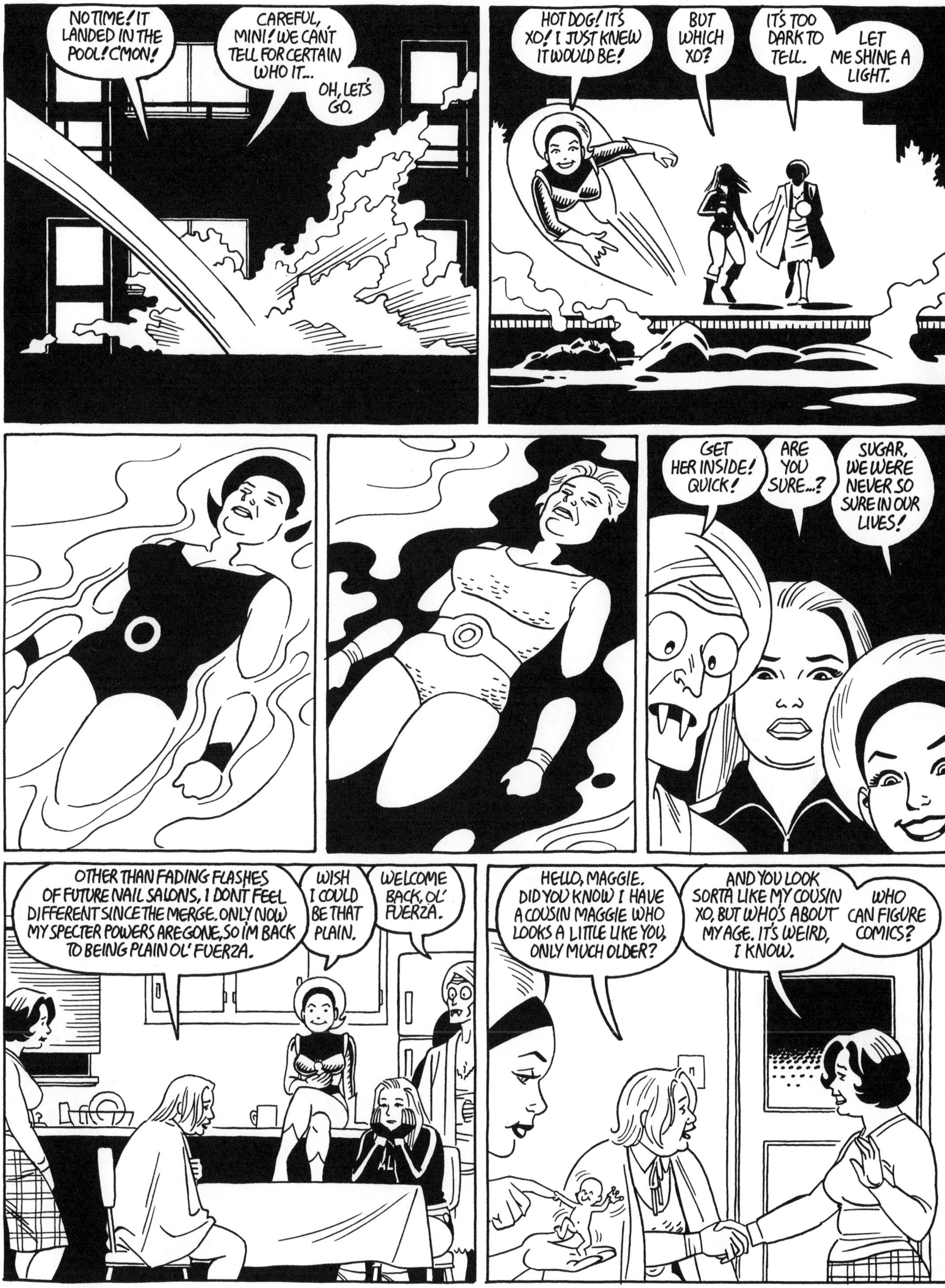
NO TIME! IT LANDED IN THE POOL! C'MON!
CAREFUL, MINI! WE CAN'T TELL FOR CERTAIN WHO IT...
OH, LET'S GO.
HOT DOG! IT'S XO! I JUST KNEW IT WOULD BE!
BUT WHICH XO?
IT'S TOO DARK TO TELL.
LET ME SHINE A LIGHT.
GET HER INSIDE! QUICK!
ARE YOU SURE...?
SUGAR, WE WERE NEVER SO SURE IN OUR LIVES!
OTHER THAN FADING FLASHES OF FUTURE NAIL SALONS, I DONT FEEL DIFFERENT SINCE THE MERGE. ONLY NOW MY SPECTER POWERS ARE GONE, SO I'M BACK TO BEING PLAIN OL' FUERZA.
WISH I COULD BE THAT PLAIN.
WELCOME BACK, OL' FUERZA.
HELLO, MAGGIE. DID YOU KNOW I HAVE A COUSIN MAGGIE WHO LOOKS A LITTLE LIKE YOU, ONLY MUCH OLDER?
AND YOU LOOK SORTA LIKE MY COUSIN XO, BUT WHO'S ABOUT MY AGE. IT'S WEIRD, I KNOW.
WHO CAN FIGURE COMICS?

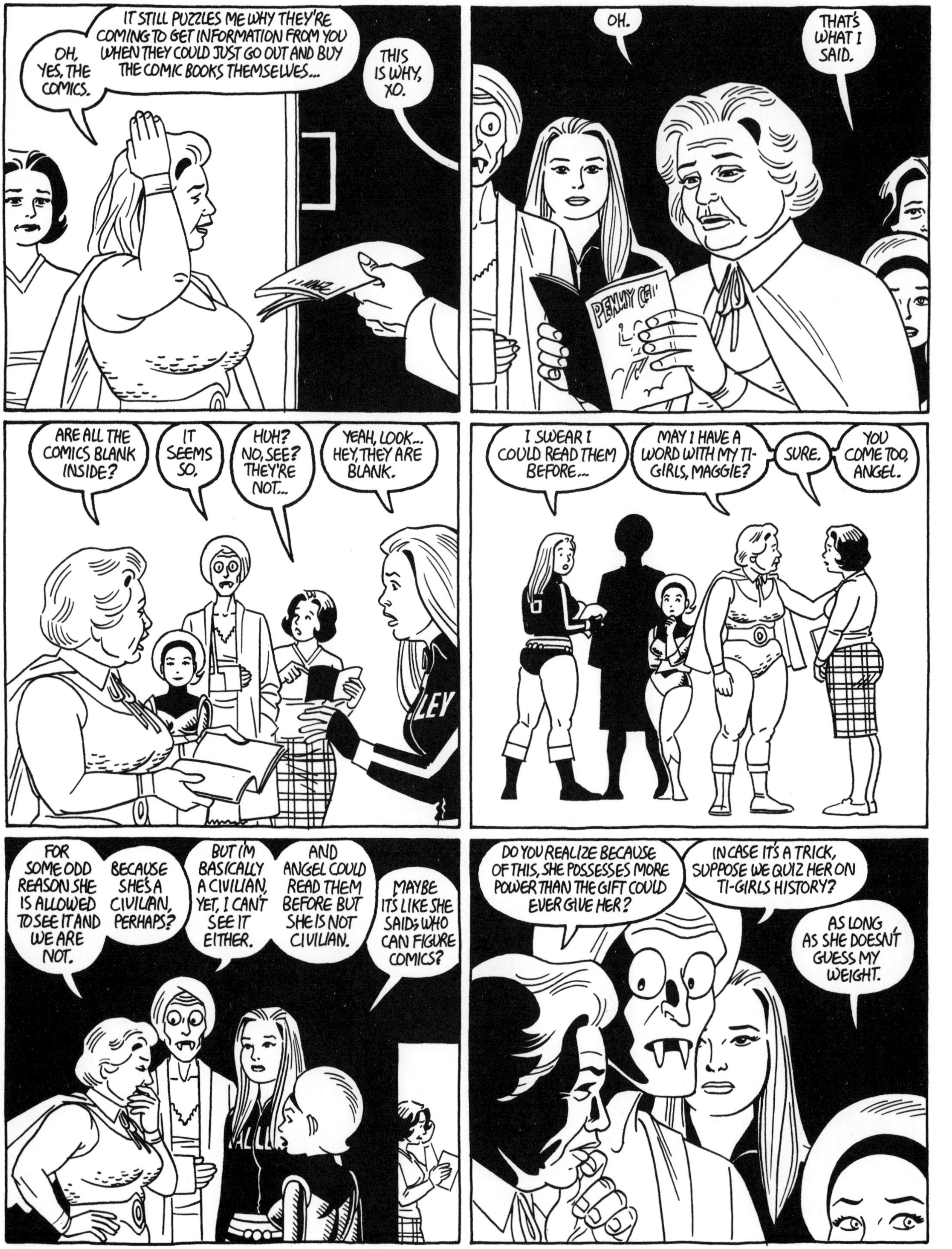
OH, YES, THE COMICS.
IT STILL PUZZLES ME WHY THEY'RE COMING TO GET INFORMATION FROM YOU WHEN THEY COULD JUST GO OUT AND BUY THE COMIC BOOKS THEMSELVES...
THIS IS WHY, XO.
OH.
THAT'S WHAT I SAID.
PENNY C
ARE ALL THE COMICS BLANK INSIDE?
IT SEEMS SO.
HUH? NO, SEE? THEY'RE NOT...
YEAH, LOOK... HEY, THEY ARE BLANK.
I SWEAR I COULD READ THEM BEFORE...
MAY I HAVE A WORD WITH MY TI-GIRLS, MAGGIE?
SURE.
YOU COME TOO, ANGEL.
FOR SOME ODD REASON SHE IS ALLOWED TO SEE IT AND WE ARE NOT.
BECAUSE SHE'S A CIVILIAN, PERHAPS?
BUT I'M BASICALLY A CIVILIAN, YET, I CAN'T SEE IT EITHER.
AND ANGEL COULD READ THEM BEFORE BUT SHE IS NOT CIVILIAN.
MAYBE IT'S LIKE SHE SAID; WHO CAN FIGURE COMICS?
DO YOU REALIZE BECAUSE OF THIS, SHE POSSESSES MORE POWER THAN THE GIFT COULD EVER GIVE HER?
IN CASE IT'S A TRICK, SUPPOSE WE QUIZ HER ON TI-GIRLS HISTORY?
AS LONG AS SHE DOESN'T GUESS MY WEIGHT.

THOUGH THE GIFT HAS EXISTED SINCE THE DAWN OF TIME, IT WASN'T UNTIL THE 20TH CENTURY SUPERHERO BOOM THAT WOMEN STARTED TO USE IT IN LARGE NUMBERS. BUT LIKE EVERYTHING ELSE, SUCCEEDING IN THE SUPER BIZ WAS DIFFICULT FOR ANYONE WHO WASN'T WHITE OR MALE OR A WHITE MALE.

IT WASN'T UNTIL THE LATE 1950'S DID THINGS START TO CHANGE WHEN ONE DAY TITAN GIRL AND MADAM TIME MET AND MADE THE BOLD DECISION TO QUIT THEIR MALE-DOMINATED SUPER TEAMS AND FORM THEIR OWN ALL-FEMALE SQUAD.

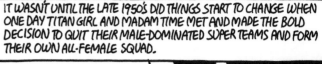

THEY WERE JOINED BY TIGER WOMAN SO THEY DECIDED TO CALL THEMSELVES THE TI-GIRLS. MISS MICRO JOINED NEXT AND CHANGED HER NAME TO TINY TAYLOR. THEY WERE READY FOR THE WORLD BUT WHAT THEY GAINED IN STRENGTH, THEY LACKED IN LEADERSHIP.

TITAN GIRL MET AND MARRIED A BRILLIANT SCIENTIST NAMED DR. ZOLAR, FAMOUS FOR ADVANCING THE CAREER OF MIRACLE WOMAN IN THE 40'S. HE WAS SOON VOTED IN (BY HIMSELF AND HIS WIFE) AS THE LEADER OF THE TI-GIRLS.

DR. ZOLAR WAS A STRIDENT MEGALOMANIAC AND AFTER A FEW YEARS OF INFIGHTING, THE TI-GIRLS COLLAPSED. TITAN GIRL RAN AWAY WITH A DRUMMER BACK EAST AND THE REST EITHER QUIT OR RETIRED, THUS LEAVING THE DOCTOR WITH EGG ON HIS FACE.

IMMEDIATELY DR. ZOLAR STARTED RECRUITING AN ALL-NEW TI-GIRLS. HE FOCUSED ON YOUNG, INFLUENTIAL MISFITS AND REJECTS FROM OTHER TEAMS, LIKE THE DIABETIC SATURNA, THE ALCOHOLIC FALCONA AND AN ILLEGAL ALIEN (IMMIGRANT) NAMED FUERZA (LATER ESPECTRA).

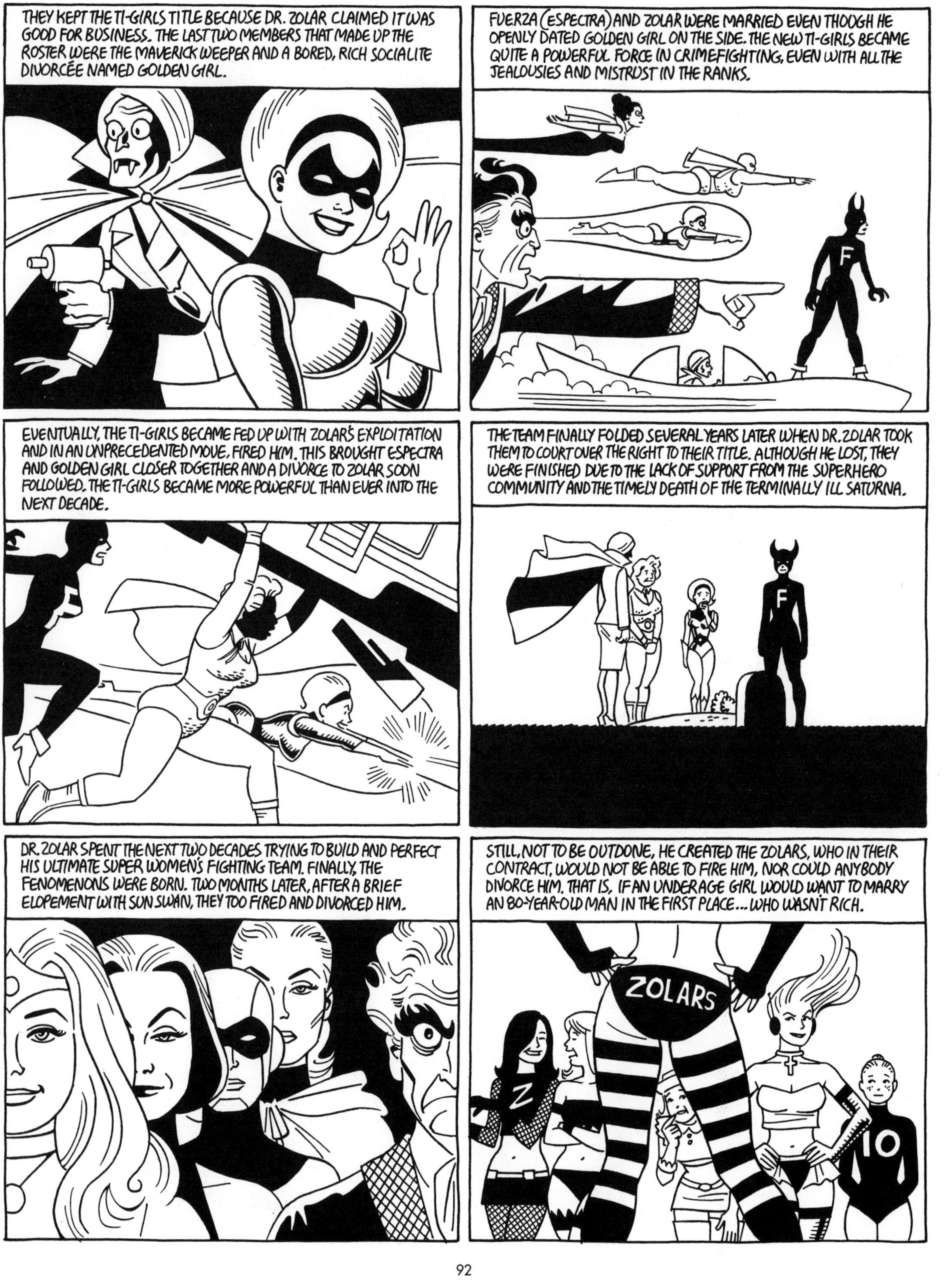
THEY KEPT THE TI-GIRLS TITLE BECAUSE DR. ZOLAR CLAIMED IT WAS GOOD FOR BUSINESS. THE LAST TWO MEMBERS THAT MADE UP THE ROSTER WERE THE MAVERICK WEEPER AND A BORED, RICH SOCIALITE DIVORCÉE NAMED GOLDEN GIRL.
FUERZA (ESPECTRA) AND ZOLAR WERE MARRIED EVEN THOUGH HE OPENLY DATED GOLDEN GIRL ON THE SIDE. THE NEW TI-GIRLS BECAME QUITE A POWERFUL FORCE IN CRIMEFIGHTING, EVEN WITH ALL THE JEALOUSIES AND MISTRUST IN THE RANKS.
EVENTUALLY, THE TI-GIRLS BECAME FED UP WITH ZOLAR'S EXPLOITATION AND IN AN UNPRECEDENTED MOVE, FIRED HIM. THIS BROUGHT ESPECTRA AND GOLDEN GIRL CLOSER TOGETHER AND A DIVORCE TO ZOLAR SOON FOLLOWED. THE TI-GIRLS BECAME MORE POWERFUL THAN EVER INTO THE NEXT DECADE.
THE TEAM FINALLY FOLDED SEVERAL YEARS LATER WHEN DR. ZOLAR TOOK THEM TO COURT OVER THE RIGHT TO THEIR TITLE. ALTHOUGH HE LOST, THEY WERE FINISHED DUE TO THE LACK OF SUPPORT FROM THE SUPERHERO COMMUNITY AND THE TIMELY DEATH OF THE TERMINALLY ILL SATURNA.
DR. ZOLAR SPENT THE NEXT TWO DECADES TRYING TO BUILD AND PERFECT HIS ULTIMATE SUPER WOMEN'S FIGHTING TEAM. FINALLY, THE FENOMENONS WERE BORN. TWO MONTHS LATER, AFTER A BRIEF ELOPEMENT WITH SUN SWAN, THEY TOO FIRED AND DIVORCED HIM.
STILL, NOT TO BE OUTDONE, HE CREATED THE ZOLARS, WHO IN THEIR CONTRACT, WOULD NOT BE ABLE TO FIRE HIM, NOR COULD ANYBODY DIVORCE HIM. THAT IS, IF AN UNDERAGE GIRL WOULD WANT TO MARRY AN 80-YEAR-OLD MAN IN THE FIRST PLACE... WHO WASN'T RICH.
ZOLARS

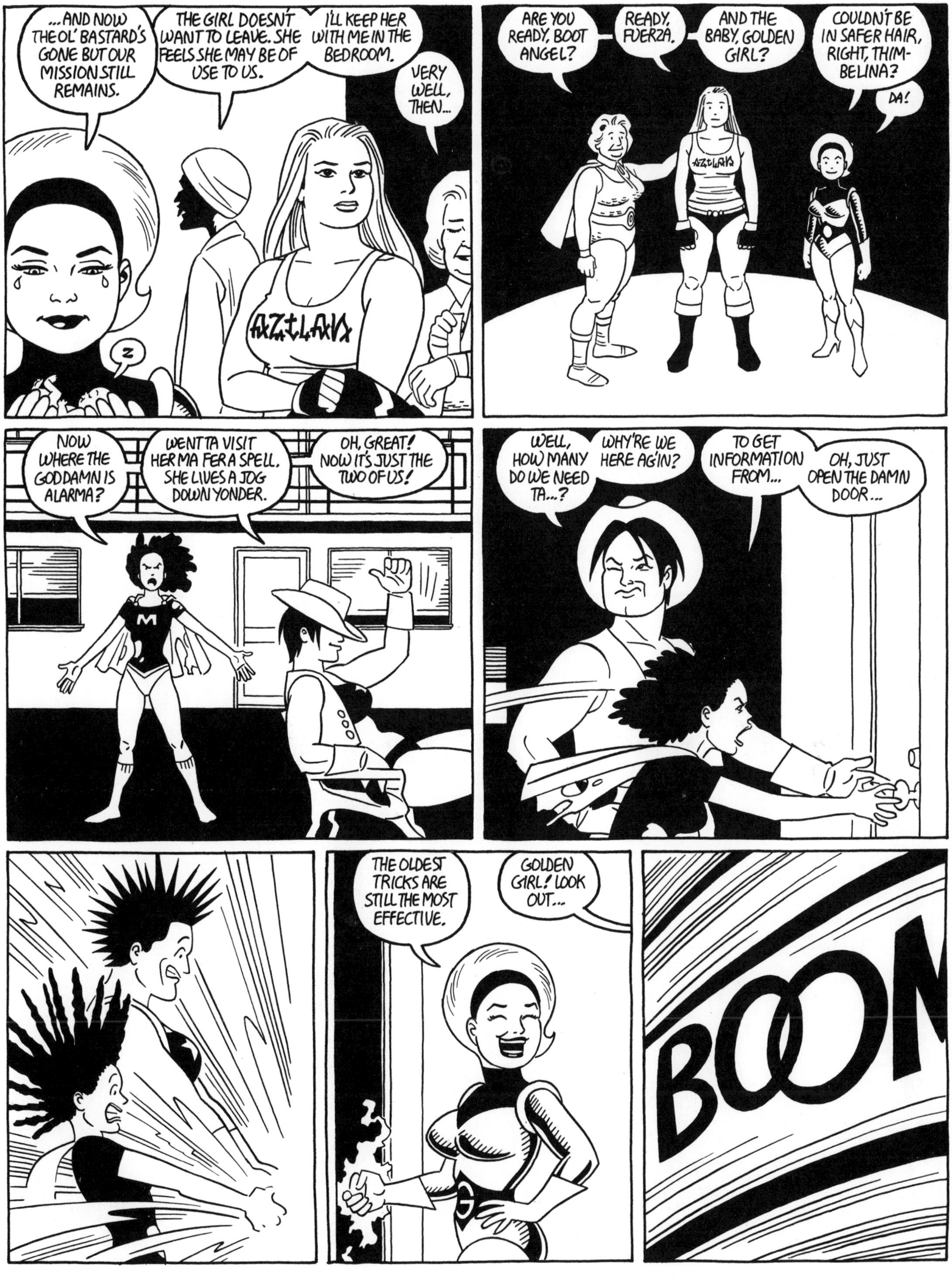
...AND NOW THE OL' BASTARD'S GONE BUT OUR MISSION STILL REMAINS.
THE GIRL DOESN'T WANT TO LEAVE. SHE FEELS SHE MAY BE OF USE TO US.
I'LL KEEP HER WITH ME IN THE BEDROOM.
VERY WELL, THEN...
Z
ARE YOU READY, BOOT ANGEL?
READY, FUERZA.
AND THE BABY, GOLDEN GIRL?
COULDN'T BE IN SAFER HAIR, RIGHT, THIMBELINA?
DA!
AZTLAN
NOW WHERE THE GODDAMN IS ALARMA?
WENTTA VISIT HER MA FER A SPELL. SHE LIVES A JOG DOWN YONDER.
OH, GREAT! NOW IT'S JUST THE TWO OF US!
WELL, HOW MANY DO WE NEED TA...?
WHY'RE WE HERE AG'IN?
TO GET INFORMATION FROM...
OH, JUST OPEN THE DAMN DOOR...
THE OLDEST TRICKS ARE STILL THE MOST EFFECTIVE.
GOLDEN GIRL! LOOK OUT...
BOOM

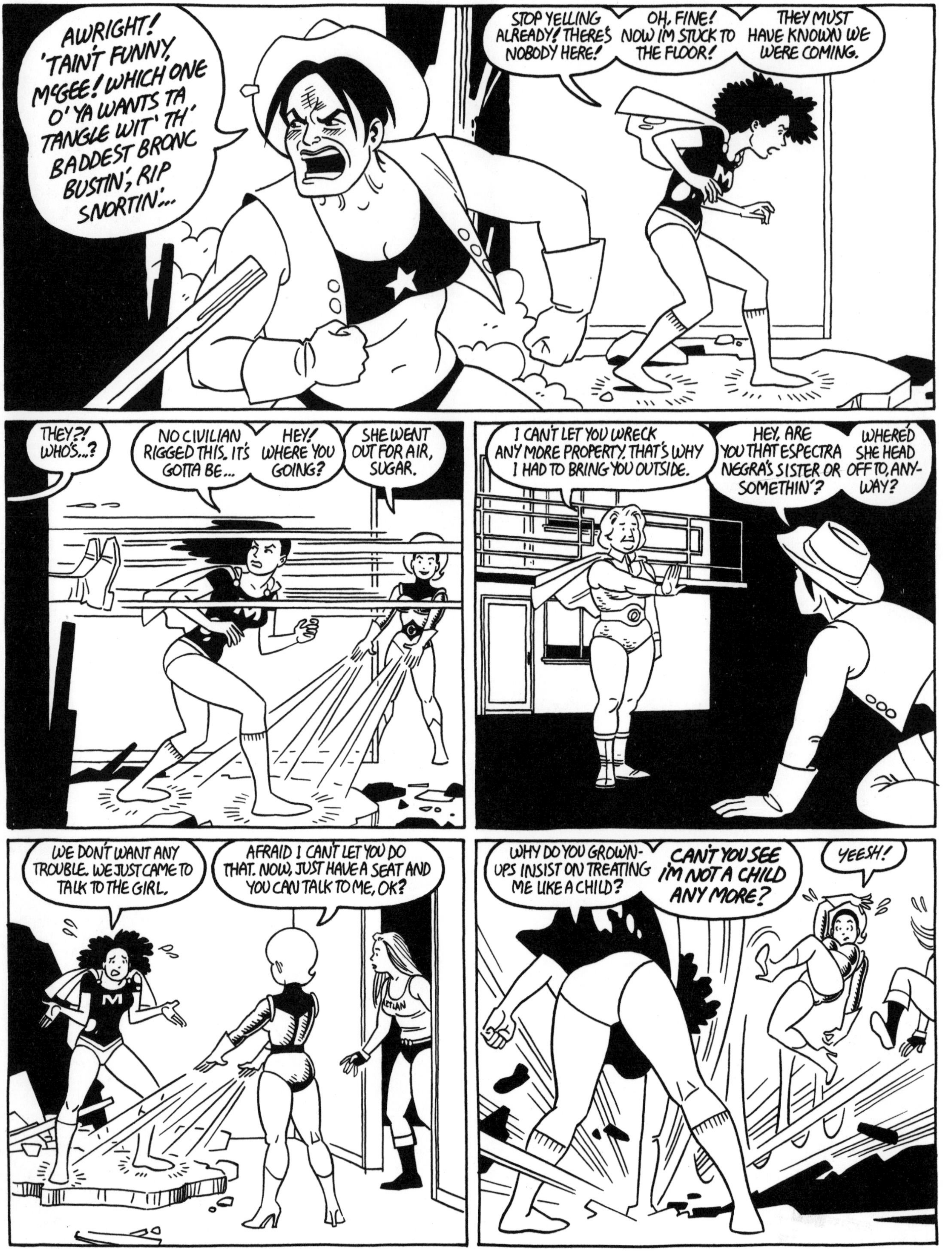
AWRIGHT! 'TAIN'T FUNNY, McGEE! WHICH ONE O' YA WANTS TA TANGLE WIT' TH' BADDEST BRONC BUSTIN', RIP SNORTIN'...
STOP YELLING ALREADY! THERE'S NOBODY HERE!
OH, FINE! NOW I'M STUCK TO THE FLOOR!
THEY MUST HAVE KNOWN WE WERE COMING.
THEY?! WHO'S...?
NO CIVILIAN RIGGED THIS. IT'S GOTTA BE...
HEY! WHERE YOU GOING?
SHE WENT OUT FOR AIR, SUGAR.
I CAN'T LET YOU WRECK ANY MORE PROPERTY. THAT'S WHY I HAD TO BRING YOU OUTSIDE.
HEY, ARE YOU THAT ESPECTRA NEGRA'S SISTER OR SOMETHIN'?
WHERE'D SHE HEAD OFF TO, ANYWAY?
WE DON'T WANT ANY TROUBLE. WE JUST CAME TO TALK TO THE GIRL.
AFRAID I CAN'T LET YOU DO THAT. NOW, JUST HAVE A SEAT AND YOU CAN TALK TO ME, OK?
WHY DO YOU GROWN-UPS INSIST ON TREATING ME LIKE A CHILD?
CAN'T YOU SEE I'M NOT A CHILD ANY MORE?
YEESH!

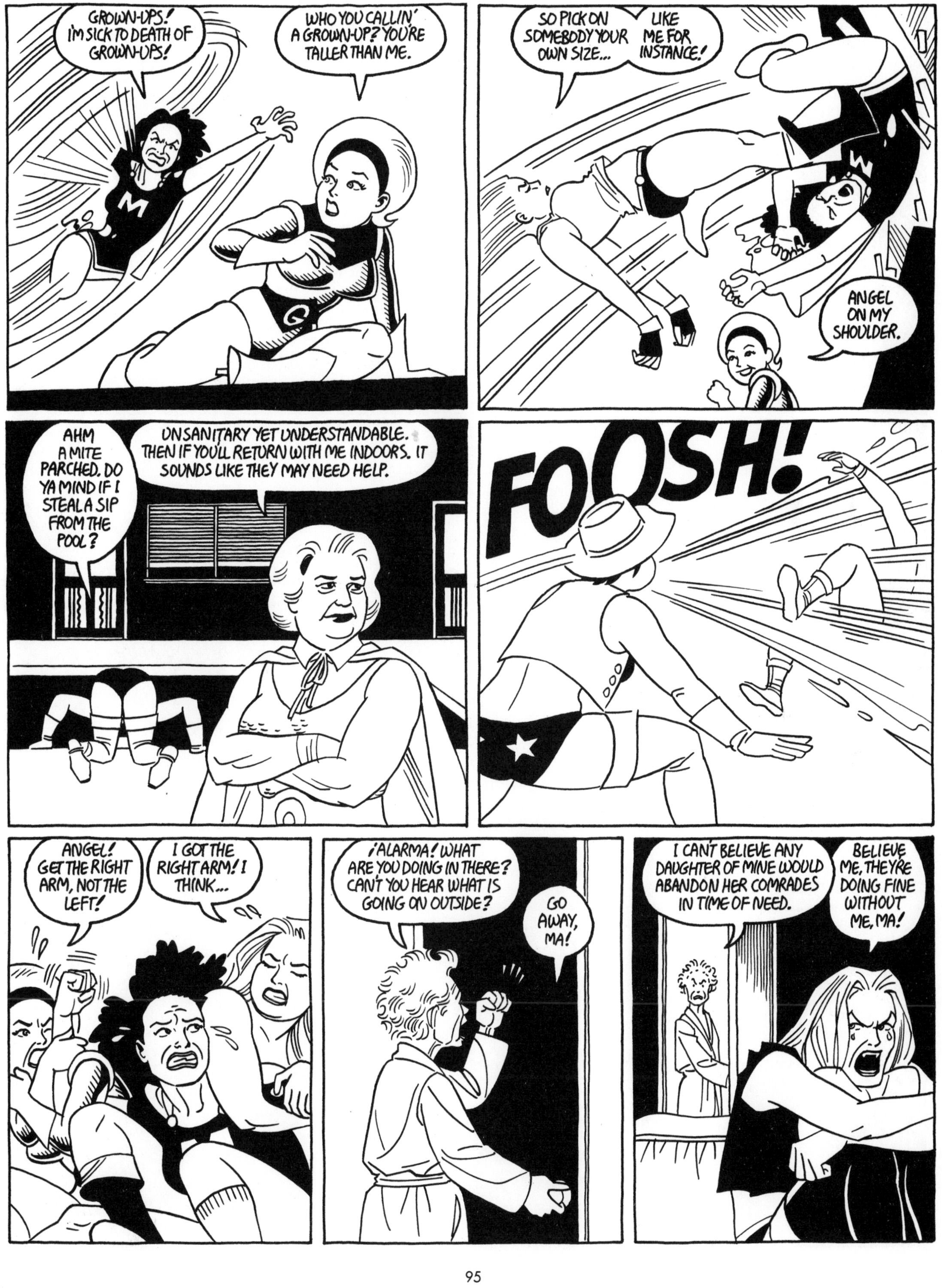
GROWN-UPS! I'M SICK TO DEATH OF GROWN-UPS!
WHO YOU CALLIN' A GROWN-UP? YOU'RE TALLER THAN ME.
SO PICK ON SOMEBODY YOUR OWN SIZE...
LIKE ME FOR INSTANCE!
ANGEL ON MY SHOULDER.
AHM A MITE PARCHED. DO YA MIND IF I STEAL A SIP FROM THE POOL?
UNSANITARY YET UNDERSTANDABLE. THEN IF YOU'LL RETURN WITH ME INDOORS. IT SOUNDS LIKE THEY MAY NEED HELP.
FOOSH!
ANGEL! GET THE RIGHT ARM, NOT THE LEFT!
I GOT THE RIGHT ARM! I THINK...
¡ALARMA! WHAT ARE YOU DOING IN THERE? CAN'T YOU HEAR WHAT IS GOING ON OUTSIDE?
GO AWAY, MA!
I CAN'T BELIEVE ANY DAUGHTER OF MINE WOULD ABANDON HER COMRADES IN TIME OF NEED.
BELIEVE ME, THEY'RE DOING FINE WITHOUT ME, MA!

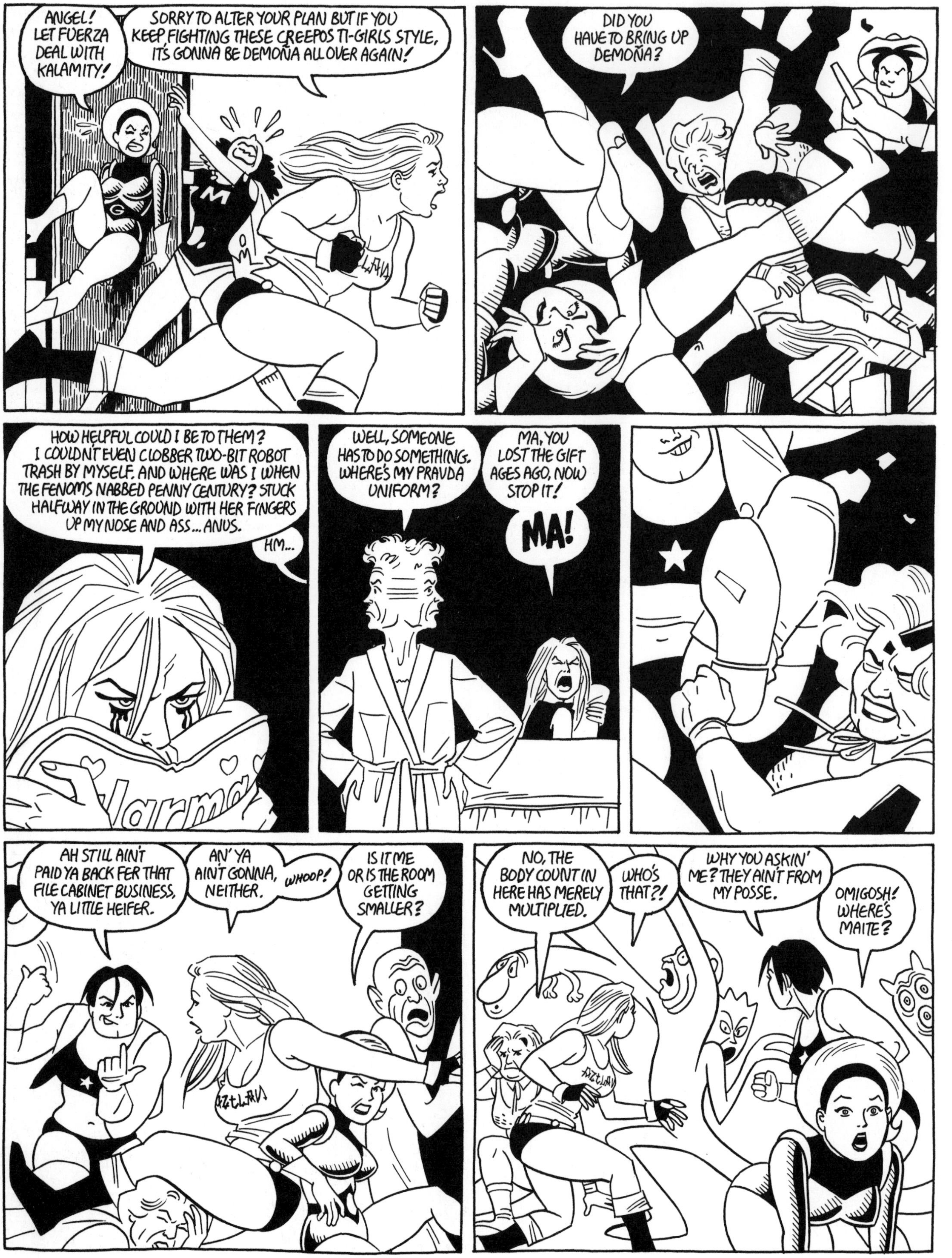
ANGEL! LET FUERZA DEAL WITH KALAMITY!
SORRY TO ALTER YOUR PLAN BUT IF YOU KEEP FIGHTING THESE CREEPOS TI-GIRLS STYLE, IT'S GONNA BE DEMOÑA ALL OVER AGAIN!
DID YOU HAVE TO BRING UP DEMOÑA?
HOW HELPFUL COULD I BE TO THEM? I COULDN'T EVEN CLOBBER TWO-BIT ROBOT TRASH BY MYSELF. AND WHERE WAS I WHEN THE FENOMS NABBED PENNY CENTURY? STUCK HALFWAY IN THE GROUND WITH HER FINGERS UP MY NOSE AND ASS... ANUS.
HM...
WELL, SOMEONE HAS TO DO SOMETHING. WHERE'S MY PRAVDA UNIFORM?
MA, YOU LOST THE GIFT AGES AGO, NOW STOP IT!
MA!
AH STILL AIN'T PAID YA BACK FER THAT FILE CABINET BUSINESS, YA LITTLE HEIFER.
AN' YA AIN'T GONNA, NEITHER.
WHOOP!
IS IT ME OR IS THE ROOM GETTING SMALLER?
NO, THE BODY COUNT IN HERE HAS MERELY MULTIPLIED.
WHO'S THAT?!
WHY YOU ASKIN' ME? THEY AIN'T FROM MY POSSE.
OMIGOSH! WHERE'S MAITE?

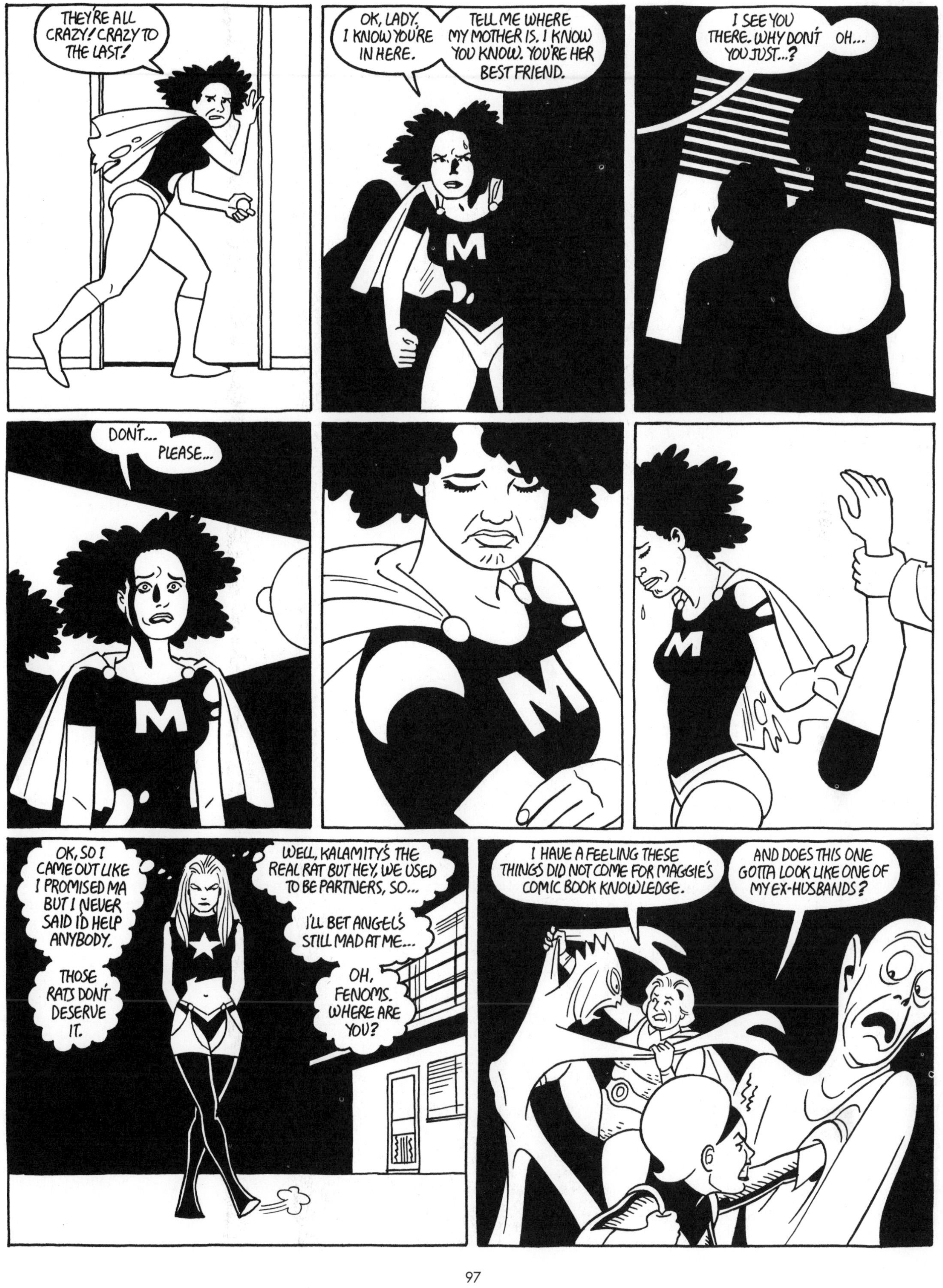
THEY'RE ALL CRAZY! CRAZY TO THE LAST!
OK, LADY, I KNOW YOU'RE IN HERE.
TELL ME WHERE MY MOTHER IS. I KNOW YOU KNOW. YOU'RE HER BEST FRIEND.
I SEE YOU THERE. WHY DON'T YOU JUST...?
OH...
DON'T...
PLEASE...
OK, SO I CAME OUT LIKE I PROMISED MA BUT I NEVER SAID I'D HELP ANYBODY.
THOSE RATS DON'T DESERVE IT.
WELL, KALAMITY'S THE REAL RAT BUT HEY, WE USED TO BE PARTNERS, SO...
I'LL BET ANGEL'S STILL MAD AT ME...
OH, FENOMS. WHERE ARE YOU?
I HAVE A FEELING THESE THINGS DID NOT COME FOR MAGGIE'S COMIC BOOK KNOWLEDGE.
AND DOES THIS ONE GOTTA LOOK LIKE ONE OF MY EX-HUSBANDS?

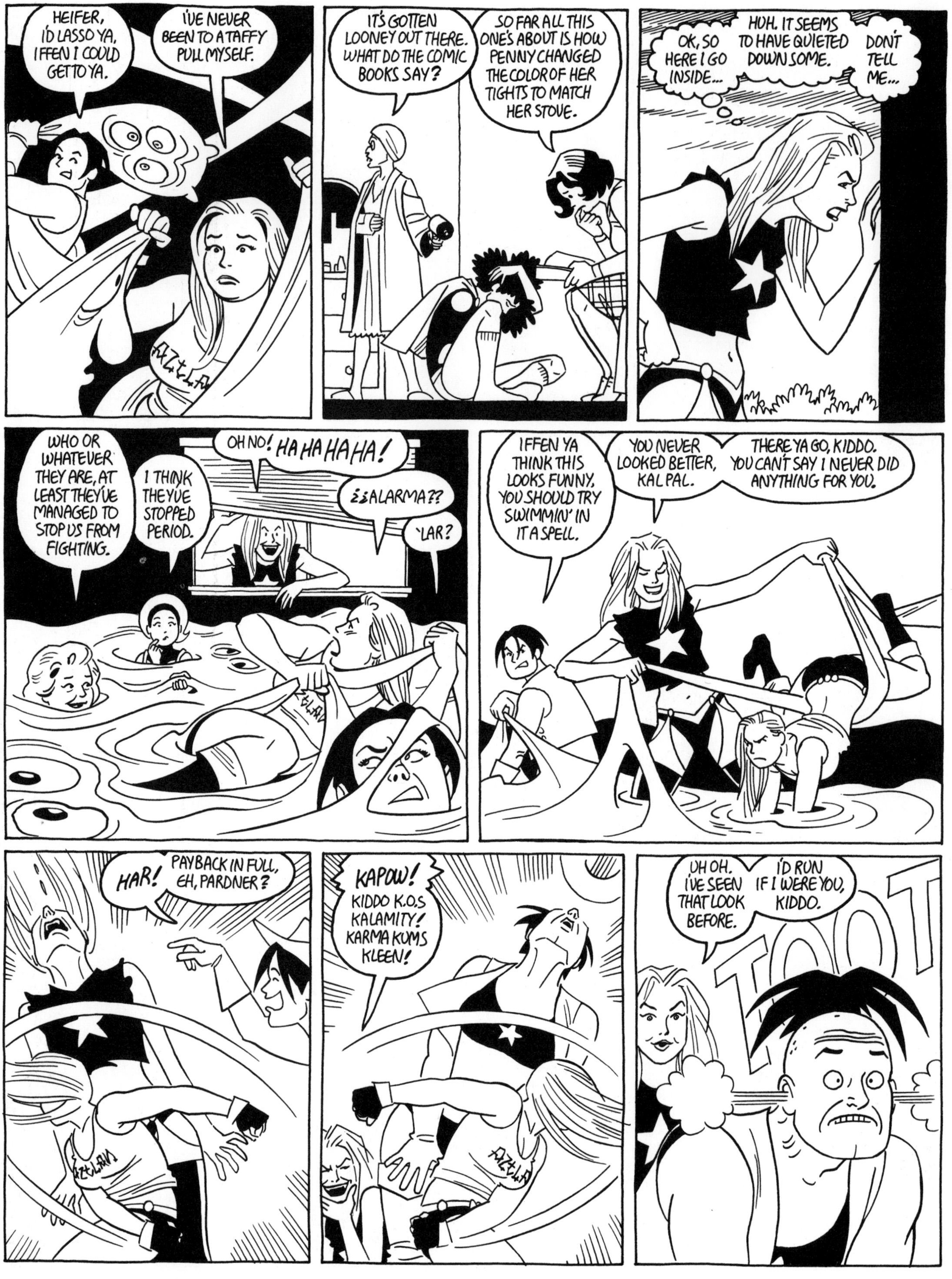
HEIFER, I'D LASSO YA, IFFEN I COULD GET TO YA.
I'VE NEVER BEEN TO A TAFFY PULL MYSELF.
IT'S GOTTEN LOONEY OUT THERE. WHAT DO THE COMIC BOOKS SAY?
SO FAR ALL THIS ONE'S ABOUT IS HOW PENNY CHANGED THE COLOR OF HER TIGHTS TO MATCH HER STOVE.
OK, SO HERE I GO INSIDE...
HUH. IT SEEMS TO HAVE QUIETED DOWN SOME.
DON'T TELL ME...
WHO OR WHATEVER THEY ARE, AT LEAST THEY'VE MANAGED TO STOP US FROM FIGHTING.
I THINK THEY'VE STOPPED PERIOD.
OH NO! HA HA HA HA!
¿¡ALARMA??
'LAR?
IFFEN YA THINK THIS LOOKS FUNNY, YOU SHOULD TRY SWIMMIN' IN IT A SPELL.
YOU NEVER LOOKED BETTER, KAL PAL.
THERE YA GO, KIDDO. YOU CAN'T SAY I NEVER DID ANYTHING FOR YOU.
HAR!
PAYBACK IN FULL, EH, PARDNER?
KAPOW!
KIDDO K.O.S KALAMITY! KARMA KUMS KLEEN!
UH OH. I'VE SEEN THAT LOOK BEFORE.
I'D RUN IF I WERE YOU, KIDDO.
TOOT

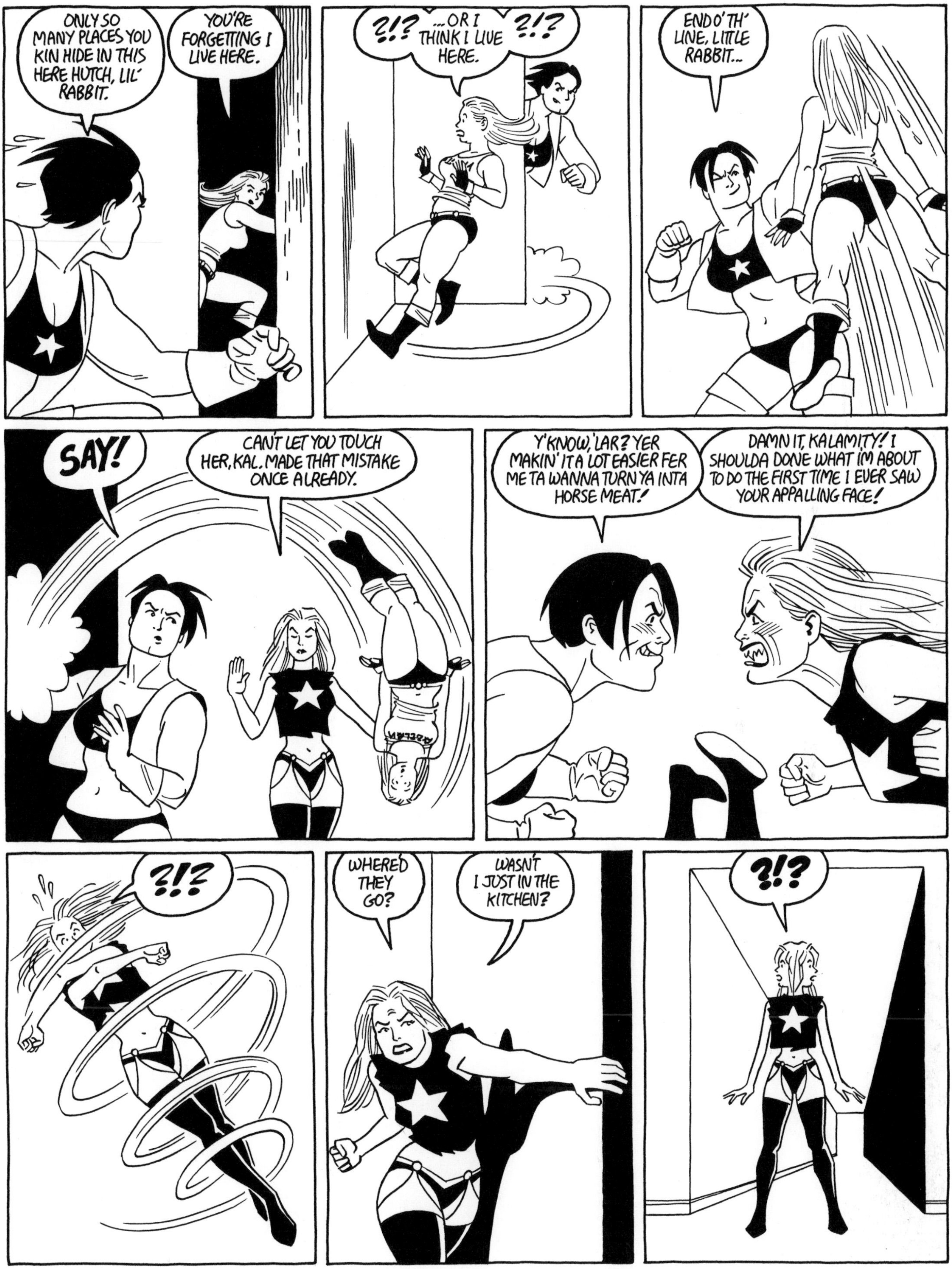
ONLY SO MANY PLACES YOU KIN HIDE IN THIS HERE HUTCH, LIL' RABBIT.
YOU'RE FORGETTING I LIVE HERE.
?!?
...OR I THINK I LIVE HERE.
?!?
END O' TH' LINE, LITTLE RABBIT...
SAY!
CAN'T LET YOU TOUCH HER, KAL. MADE THAT MISTAKE ONCE ALREADY.
Y'KNOW, 'LAR? YER MAKIN' IT A LOT EASIER FER ME TA WANNA TURN YA INTA HORSE MEAT!
DAMN IT, KALAMITY! I SHOULDA DONE WHAT I'M ABOUT TO DO THE FIRST TIME I EVER SAW YOUR APPALLING FACE!
?!?
WHERE'D THEY GO?
WASN'T I JUST IN THE KITCHEN?
?!?

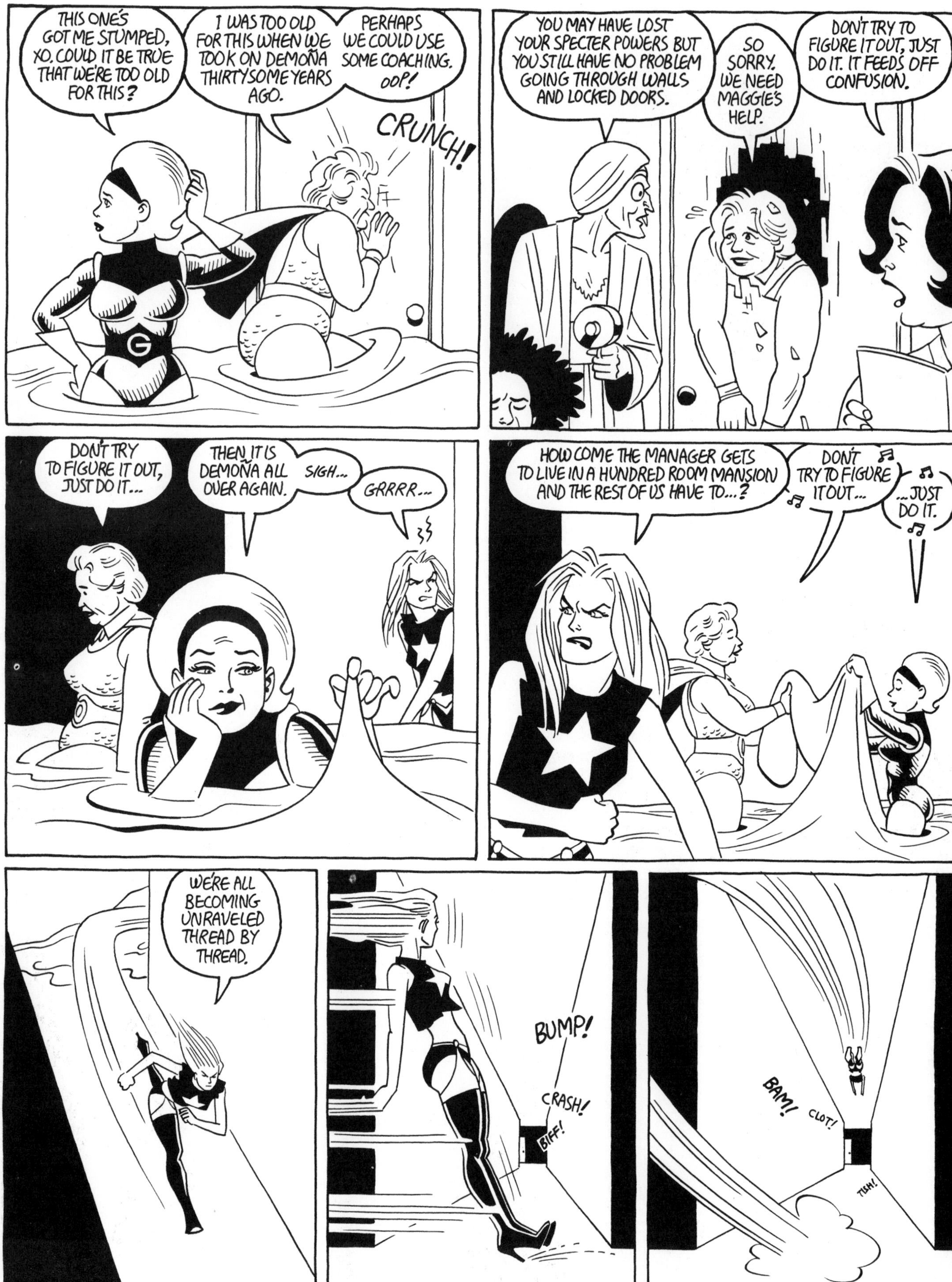

THIS ONE'S GOT ME STUMPED, XO. COULD IT BE TRUE THAT WE'RE TOO OLD FOR THIS?
I WAS TOO OLD FOR THIS WHEN WE TOOK ON DEMOÑA THIRTYSOME YEARS AGO.
PERHAPS WE COULD USE SOME COACHING. OOP!
CRUNCH!
YOU MAY HAVE LOST YOUR SPECTER POWERS BUT YOU STILL HAVE NO PROBLEM GOING THROUGH WALLS AND LOCKED DOORS.
SO SORRY. WE NEED MAGGIE'S HELP.
DON'T TRY TO FIGURE IT OUT, JUST DO IT. IT FEEDS OFF CONFUSION.
DON'T TRY TO FIGURE IT OUT, JUST DO IT...
THEN, IT IS DEMOÑA ALL OVER AGAIN.
SIGH...
GRRRR...
HOW COME THE MANAGER GETS TO LIVE IN A HUNDRED ROOM MANSION AND THE REST OF US HAVE TO...?
DON'T TRY TO FIGURE IT OUT...
...JUST DO IT.
WE'RE ALL BECOMING UNRAVELED THREAD BY THREAD.
BUMP!
CRASH!
BIFF!
BAM!
CLOT!
TISH!

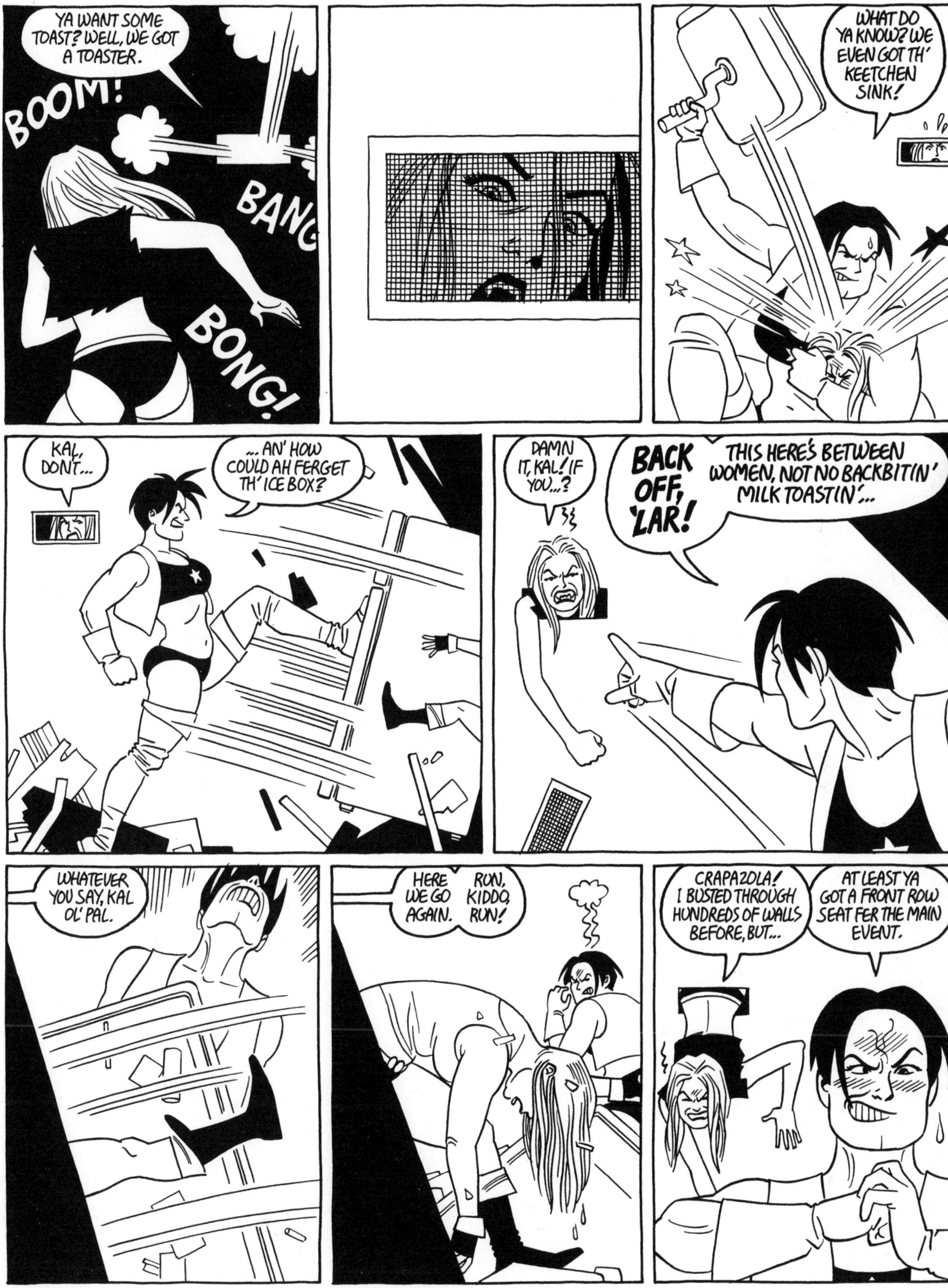

YA WANT SOME TOAST? WELL, WE GOT A TOASTER.
BOOM!
BANG
BONG!
WHAT DO YA KNOW? WE EVEN GOT TH' KEETCHEN SINK!
KAL, DON'T...
... AN' HOW COULD AH FERGET TH' ICE BOX?
DAMN IT, KAL! IF YOU...?
BACK OFF, 'LAR!
THIS HERE'S BETWEEN WOMEN, NOT NO BACKBITIN' MILK TOASTIN'...
WHATEVER YOU SAY, KAL OL' PAL.
HERE WE GO AGAIN.
RUN, KIDDO, RUN!
CRAPAZOLA! I BUSTED THROUGH HUNDREDS OF WALLS BEFORE, BUT...
AT LEAST YA GOT A FRONT ROW SEAT FER THE MAIN EVENT.

NO, KIDDO! DON'T...
SO, YA WANNA BOX, DO YA?
WHAT'S AZTLAN ANYWAY, SOME KINDA WETBACK SHIT?
AZTLAN
!!!
KLOK!
LOOK OUT! SHE'S ON RUBBER LEG STREET!
GANGWAY, KIDDO!
AZTLAN
BLOOM!
OK, WE GOT HER, ALARMA!
BUT GIVE ME A TURN! THIS BATHROOM'S EVEN TOO CROWDED FOR ME AN' MAGGIE!
BIFF!
SOK!
OK, GO. STAY ON HER, KIDDO.
GOT IT!
THEY'RE NOT GOING TO STOP UNTIL SOMEONE GETS HURT. TSK!
AH, YOUTH, BY CRACKY.
OK, TAKE FIVE, KIDDO!
BAP BAP BAP BAP
BAP
BAP BAP BAP
BAM
OK, GO!
FIVE SECONDS, NOT MINUTES!
AZTLAN

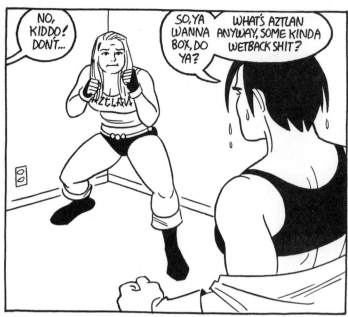

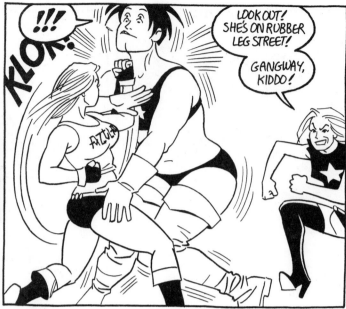

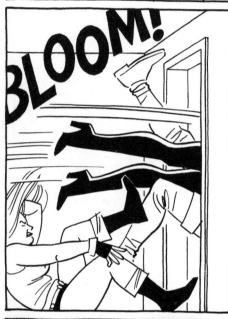

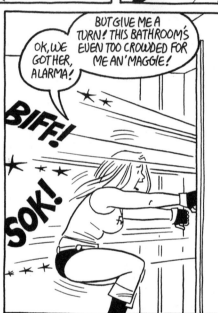

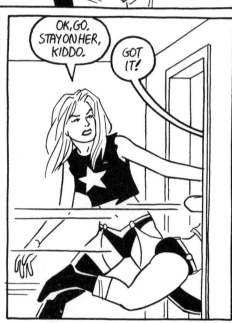

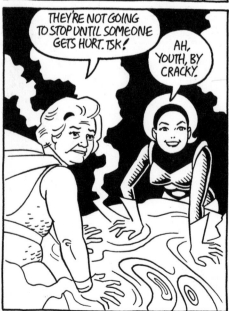

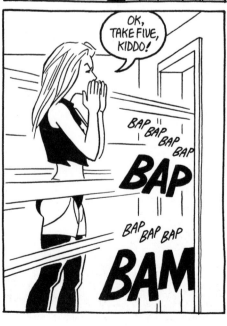

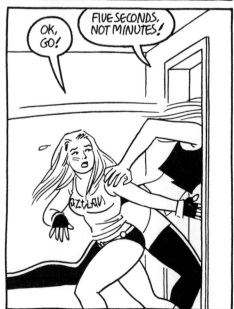

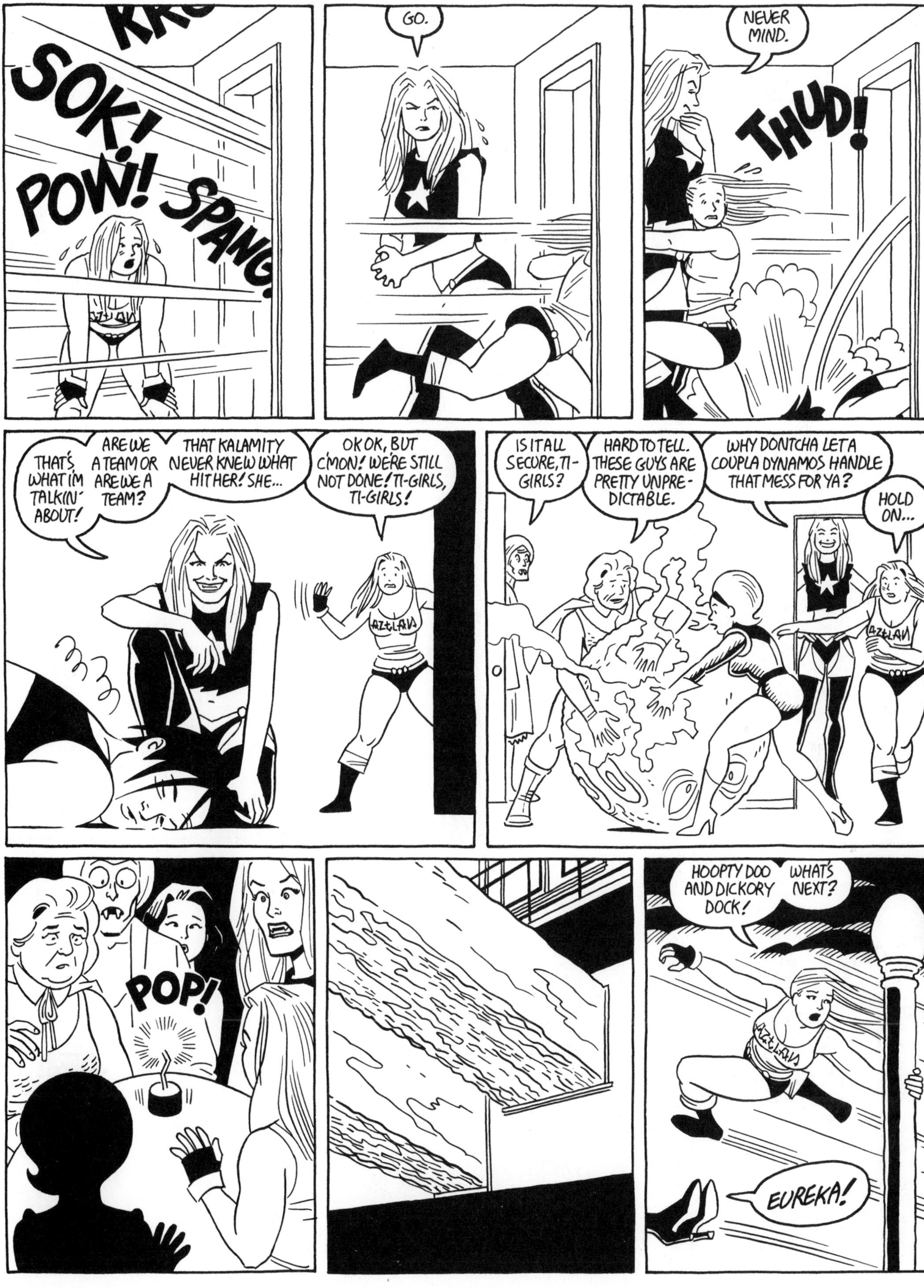
KRG
SOK!
POW!
SPANG!
GO.
NEVER MIND.
THUD!
THAT'S WHAT I'M TALKIN' ABOUT!
ARE WE A TEAM OR ARE WE A TEAM?
THAT KALAMITY NEVER KNEW WHAT HIT HER! SHE...
OK OK, BUT C'MON! WE'RE STILL NOT DONE! TI-GIRLS, TI-GIRLS!
AZTLAN
IS IT ALL SECURE, TI-GIRLS?
HARD TO TELL. THESE GUYS ARE PRETTY UNPREDICTABLE.
WHY DONTCHA LET A COUPLA DYNAMOS HANDLE THAT MESS FOR YA?
HOLD ON...
POP!
HOOPTY DOO AND DICKORY DOCK!
WHAT'S NEXT?
EUREKA!

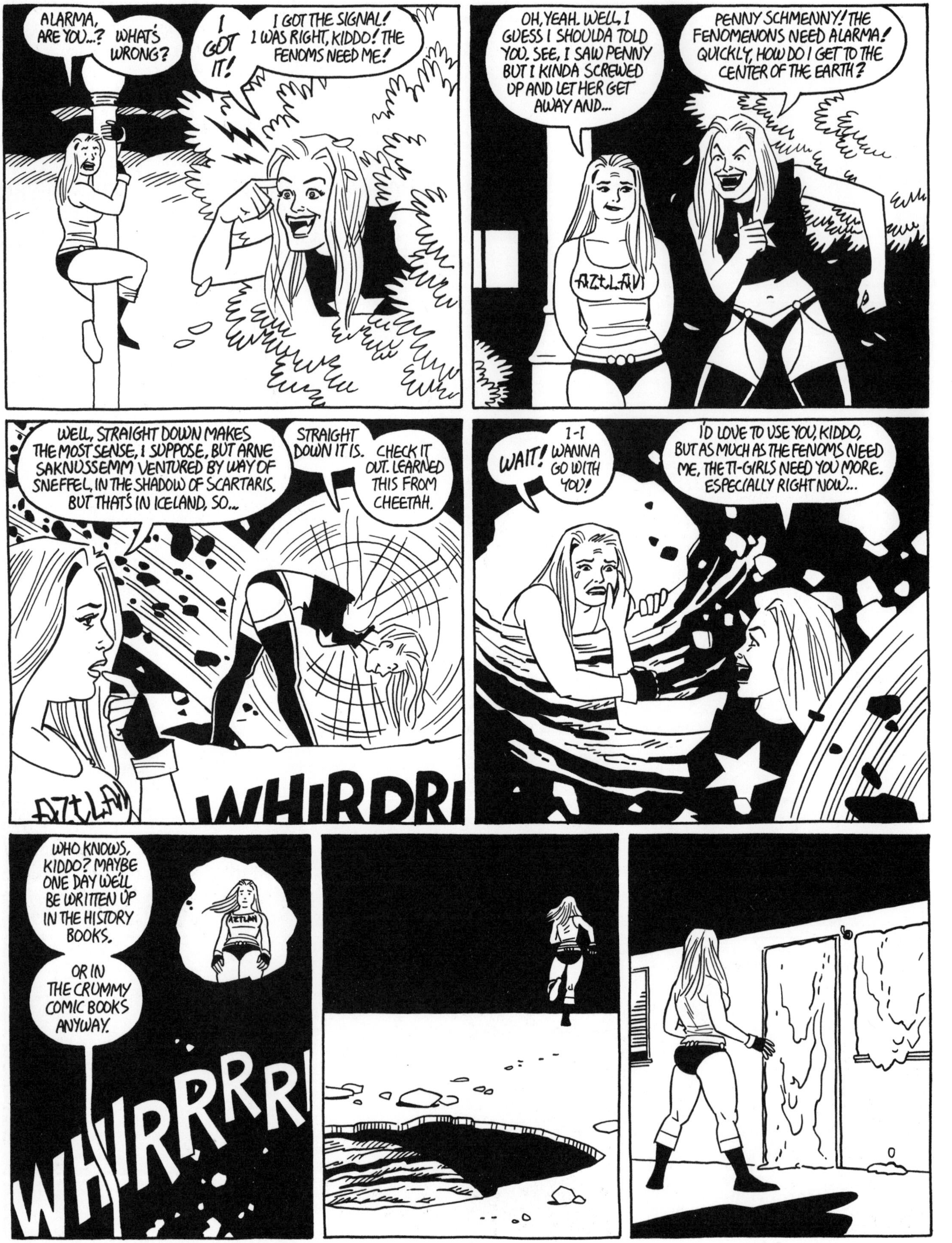

ALARMA, ARE YOU...?
WHAT'S WRONG?
I GOT IT!
I GOT THE SIGNAL! I WAS RIGHT, KIDDO! THE FENOMS NEED ME!
OH, YEAH. WELL, I GUESS I SHOULDA TOLD YOU. SEE, I SAW PENNY BUT I KINDA SCREWED UP AND LET HER GET AWAY AND...
PENNY SCHMENNY! THE FENOMENONS NEED ALARMA! QUICKLY, HOW DO I GET TO THE CENTER OF THE EARTH?
AZTLAN
WELL, STRAIGHT DOWN MAKES THE MOST SENSE, I SUPPOSE, BUT ARNE SAKNUSSEMM VENTURED BY WAY OF SNEFFEL, IN THE SHADOW OF SCARTARIS. BUT THAT'S IN ICELAND, SO...
STRAIGHT DOWN IT IS.
CHECK IT OUT. LEARNED THIS FROM CHEETAH.
AZTLAN
WHIRRR!
WAIT!
I-I WANNA GO WITH YOU!
I'D LOVE TO USE YOU, KIDDO, BUT AS MUCH AS THE FENOMS NEED ME, THE TI-GIRLS NEED YOU MORE. ESPECIALLY RIGHT NOW...
WHO KNOWS, KIDDO? MAYBE ONE DAY WE'LL BE WRITTEN UP IN THE HISTORY BOOKS.
OR IN THE CRUMMY COMIC BOOKS ANYWAY.
AZTLAN
WHIRRRRR!

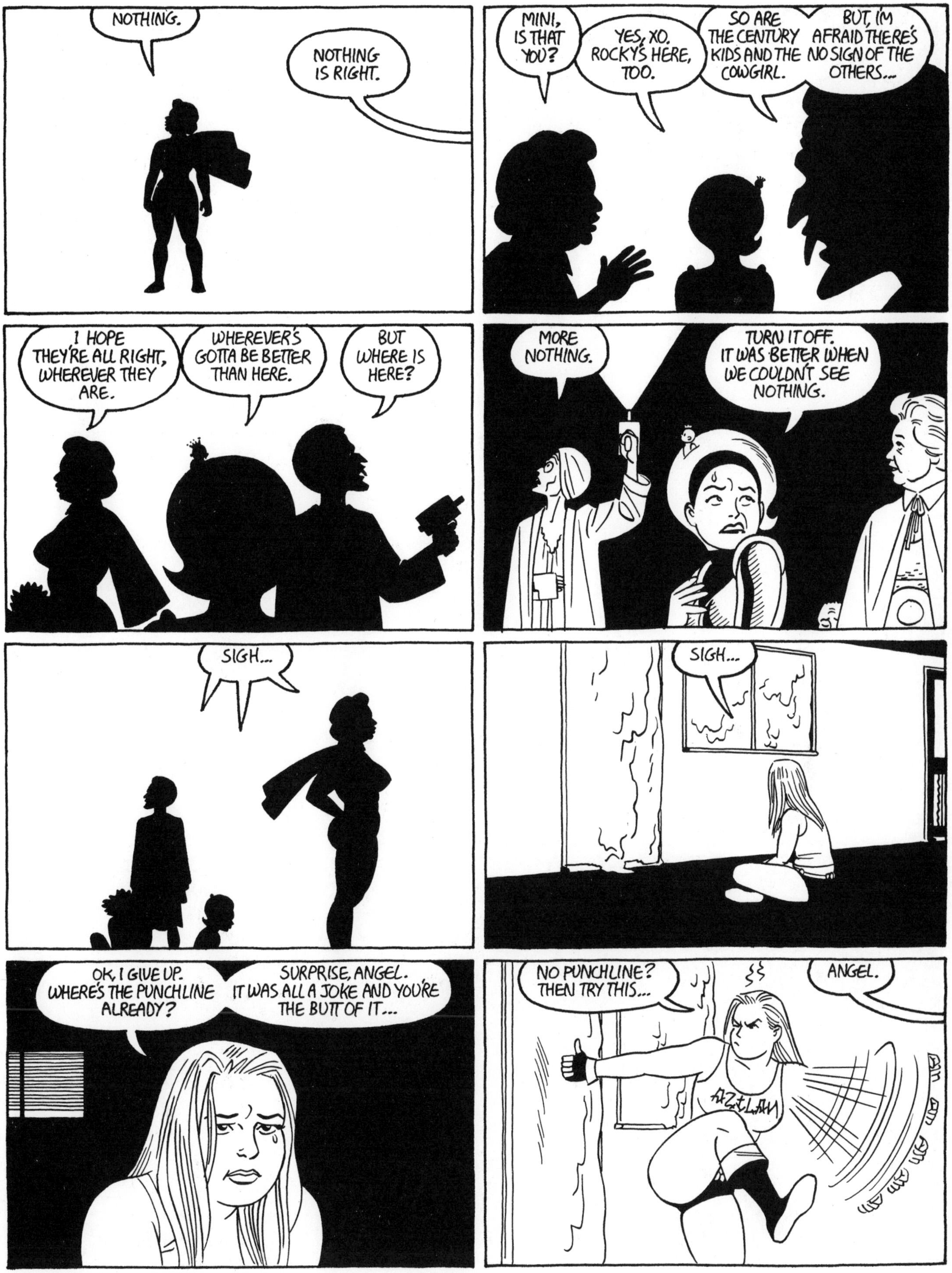
NOTHING.
NOTHING IS RIGHT.
MINI, IS THAT YOU?
YES, XO. ROCKY'S HERE, TOO.
SO ARE THE CENTURY KIDS AND THE COWGIRL.
BUT, I'M AFRAID THERE'S NO SIGN OF THE OTHERS...
I HOPE THEY'RE ALL RIGHT, WHEREVER THEY ARE.
WHEREVER'S GOTTA BE BETTER THAN HERE.
BUT WHERE IS HERE?
MORE NOTHING.
TURN IT OFF. IT WAS BETTER WHEN WE COULDN'T SEE NOTHING.
SIGH...
SIGH...
OK, I GIVE UP. WHERE'S THE PUNCHLINE ALREADY?
SURPRISE, ANGEL. IT WAS ALL A JOKE AND YOU'RE THE BUTT OF IT...
NO PUNCHLINE? THEN TRY THIS...
ANGEL.
AZTLAN

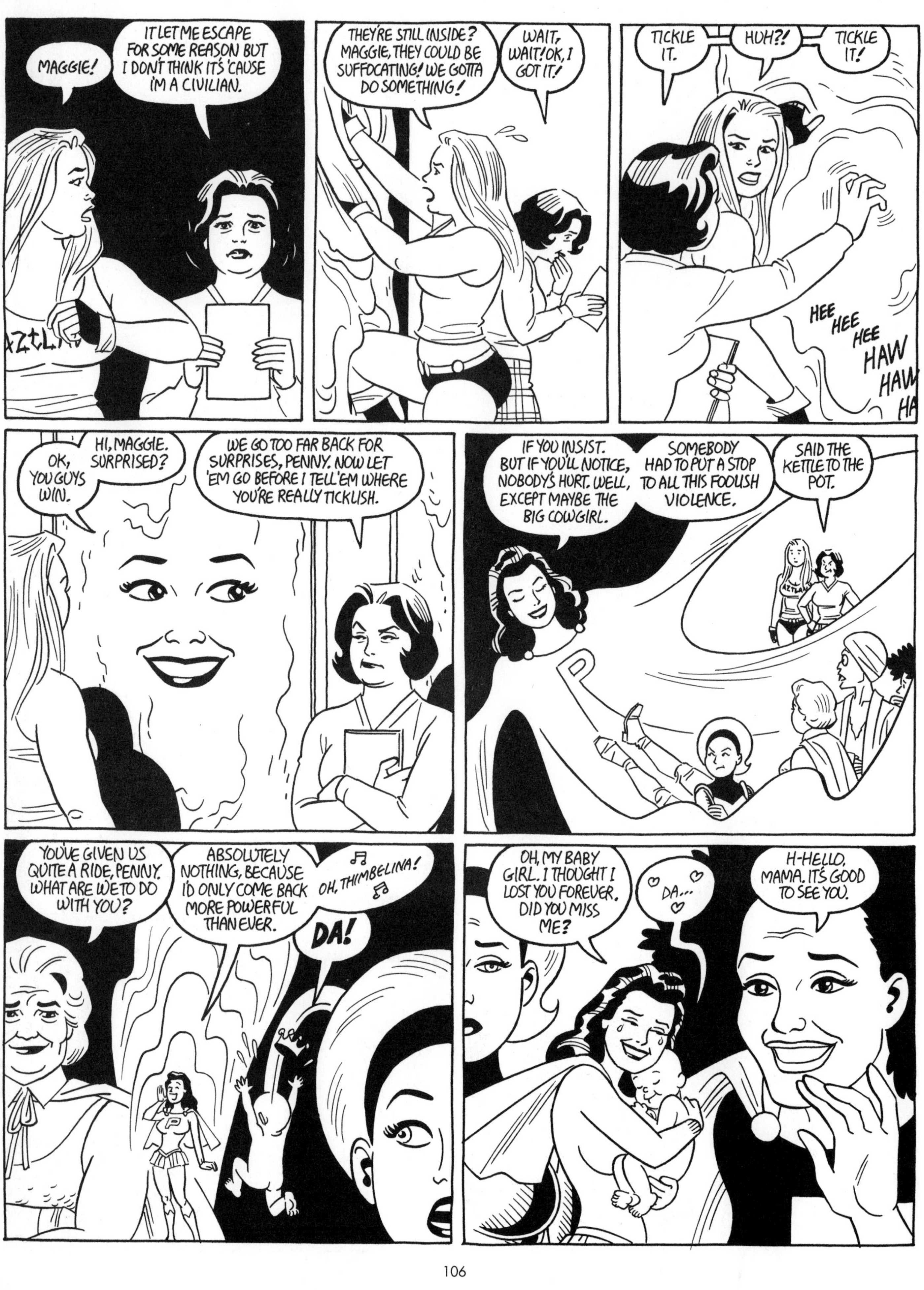
MAGGIE!
IT LET ME ESCAPE FOR SOME REASON BUT I DON'T THINK IT'S 'CAUSE I'M A CIVILIAN.
AZTLAN
THEY'RE STILL INSIDE? MAGGIE, THEY COULD BE SUFFOCATING! WE GOTTA DO SOMETHING!
WAIT, WAIT! OK, I GOT IT!
TICKLE IT.
HUH?!
TICKLE IT!
HEE HEE HEE HAW HAW HA
OK, YOU GUYS WIN.
HI, MAGGIE. SURPRISED?
WE GO TOO FAR BACK FOR SURPRISES, PENNY. NOW LET 'EM GO BEFORE I TELL 'EM WHERE YOU'RE REALLY TICKLISH.
IF YOU INSIST. BUT IF YOU'LL NOTICE, NOBODY'S HURT. WELL, EXCEPT MAYBE THE BIG COWGIRL.
SOMEBODY HAD TO PUT A STOP TO ALL THIS FOOLISH VIOLENCE.
SAID THE KETTLE TO THE POT.
YOU'VE GIVEN US QUITE A RIDE, PENNY. WHAT ARE WE TO DO WITH YOU?
ABSOLUTELY NOTHING, BECAUSE I'D ONLY COME BACK MORE POWERFUL THAN EVER.
OH, THIMBELINA!
DA!
OH, MY BABY GIRL. I THOUGHT I LOST YOU FOREVER. DID YOU MISS ME?
DA...
H-HELLO, MAMA. IT'S GOOD TO SEE YOU.

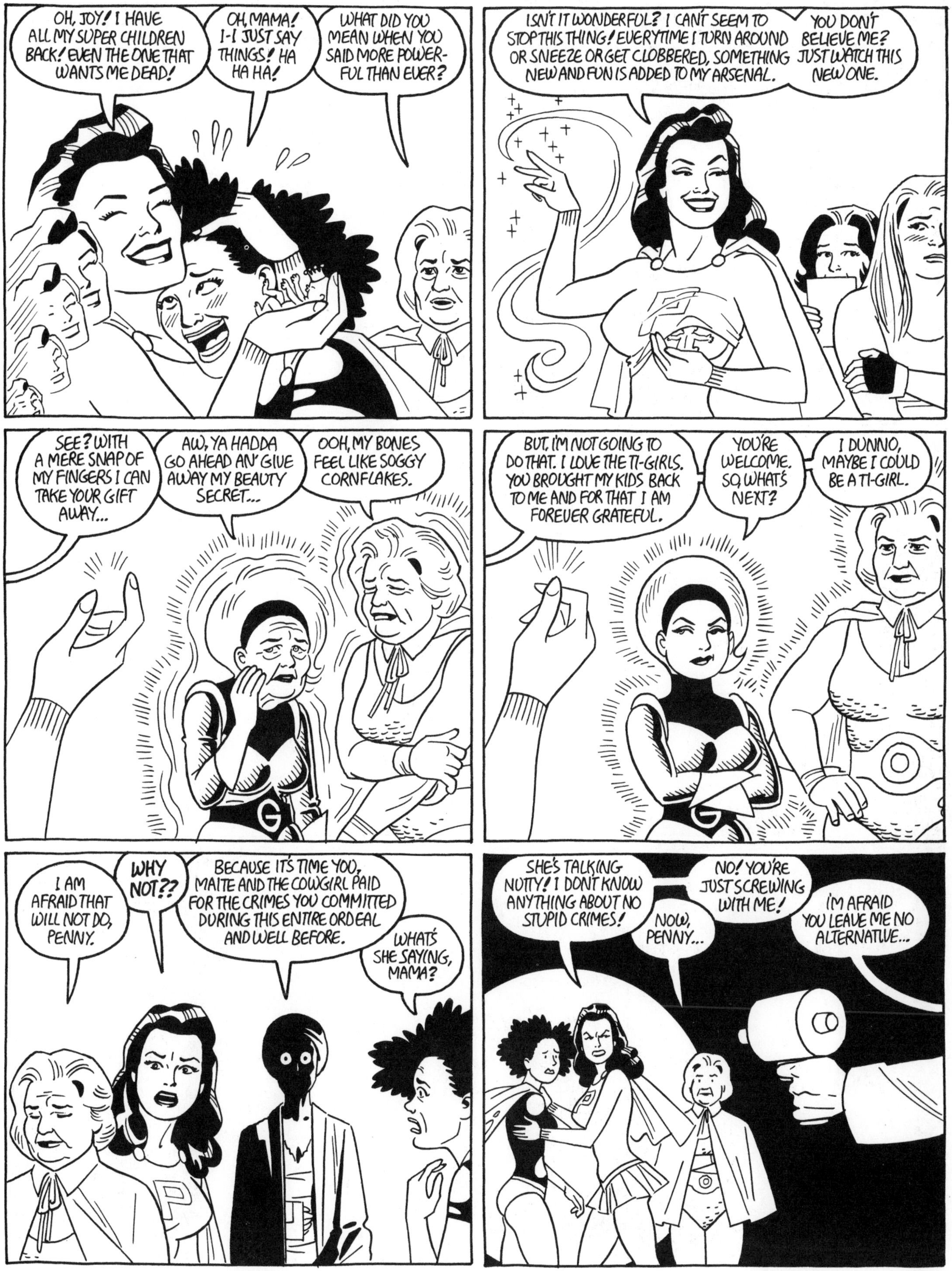
OH, JOY! I HAVE ALL MY SUPER CHILDREN BACK! EVEN THE ONE THAT WANTS ME DEAD!
OH, MAMA! I-I JUST SAY THINGS! HA HA HA!
WHAT DID YOU MEAN WHEN YOU SAID MORE POWERFUL THAN EVER?
ISN'T IT WONDERFUL? I CAN'T SEEM TO STOP THIS THING! EVERYTIME I TURN AROUND OR SNEEZE OR GET CLOBBERED, SOMETHING NEW AND FUN IS ADDED TO MY ARSENAL.
YOU DON'T BELIEVE ME? JUST WATCH THIS NEW ONE.
SEE? WITH A MERE SNAP OF MY FINGERS I CAN TAKE YOUR GIFT AWAY...
AW, YA HADDA GO AHEAD AN' GIVE AWAY MY BEAUTY SECRET...
OOH, MY BONES FEEL LIKE SOGGY CORNFLAKES.
BUT, I'M NOT GOING TO DO THAT. I LOVE THE TI-GIRLS. YOU BROUGHT MY KIDS BACK TO ME AND FOR THAT I AM FOREVER GRATEFUL.
YOU'RE WELCOME. SO, WHAT'S NEXT?
I DUNNO, MAYBE I COULD BE A TI-GIRL.
I AM AFRAID THAT WILL NOT DO, PENNY.
WHY NOT??
BECAUSE IT'S TIME YOU, MAITE AND THE COWGIRL PAID FOR THE CRIMES YOU COMMITTED DURING THIS ENTIRE ORDEAL AND WELL BEFORE.
WHAT'S SHE SAYING, MAMA?
SHE'S TALKING NUTTY! I DON'T KNOW ANYTHING ABOUT NO STUPID CRIMES!
NO! YOU'RE JUST SCREWING WITH ME!
NOW, PENNY...
I'M AFRAID YOU LEAVE ME NO ALTERNATIVE...

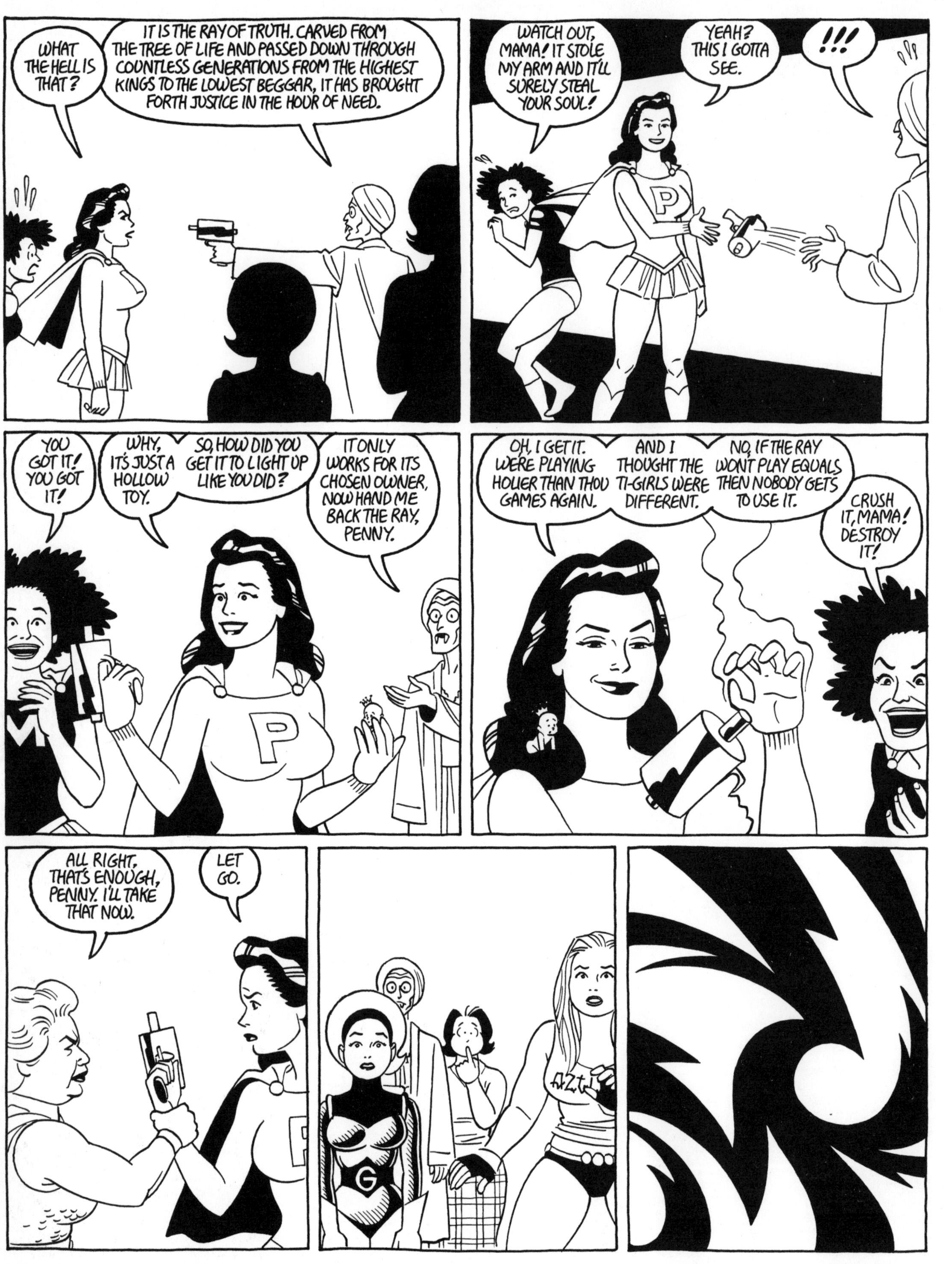
WHAT THE HELL IS THAT?
IT IS THE RAY OF TRUTH. CARVED FROM THE TREE OF LIFE AND PASSED DOWN THROUGH COUNTLESS GENERATIONS FROM THE HIGHEST KINGS TO THE LOWEST BEGGAR, IT HAS BROUGHT FORTH JUSTICE IN THE HOUR OF NEED.
WATCH OUT, MAMA! IT STOLE MY ARM AND IT'LL SURELY STEAL YOUR SOUL!
YEAH? THIS I GOTTA SEE.
!!!
YOU GOT IT! YOU GOT IT!
WHY, IT'S JUST A HOLLOW TOY.
SO, HOW DID YOU GET IT TO LIGHT UP LIKE YOU DID?
IT ONLY WORKS FOR ITS CHOSEN OWNER, NOW HAND ME BACK THE RAY, PENNY.
OH, I GET IT. WE'RE PLAYING HOLIER THAN THOU GAMES AGAIN.
AND I THOUGHT THE TI-GIRLS WERE DIFFERENT.
NO, IF THE RAY WON'T PLAY EQUALS THEN NOBODY GETS TO USE IT.
CRUSH IT, MAMA! DESTROY IT!
ALL RIGHT, THAT'S ENOUGH, PENNY. I'LL TAKE THAT NOW.
LET GO.
P
G

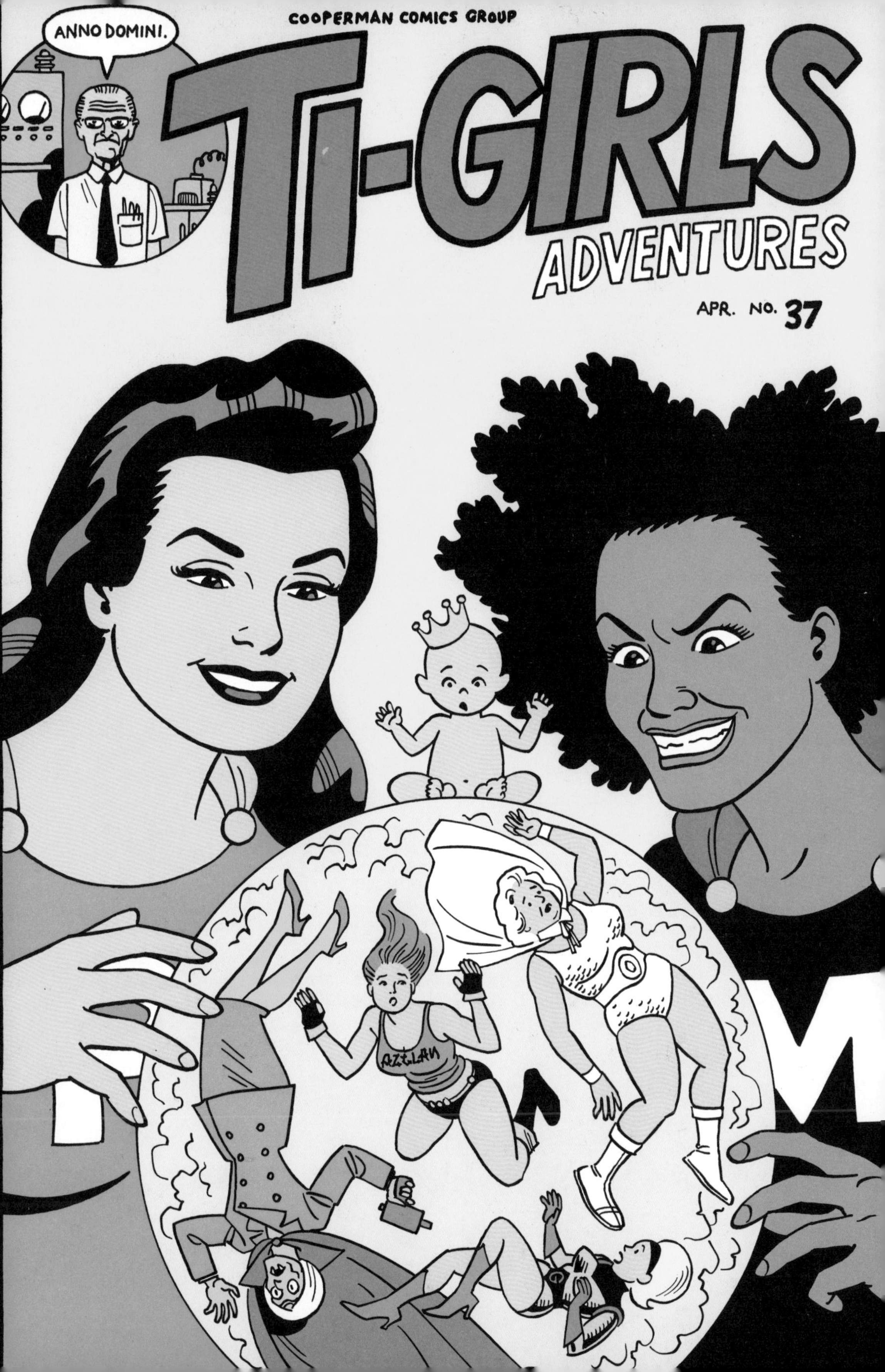
COOPERMAN COMICS GROUP
ANNO DOMINI.
TI-GIRLS
ADVENTURES
APR. NO. 37
AZTLAN

PART 5
RIDICULUM!!!
HOLY COW! ONE MORE EXPLOSION AND I SWEAR I'M PACKING MY BAGS AND MOVING TO CANADA!
WHERE DID THEY GO? DID THE RAY BLOW THEM TO PIECES?
NO, THEY WENT STRAIGHT THROUGH THE ROOF...
ALREADY MILES OUT OF SIGHT.
MY POOR UPSTAIRS TENANT. WE JUST HAD THAT CARPET PUT IN.
MAMA...?
MAMA, DON'T LEAVE ME WITH THESE PEOPLE!
OH OH, RUNAWAY NUT.
HOLD THE FORT, GIRLS.
'FRAID WE CAN'T LET YOU GO EITHER, KID.
BUT, MAMA...!
HEY, WHAT'S THAT?

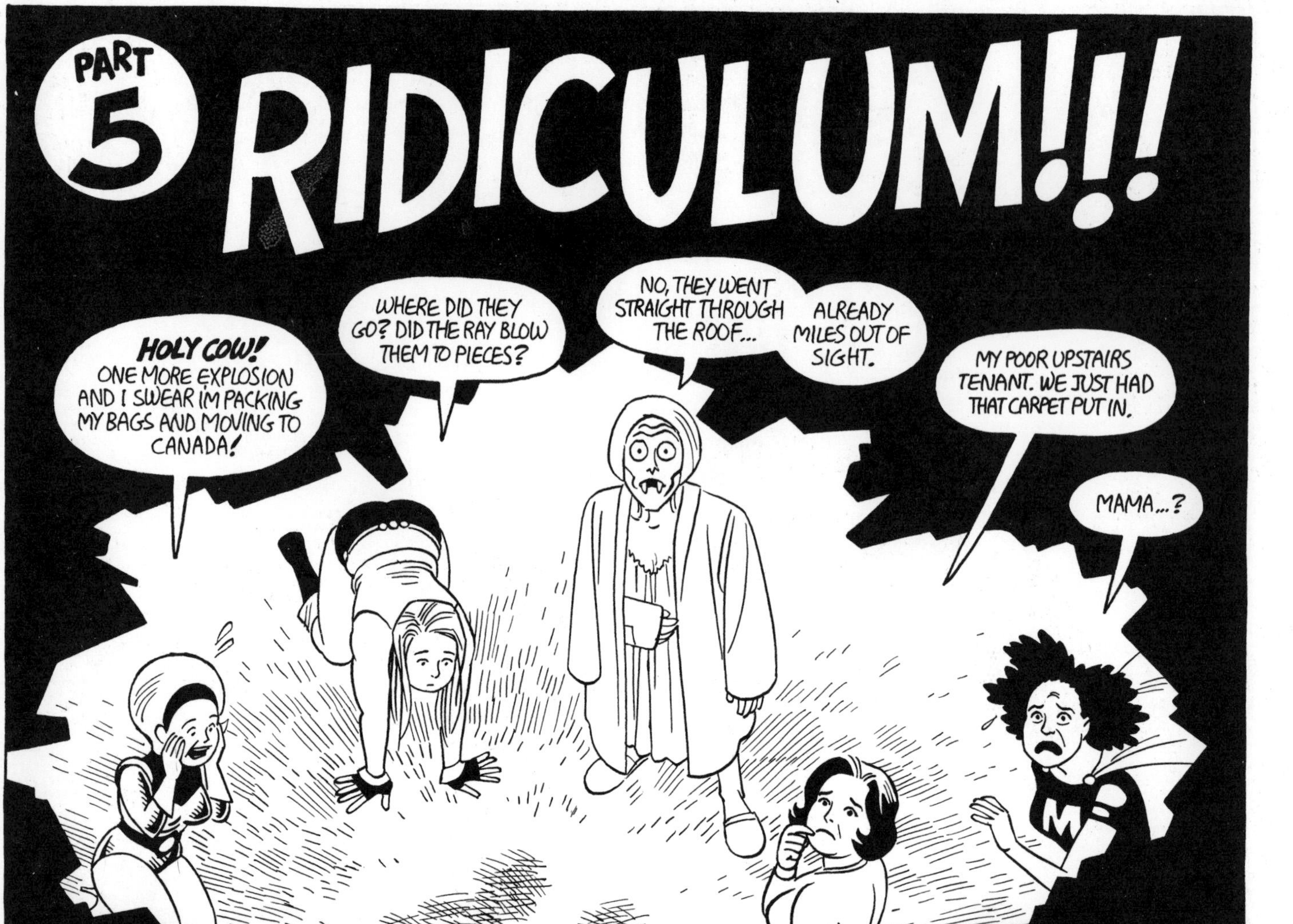

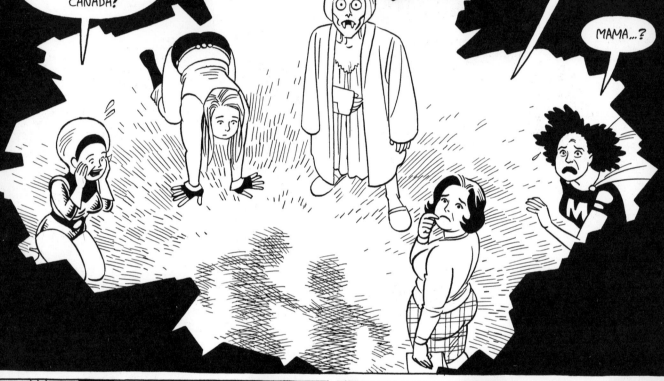

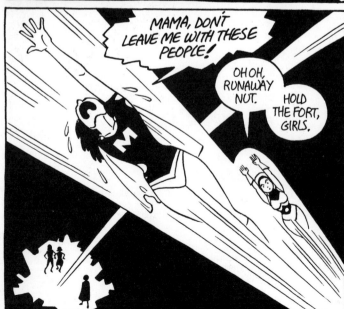

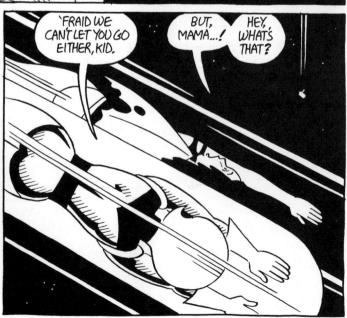

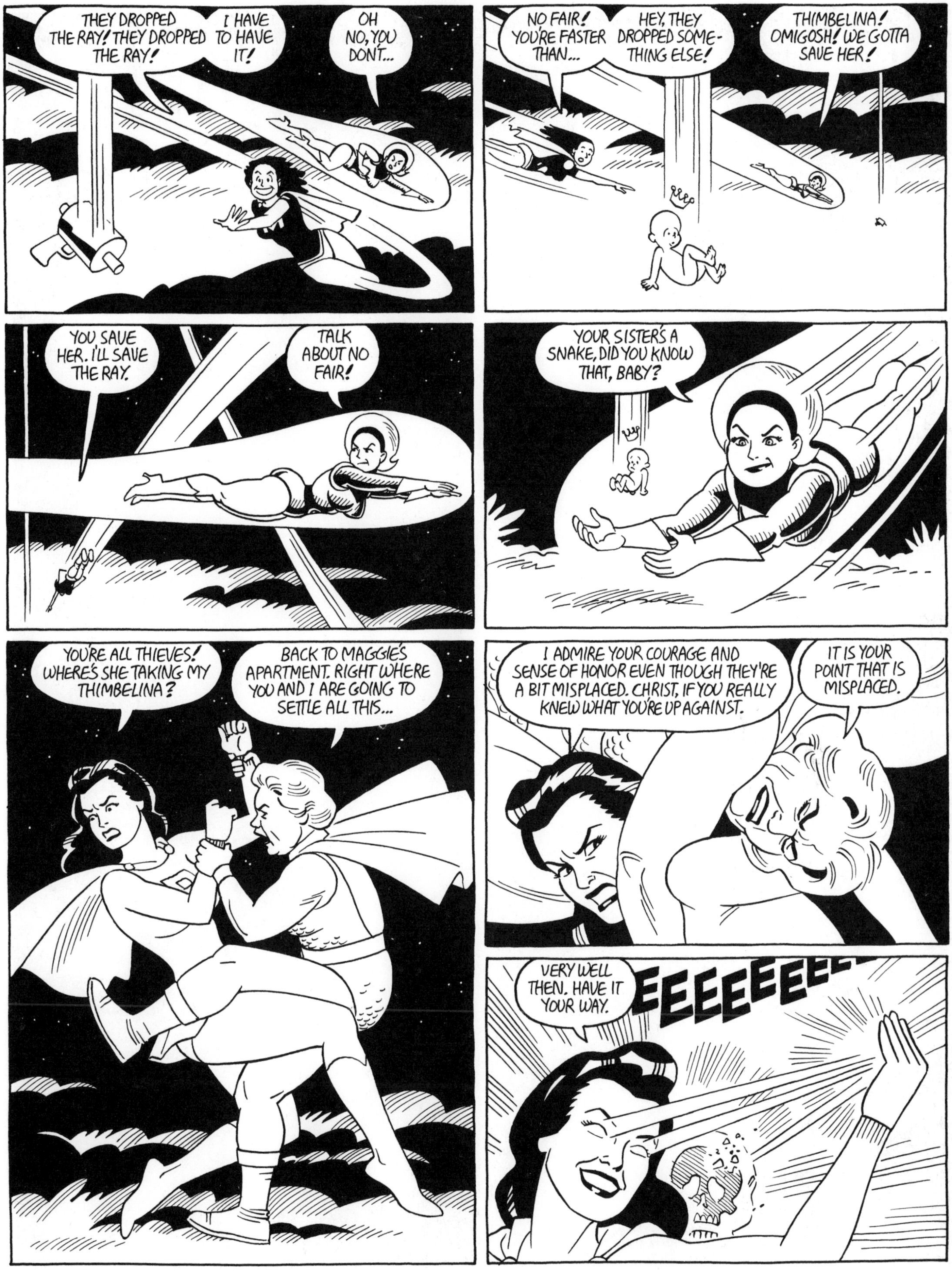
THEY DROPPED THE RAY! THEY DROPPED THE RAY!
I HAVE TO HAVE IT!
OH NO, YOU DON'T...
NO FAIR! YOU'RE FASTER THAN...
HEY, THEY DROPPED SOME-THING ELSE!
THIMBELINA! OMIGOSH! WE GOTTA SAVE HER!
YOU SAVE HER. I'LL SAVE THE RAY.
TALK ABOUT NO FAIR!
YOUR SISTER'S A SNAKE, DID YOU KNOW THAT, BABY?
YOU'RE ALL THIEVES! WHERE'S SHE TAKING MY THIMBELINA?
BACK TO MAGGIE'S APARTMENT. RIGHT WHERE YOU AND I ARE GOING TO SETTLE ALL THIS...
I ADMIRE YOUR COURAGE AND SENSE OF HONOR EVEN THOUGH THEY'RE A BIT MISPLACED. CHRIST, IF YOU REALLY KNEW WHAT YOU'RE UP AGAINST.
IT IS YOUR POINT THAT IS MISPLACED.
VERY WELL THEN. HAVE IT YOUR WAY.
EEEEEEEEE

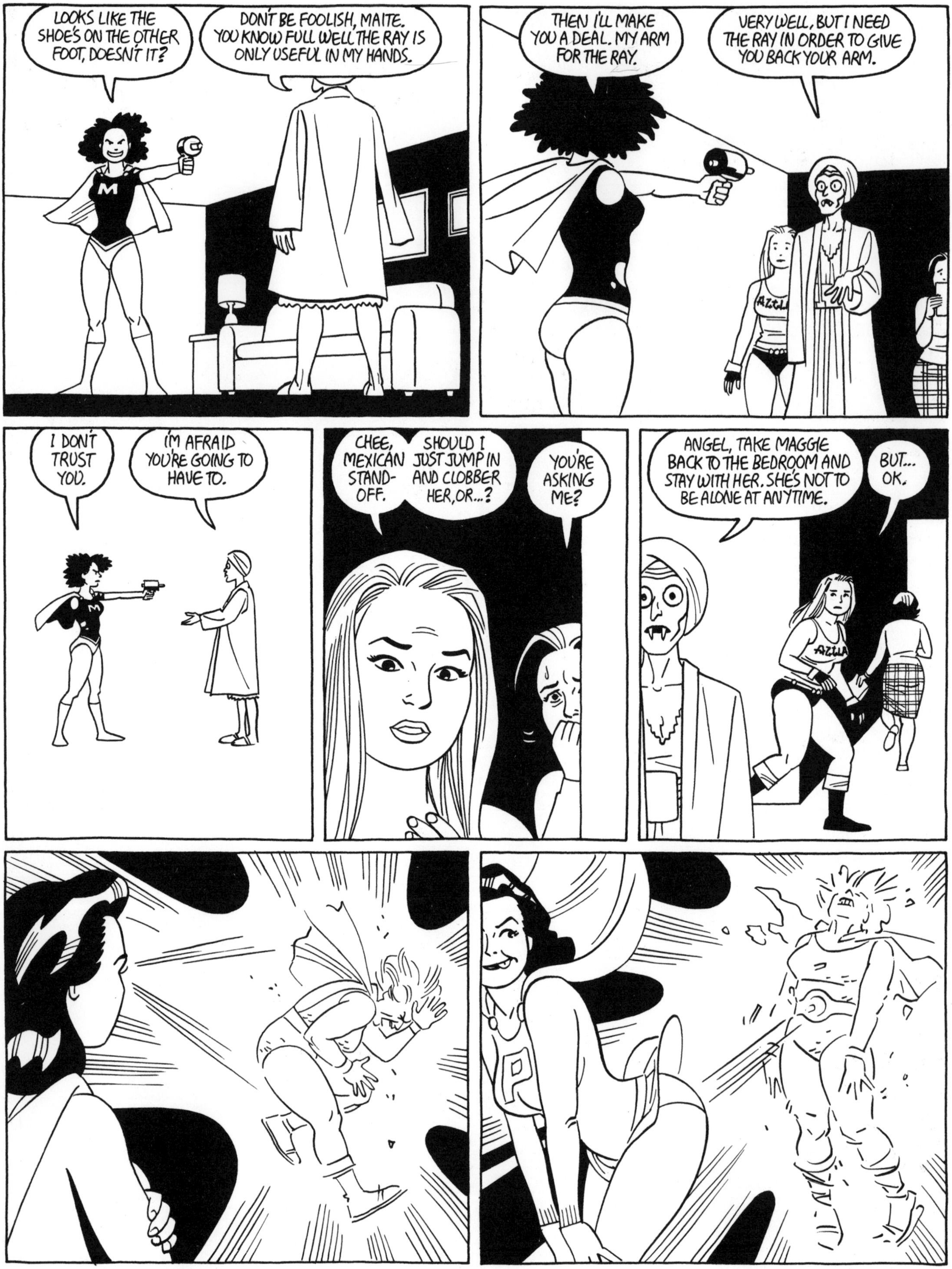
LOOKS LIKE THE SHOE'S ON THE OTHER FOOT, DOESN'T IT?
DON'T BE FOOLISH, MAITE. YOU KNOW FULL WELL THE RAY IS ONLY USEFUL IN MY HANDS.
THEN I'LL MAKE YOU A DEAL. MY ARM FOR THE RAY.
VERY WELL, BUT I NEED THE RAY IN ORDER TO GIVE YOU BACK YOUR ARM.
I DON'T TRUST YOU.
I'M AFRAID YOU'RE GOING TO HAVE TO.
CHEE, MEXICAN STAND-OFF.
SHOULD I JUST JUMP IN AND CLOBBER HER, OR...?
YOU'RE ASKING ME?
ANGEL, TAKE MAGGIE BACK TO THE BEDROOM AND STAY WITH HER. SHE'S NOT TO BE ALONE AT ANYTIME.
BUT... OK.

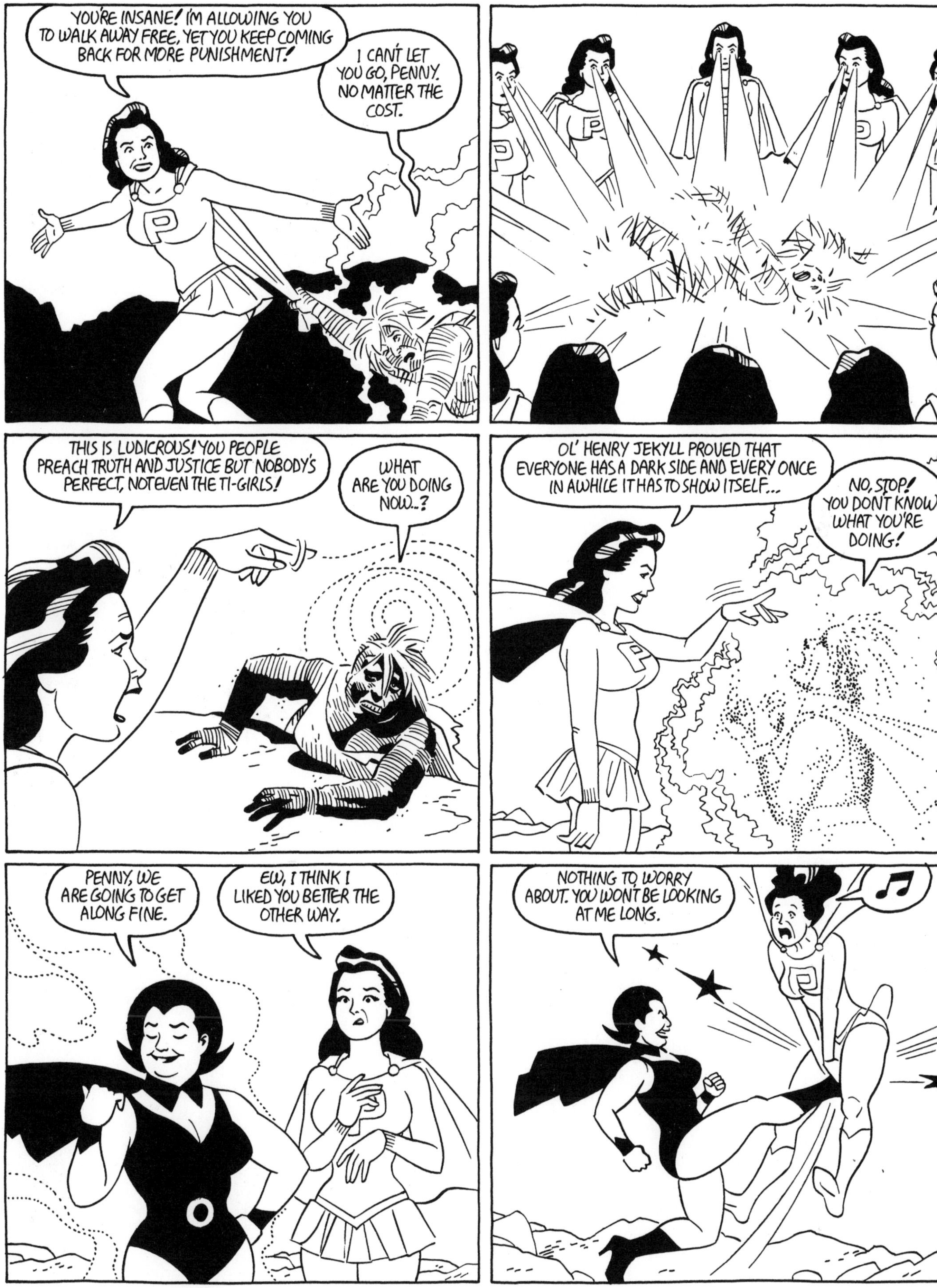
YOU'RE INSANE! I'M ALLOWING YOU TO WALK AWAY FREE, YET YOU KEEP COMING BACK FOR MORE PUNISHMENT!
I CAN'T LET YOU GO, PENNY. NO MATTER THE COST.
THIS IS LUDICROUS! YOU PEOPLE PREACH TRUTH AND JUSTICE BUT NOBODY'S PERFECT, NOT EVEN THE TI-GIRLS!
WHAT ARE YOU DOING NOW..?
OL' HENRY JEKYLL PROVED THAT EVERYONE HAS A DARK SIDE AND EVERY ONCE IN AWHILE IT HAS TO SHOW ITSELF...
NO, STOP! YOU DON'T KNOW WHAT YOU'RE DOING!
PENNY, WE ARE GOING TO GET ALONG FINE.
EW, I THINK I LIKED YOU BETTER THE OTHER WAY.
NOTHING TO WORRY ABOUT. YOU WON'T BE LOOKING AT ME LONG.

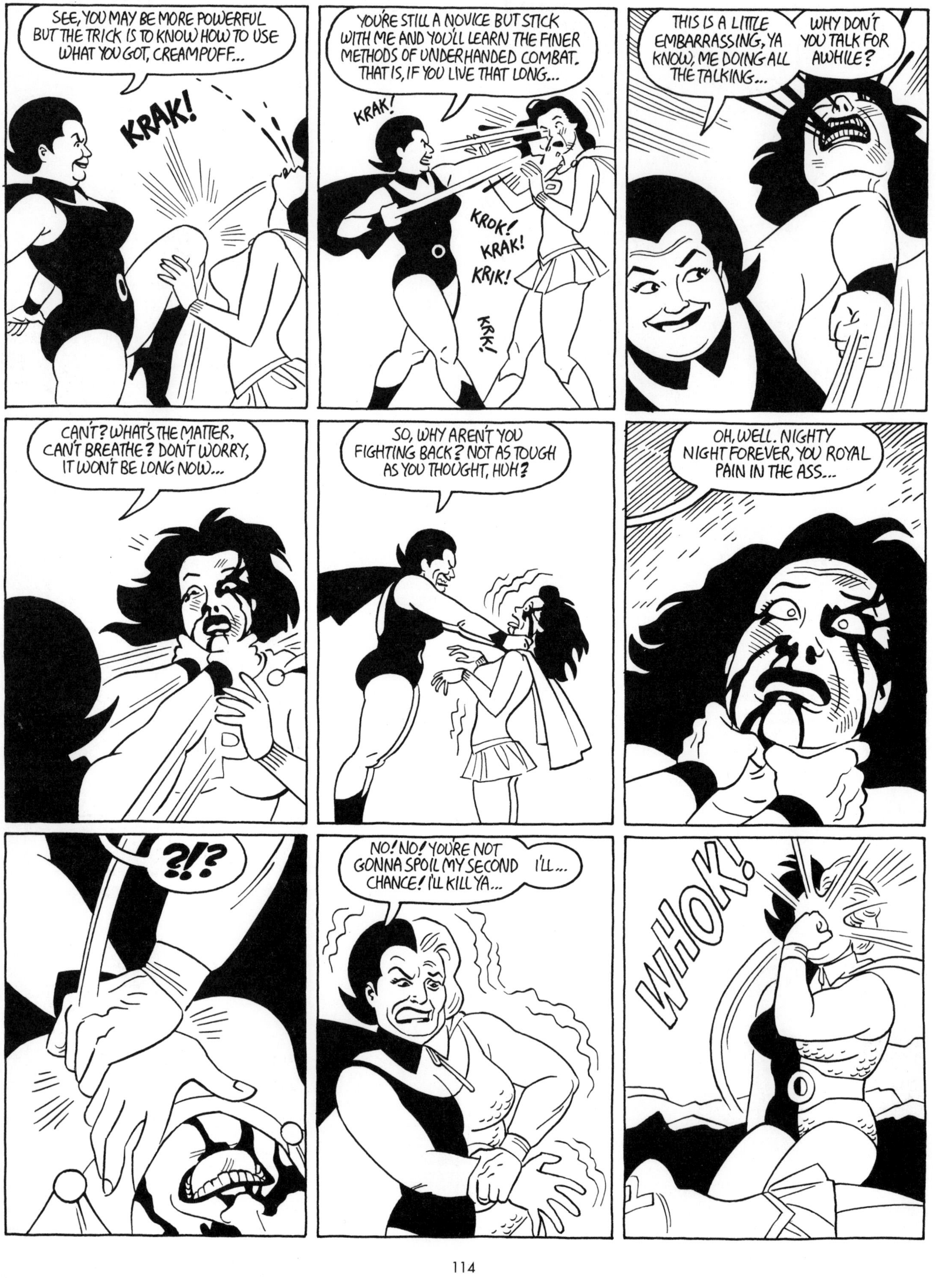
SEE, YOU MAY BE MORE POWERFUL BUT THE TRICK IS TO KNOW HOW TO USE WHAT YOU GOT, CREAMPUFF...
KRAK!
YOU'RE STILL A NOVICE BUT STICK WITH ME AND YOU'LL LEARN THE FINER METHODS OF UNDERHANDED COMBAT. THAT IS, IF YOU LIVE THAT LONG...
KRAK!
KROK!
KRAK!
KRIK!
KRIK!
THIS IS A LITTLE EMBARRASSING, YA KNOW, ME DOING ALL THE TALKING...
WHY DON'T YOU TALK FOR AWHILE?
CAN'T? WHAT'S THE MATTER, CAN'T BREATHE? DON'T WORRY, IT WON'T BE LONG NOW...
SO, WHY AREN'T YOU FIGHTING BACK? NOT AS TOUGH AS YOU THOUGHT, HUH?
OH, WELL. NIGHTY NIGHT FOREVER, YOU ROYAL PAIN IN THE ASS...
?!?
NO! NO! YOU'RE NOT GONNA SPOIL MY SECOND CHANCE! I'LL KILL YA...
I'LL...
WHOK!

WELL, THAT WAS CERTAINLY INTERESTING.

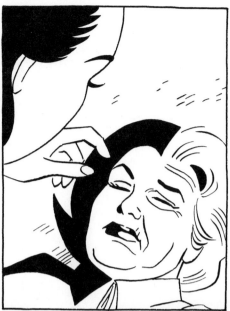

EW!

NO MORE DARK STUFF.

YOU CAN REST EASY NOW.

STILL NO SOUND, ANGEL?

NO. I WISH THE WEEPER WOULD LET ME HELP.

THE POWER OF THE RAY IS TOO UNPREDICTABLE, ESPECIALLY IN THE WRONG HANDS. NOT EVEN WEEPER HERSELF KNOWS ITS LIMITS.

WHAT ABOUT YOU? WHAT DO THE COMICS SAY?

"ONE CHRISTMAS, WHEN THE WEEPER WAS A LITTLE GIRL, SANTA CLAUS BROUGHT HER SISTERS EACH A DOLL BUT ALL SHE GOT WAS A CHEAP TOY GUN. SHE FELT THIS WAS A VERY CRUEL JOKE AND IMMEDIATELY WANTED TO THROW IT AWAY.

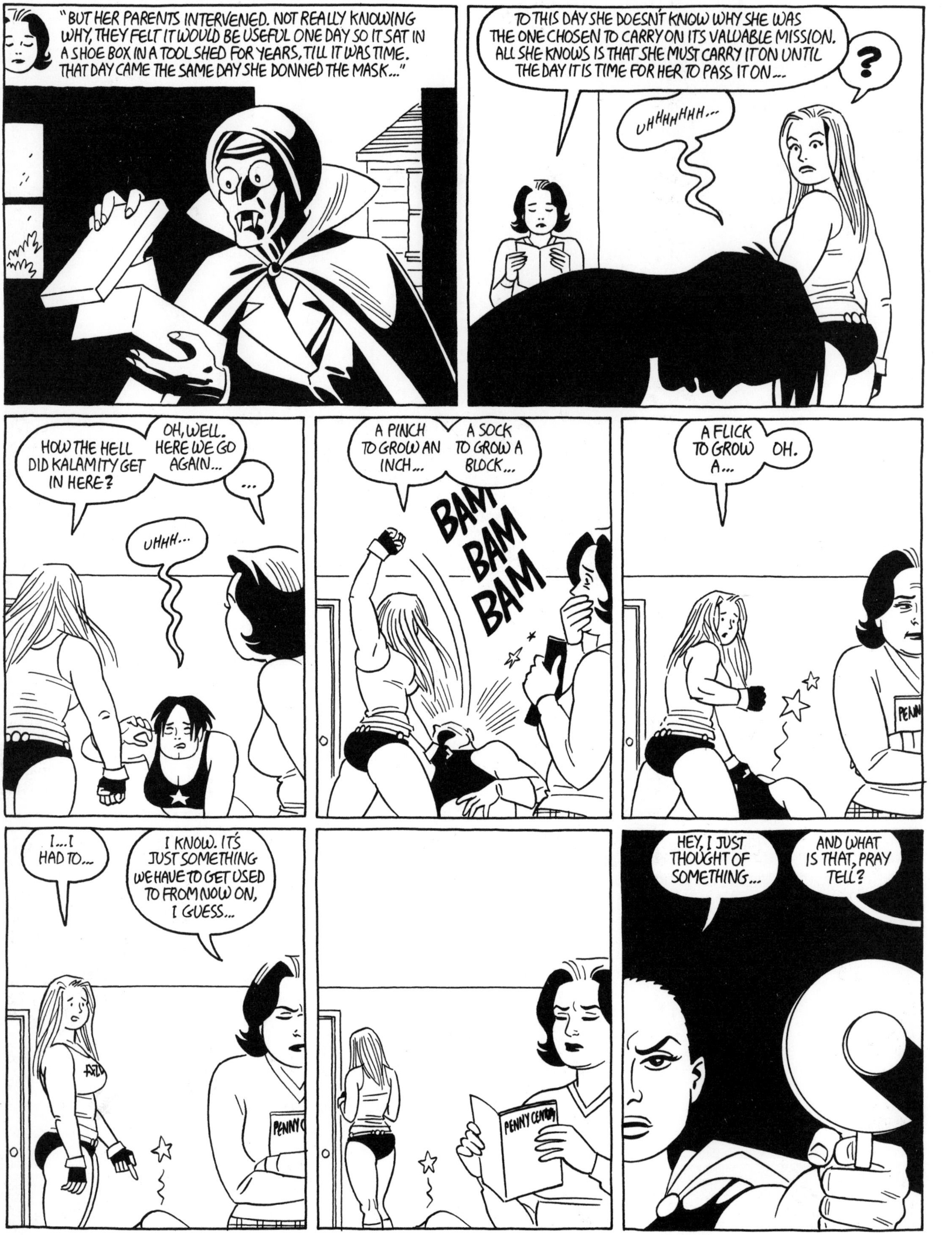
"BUT HER PARENTS INTERVENED. NOT REALLY KNOWING WHY, THEY FELT IT WOULD BE USEFUL ONE DAY SO IT SAT IN A SHOE BOX IN A TOOL SHED FOR YEARS, TILL IT WAS TIME. THAT DAY CAME THE SAME DAY SHE DONNED THE MASK..."
TO THIS DAY SHE DOESN'T KNOW WHY SHE WAS THE ONE CHOSEN TO CARRY ON ITS VALUABLE MISSION. ALL SHE KNOWS IS THAT SHE MUST CARRY IT ON UNTIL THE DAY IT IS TIME FOR HER TO PASS IT ON...
?
UHHHHHHH...
HOW THE HELL DID KALAMITY GET IN HERE?
OH, WELL. HERE WE GO AGAIN...
...
UHHH...
A PINCH TO GROW AN INCH...
A SOCK TO GROW A BLOCK...
BAM BAM BAM
A FLICK TO GROW A...
OH.
PENN
I...I HAD TO...
I KNOW. IT'S JUST SOMETHING WE HAVE TO GET USED TO FROM NOW ON, I GUESS...
PENNY C
PENNY CENTURY
HEY, I JUST THOUGHT OF SOMETHING...
AND WHAT IS THAT, PRAY TELL?

LAST TIME YOU TOLD ME MY ARM WAS NEVER GONE TO BEGIN WITH.
THAT'S RIGHT, I DID.
THEN ALL I GOTTA DO IS BELIEVE IT'S STILL HERE AND... AND...
WAH!
HOW COME I CAN'T DO IT?
...THEN I STRIKE.
?!?
???
NO FAIR!
NO FAIR? WE'RE BOTH ONE-ARMED, YOUR SUPER STRENGTH AGAINST MY JUJITSU, THE JAPANESE METHOD OF USING THE STRENGTH AND WEIGHT OF AN ADVERSARY TO DISABLE HER. I'D SAY IT'S MORE THAN FAIR.
LET'S HOPE, YOUR SILLY BIG SISTER HASN'T DONE ANYTHING FOOLISH WITH THE RAY.
DA?
MAMA DA?
XOCHITL DA!

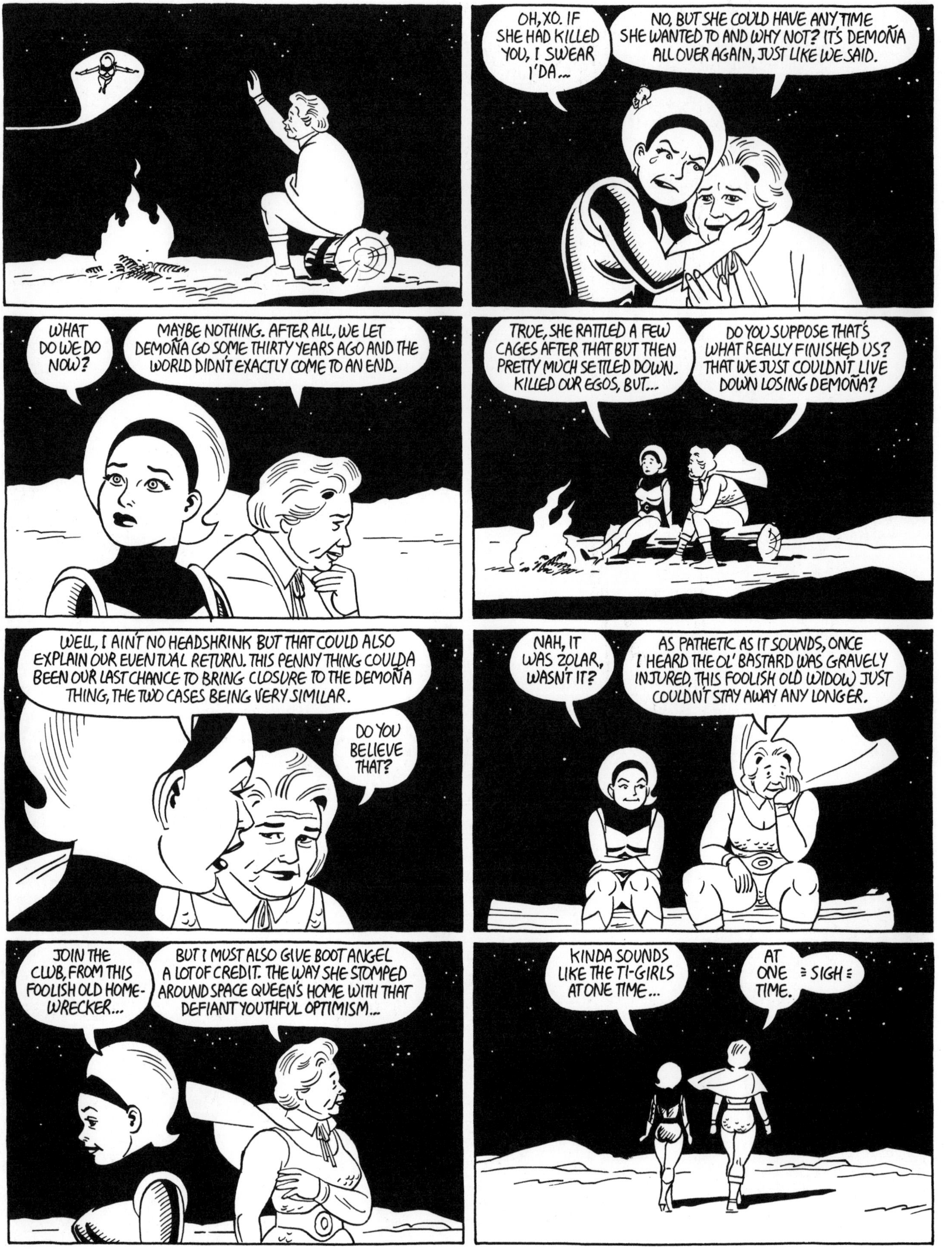
OH, XO. IF SHE HAD KILLED YOU, I SWEAR I'DA...
NO, BUT SHE COULD HAVE ANY TIME SHE WANTED TO AND WHY NOT? IT'S DEMOÑA ALL OVER AGAIN, JUST LIKE WE SAID.
WHAT DO WE DO NOW?
MAYBE NOTHING. AFTER ALL, WE LET DEMOÑA GO SOME THIRTY YEARS AGO AND THE WORLD DIDN'T EXACTLY COME TO AN END.
TRUE, SHE RATTLED A FEW CAGES AFTER THAT BUT THEN PRETTY MUCH SETTLED DOWN. KILLED OUR EGOS, BUT...
DO YOU SUPPOSE THAT'S WHAT REALLY FINISHED US? THAT WE JUST COULDN'T LIVE DOWN LOSING DEMOÑA?
WELL, I AIN'T NO HEADSHRINK BUT THAT COULD ALSO EXPLAIN OUR EVENTUAL RETURN. THIS PENNY THING COULDA BEEN OUR LAST CHANCE TO BRING CLOSURE TO THE DEMOÑA THING, THE TWO CASES BEING VERY SIMILAR.
DO YOU BELIEVE THAT?
NAH, IT WAS ZOLAR, WASN'T IT?
AS PATHETIC AS IT SOUNDS, ONCE I HEARD THE OL' BASTARD WAS GRAVELY INJURED, THIS FOOLISH OLD WIDOW JUST COULDN'T STAY AWAY ANY LONGER.
JOIN THE CLUB, FROM THIS FOOLISH OLD HOME-WRECKER...
BUT I MUST ALSO GIVE BOOT ANGEL A LOT OF CREDIT. THE WAY SHE STOMPED AROUND SPACE QUEEN'S HOME WITH THAT DEFIANT YOUTHFUL OPTIMISM...
KINDA SOUNDS LIKE THE TI-GIRLS AT ONE TIME...
AT ONE TIME.
SIGH

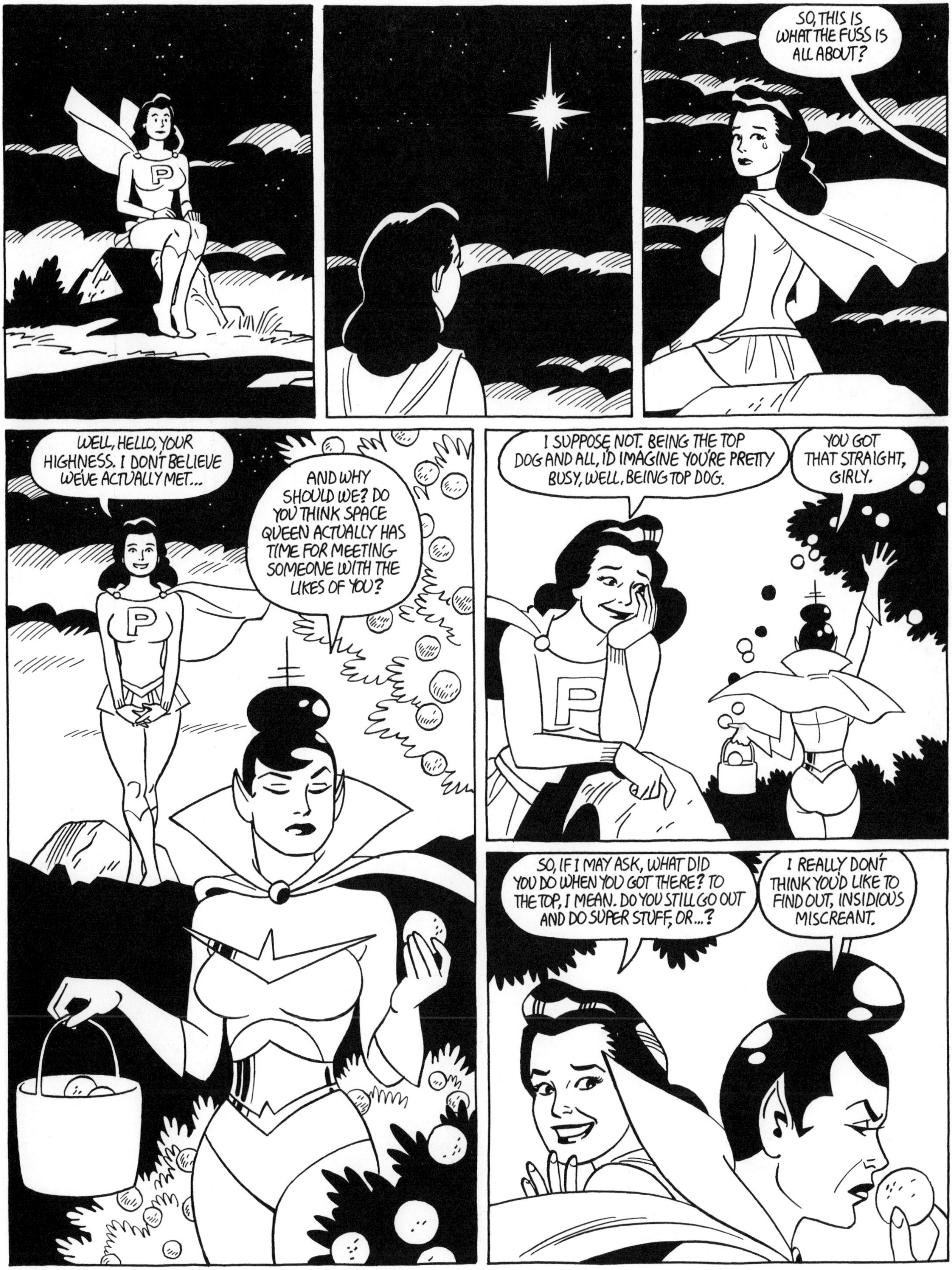

SO, THIS IS WHAT THE FUSS IS ALL ABOUT?
WELL, HELLO, YOUR HIGHNESS. I DON'T BELIEVE WE'VE ACTUALLY MET...
AND WHY SHOULD WE? DO YOU THINK SPACE QUEEN ACTUALLY HAS TIME FOR MEETING SOMEONE WITH THE LIKES OF YOU?
I SUPPOSE NOT. BEING THE TOP DOG AND ALL, I'D IMAGINE YOU'RE PRETTY BUSY, WELL, BEING TOP DOG.
YOU GOT THAT STRAIGHT, GIRLY.
SO, IF I MAY ASK, WHAT DID YOU DO WHEN YOU GOT THERE? TO THE TOP, I MEAN. DO YOU STILL GO OUT AND DO SUPER STUFF, OR...?
I REALLY DON'T THINK YOU'D LIKE TO FIND OUT, INSIDIOUS MISCREANT.

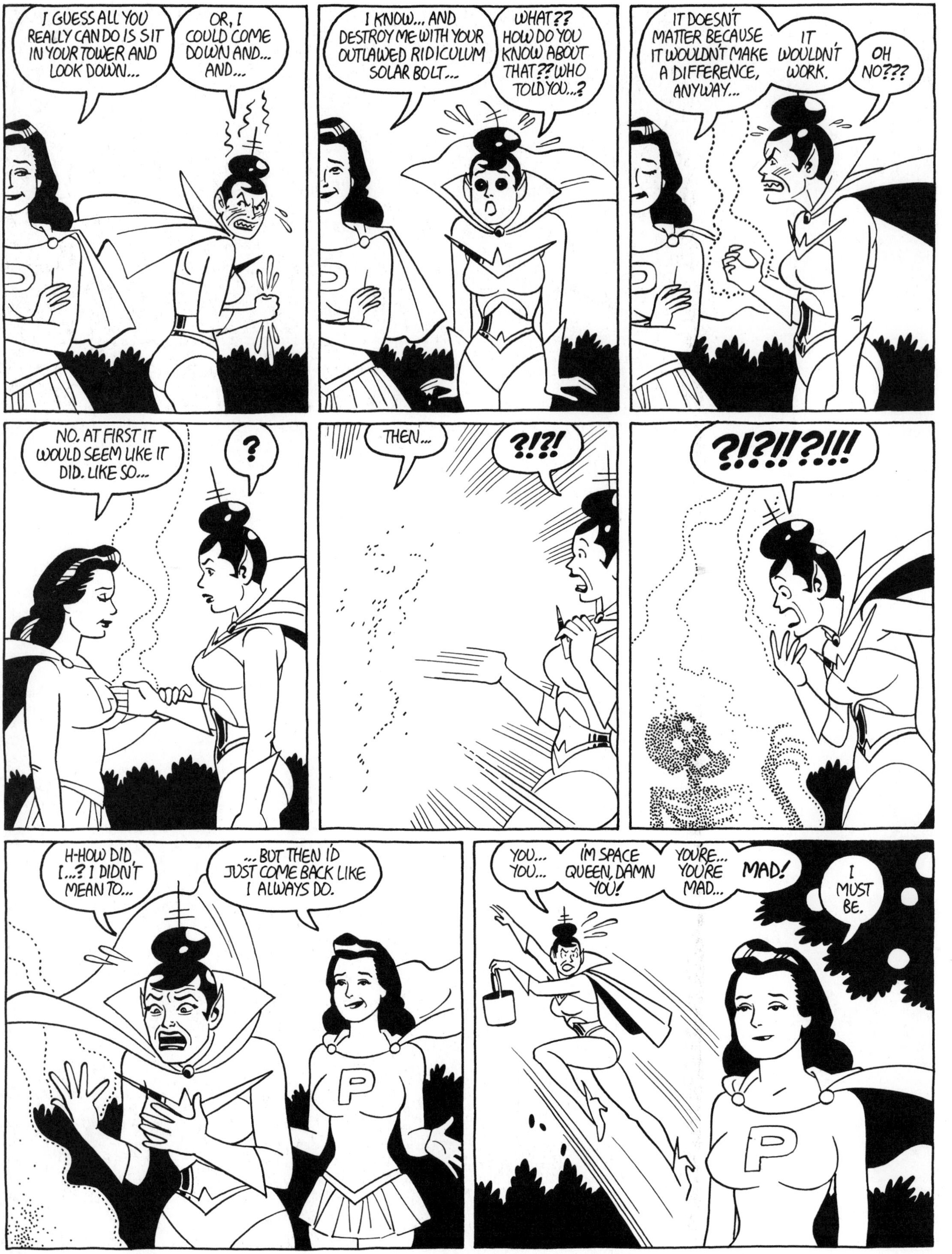
I GUESS ALL YOU REALLY CAN DO IS SIT IN YOUR TOWER AND LOOK DOWN...
OR, I COULD COME DOWN AND... AND...
I KNOW... AND DESTROY ME WITH YOUR OUTLAWED RIDICULUM SOLAR BOLT...
WHAT?? HOW DO YOU KNOW ABOUT THAT?? WHO TOLD YOU...?
IT DOESN'T MATTER BECAUSE IT WOULDN'T MAKE A DIFFERENCE, ANYWAY...
IT WOULDN'T WORK.
OH NO???
NO. AT FIRST IT WOULD SEEM LIKE IT DID. LIKE SO...
?
THEN...
?!?!
?!?!!?!!!
H-HOW DID I...? I DIDN'T MEAN TO...
...BUT THEN I'D JUST COME BACK LIKE I ALWAYS DO.
YOU... YOU...
I'M SPACE QUEEN, DAMN YOU!
YOU'RE... YOU'RE MAD...
MAD!
I MUST BE.

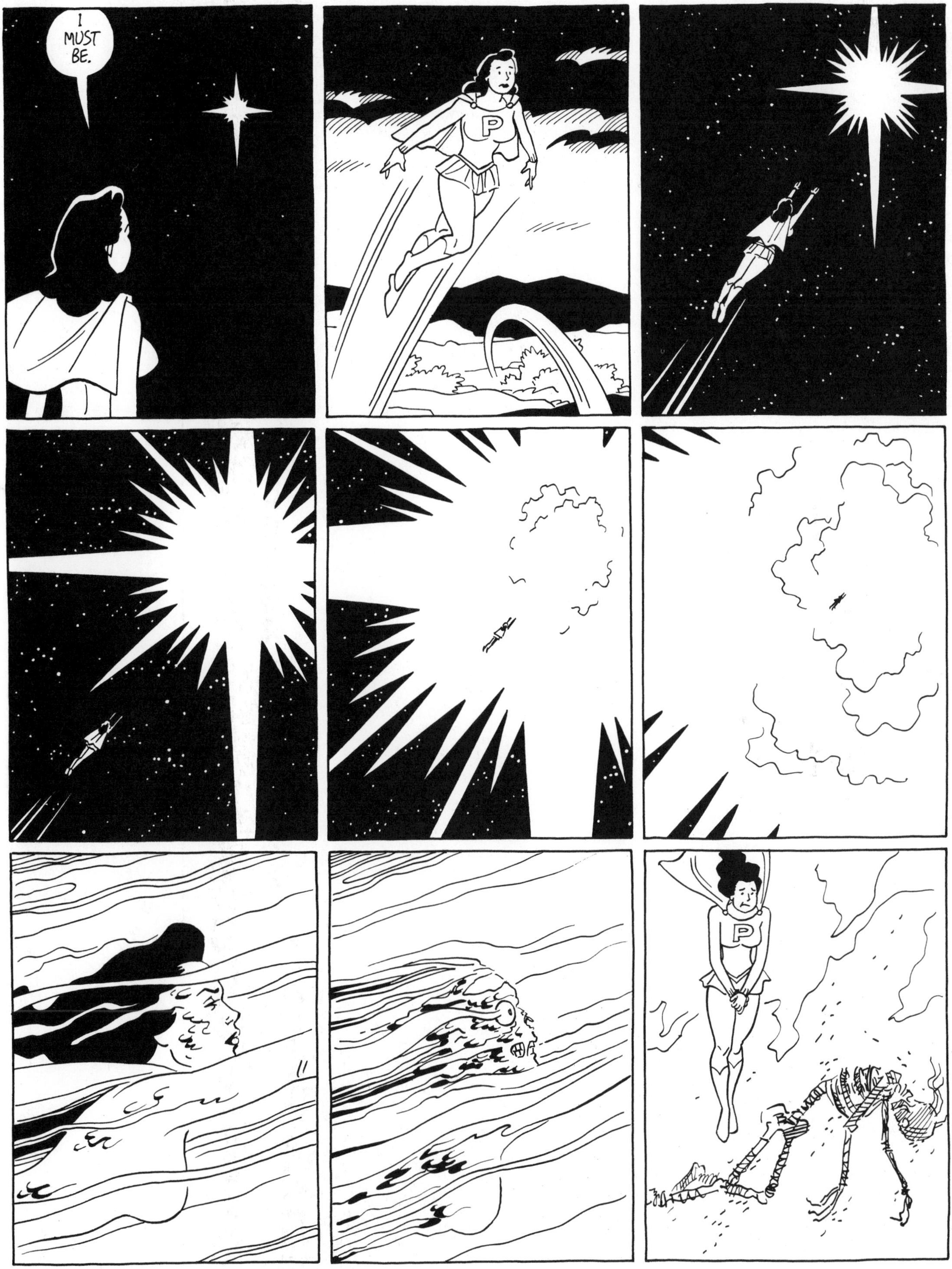
I MUST BE.

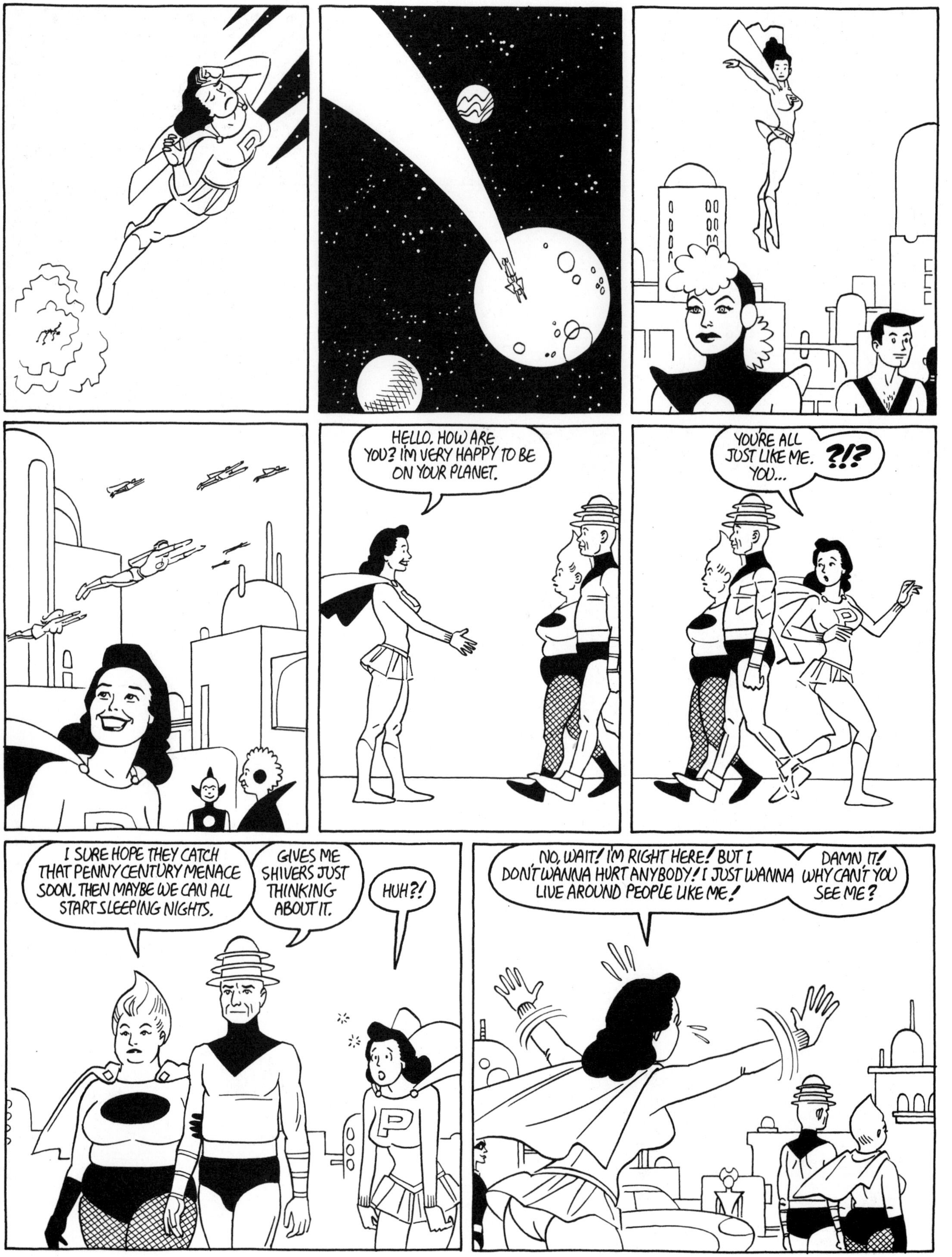
HELLO. HOW ARE YOU? I'M VERY HAPPY TO BE ON YOUR PLANET.
YOU'RE ALL JUST LIKE ME. YOU...
?!?
I SURE HOPE THEY CATCH THAT PENNY CENTURY MENACE SOON. THEN MAYBE WE CAN ALL START SLEEPING NIGHTS.
GIVES ME SHIVERS JUST THINKING ABOUT IT.
HUH?!
NO, WAIT! I'M RIGHT HERE! BUT I DON'T WANNA HURT ANYBODY! I JUST WANNA LIVE AROUND PEOPLE LIKE ME!
DAMN IT! WHY CAN'T YOU SEE ME?

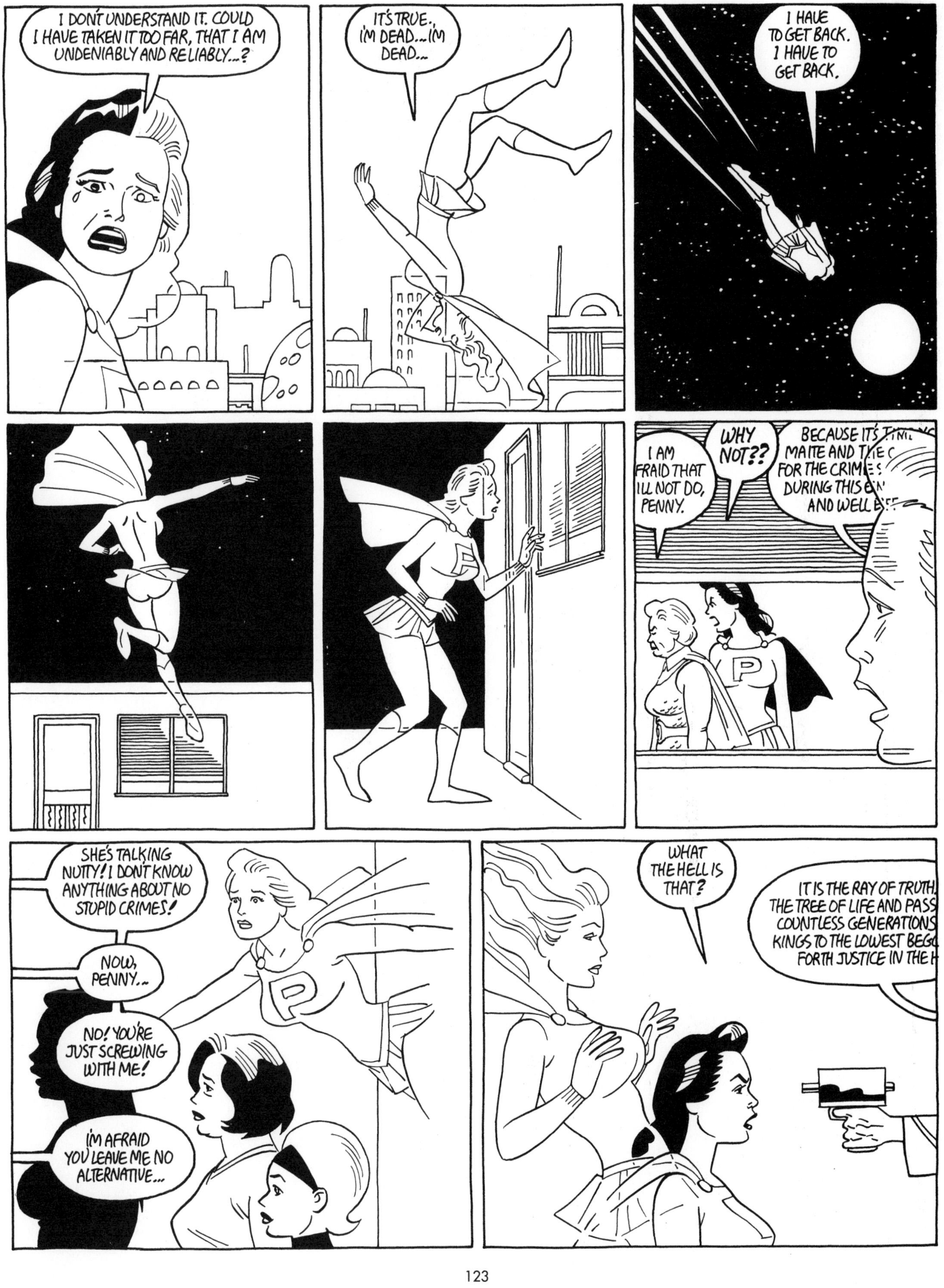
I DON'T UNDERSTAND IT. COULD I HAVE TAKEN IT TOO FAR, THAT I AM UNDENIABLY AND RELIABLY...?
IT'S TRUE.. I'M DEAD... I'M DEAD...
I HAVE TO GET BACK. I HAVE TO GET BACK.
I AM FRAID THAT ILL NOT DO, PENNY.
WHY NOT??
BECAUSE IT'S
MAITE AND THE
FOR THE CRIMES
DURING THIS
AND WELL
SHE'S TALKING NUTTY! I DON'T KNOW ANYTHING ABOUT NO STUPID CRIMES!
NOW, PENNY...
NO! YOU'RE JUST SCREWING WITH ME!
I'M AFRAID YOU LEAVE ME NO ALTERNATIVE...
WHAT THE HELL IS THAT?
IT IS THE RAY OF TRUTH,
THE TREE OF LIFE AND
COUNTLESS GENERATIONS
KINGS TO THE LOWEST
FORTH JUSTICE IN THE

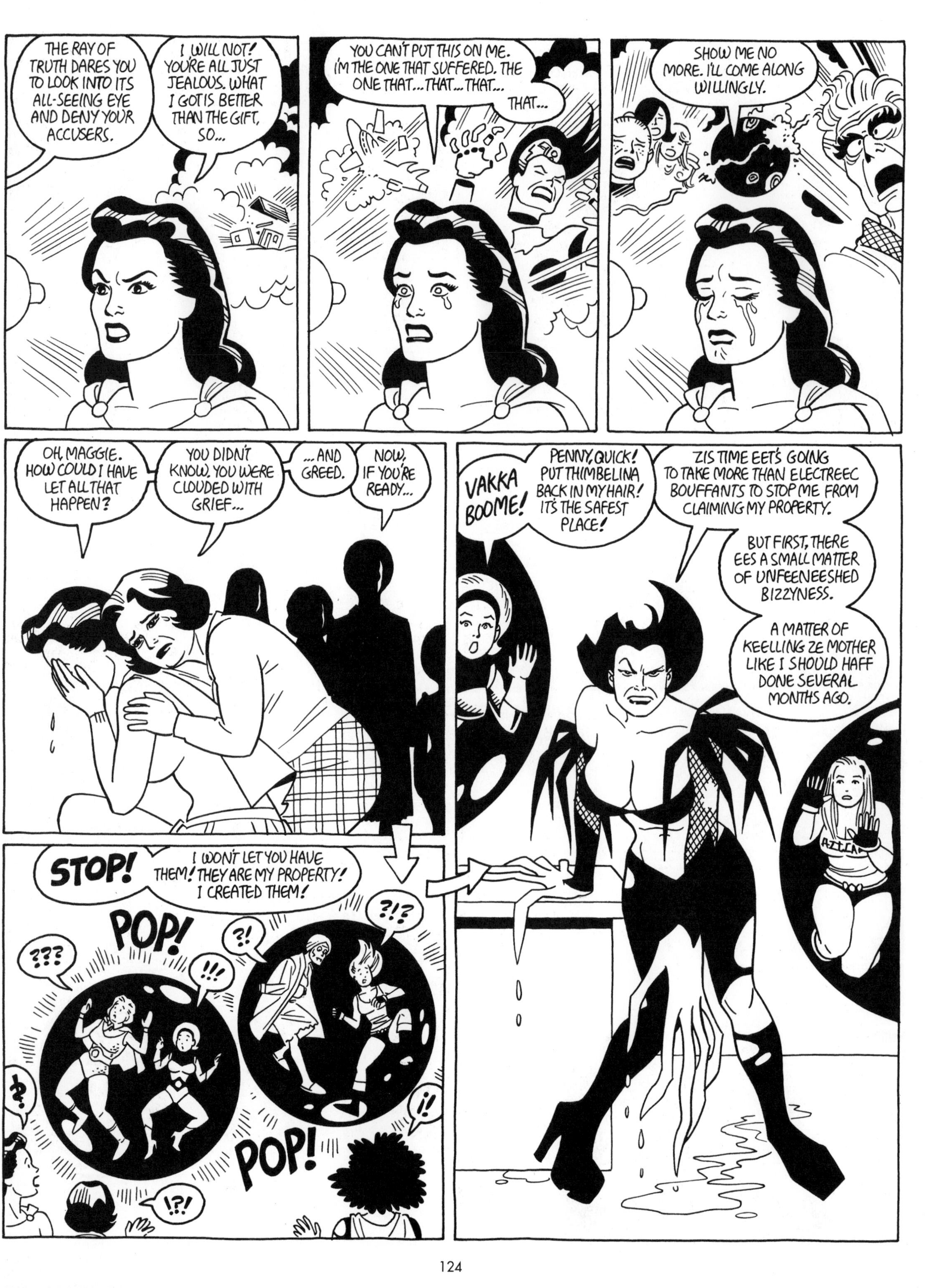

THE RAY OF TRUTH DARES YOU TO LOOK INTO ITS ALL-SEEING EYE AND DENY YOUR ACCUSERS.
I WILL NOT! YOU'RE ALL JUST JEALOUS. WHAT I GOT IS BETTER THAN THE GIFT, SO...
YOU CAN'T PUT THIS ON ME. I'M THE ONE THAT SUFFERED. THE ONE THAT... THAT... THAT...
THAT...
SHOW ME NO MORE. I'LL COME ALONG WILLINGLY.
OH, MAGGIE. HOW COULD I HAVE LET ALL THAT HAPPEN?
YOU DIDN'T KNOW. YOU WERE CLOUDED WITH GRIEF...
...AND GREED.
NOW, IF YOU'RE READY...
VAKKA BOOME!
PENNY, QUICK! PUT THIMBELINA BACK IN MY HAIR! IT'S THE SAFEST PLACE!
ZIS TIME EET'S GOING TO TAKE MORE THAN ELECTREEC BOUFFANTS TO STOP ME FROM CLAIMING MY PROPERTY.
BUT FIRST, THERE EES A SMALL MATTER OF UNFEENEESHED BIZZYNESS.
A MATTER OF KEELLING ZE MOTHER LIKE I SHOULD HAFF DONE SEVERAL MONTHS AGO.
STOP!
I WON'T LET YOU HAVE THEM! THEY ARE MY PROPERTY! I CREATED THEM!
POP!
???
!!!
?!
?!?
¿?
¡!
POP!
!?!

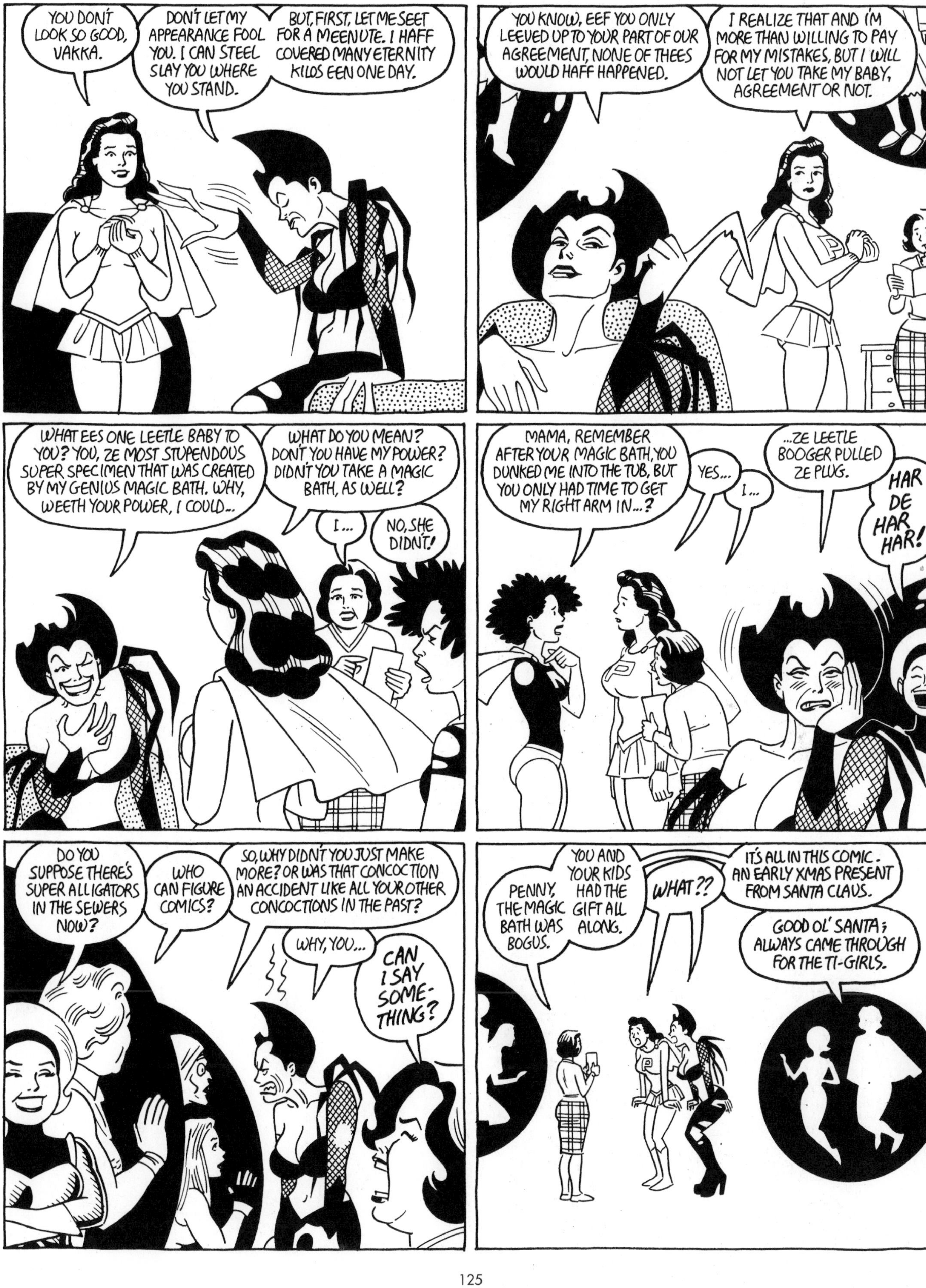

YOU DON'T LOOK SO GOOD, VAKKA.
DON'T LET MY APPEARANCE FOOL YOU. I CAN STEEL SLAY YOU WHERE YOU STAND.
BUT, FIRST, LET ME SEET FOR A MEENUTE. I HAFF COVERED MANY ETERNITY KILOS EEN ONE DAY.
YOU KNOW, EEF YOU ONLY LEEVED UP TO YOUR PART OF OUR AGREEMENT, NONE OF THEES WOULD HAFF HAPPENED.
I REALIZE THAT AND I'M MORE THAN WILLING TO PAY FOR MY MISTAKES, BUT I WILL NOT LET YOU TAKE MY BABY, AGREEMENT OR NOT.
WHAT EES ONE LEETLE BABY TO YOU? YOU, ZE MOST STUPENDOUS SUPER SPECIMEN THAT WAS CREATED BY MY GENIUS MAGIC BATH. WHY, WEETH YOUR POWER, I COULD...
WHAT DO YOU MEAN? DON'T YOU HAVE MY POWER? DIDN'T YOU TAKE A MAGIC BATH, AS WELL?
I...
NO, SHE DIDN'T!
MAMA, REMEMBER AFTER YOUR MAGIC BATH, YOU DUNKED ME INTO THE TUB, BUT YOU ONLY HAD TIME TO GET MY RIGHT ARM IN...?
YES...
I...
...ZE LEETLE BOOGER PULLED ZE PLUG.
HAR DE HAR HAR!
DO YOU SUPPOSE THERE'S SUPER ALLIGATORS IN THE SEWERS NOW?
WHO CAN FIGURE COMICS?
SO, WHY DIDN'T YOU JUST MAKE MORE? OR WAS THAT CONCOCTION AN ACCIDENT LIKE ALL YOUR OTHER CONCOCTIONS IN THE PAST?
WHY, YOU...
CAN I SAY SOME-THING?
PENNY, THE MAGIC BATH WAS BOGUS.
YOU AND YOUR KIDS HAD THE GIFT ALL ALONG.
WHAT??
IT'S ALL IN THIS COMIC. AN EARLY XMAS PRESENT FROM SANTA CLAUS.
GOOD OL' SANTA; ALWAYS CAME THROUGH FOR THE TI-GIRLS.

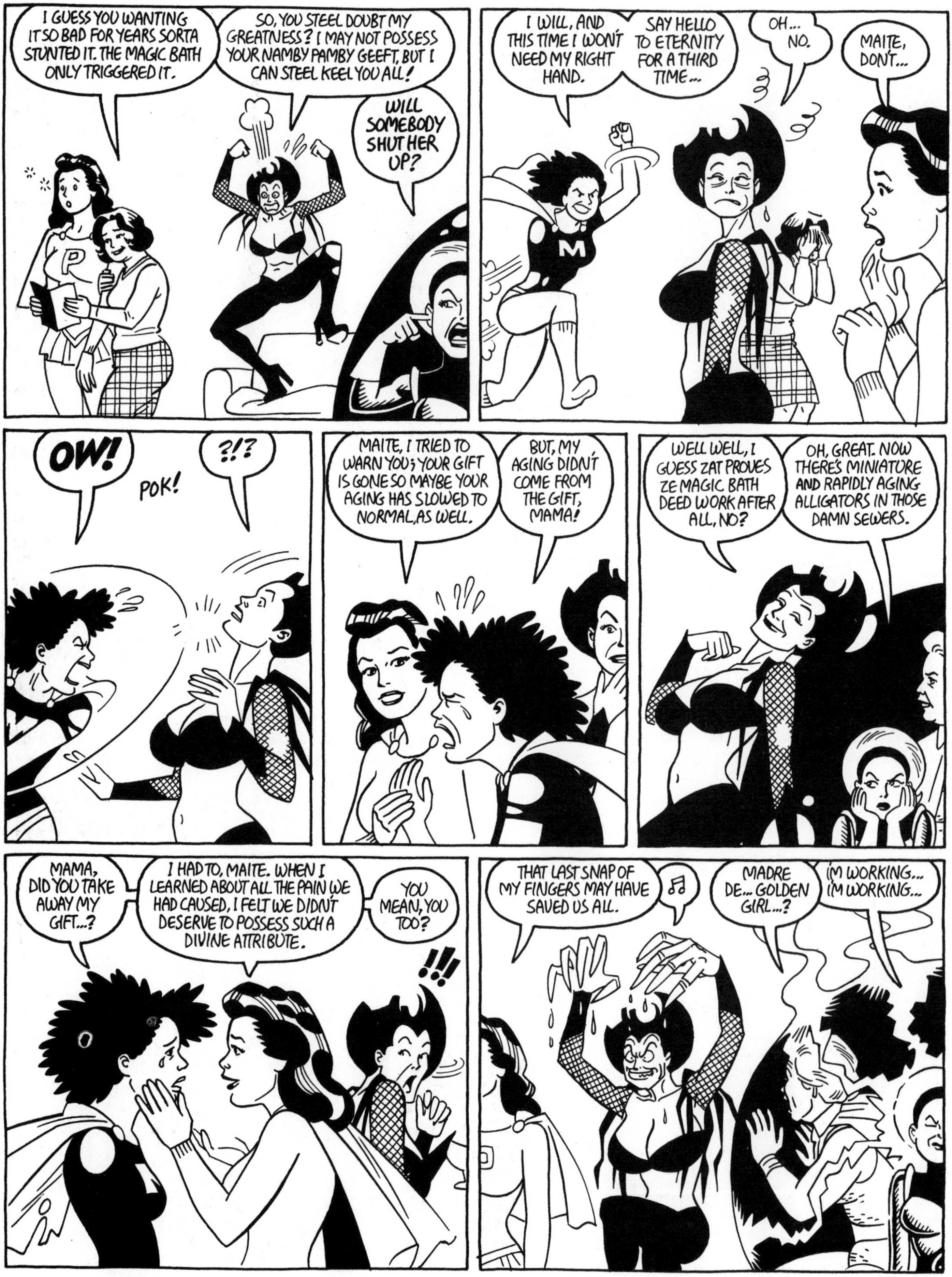

I GUESS YOU WANTING IT SO BAD FOR YEARS SORTA STUNTED IT. THE MAGIC BATH ONLY TRIGGERED IT.
SO, YOU STEEL DOUBT MY GREATNESS? I MAY NOT POSSESS YOUR NAMBY PAMBY GEEFT, BUT I CAN STEEL KEEL YOU ALL!
WILL SOMEBODY SHUT HER UP?
I WILL, AND THIS TIME I WON'T NEED MY RIGHT HAND.
SAY HELLO TO ETERNITY FOR A THIRD TIME...
OH... NO.
MAITE, DON'T...
OW!
POK!
?!?
MAITE, I TRIED TO WARN YOU; YOUR GIFT IS GONE SO MAYBE YOUR AGING HAS SLOWED TO NORMAL, AS WELL.
BUT, MY AGING DIDN'T COME FROM THE GIFT, MAMA!
WELL WELL, I GUESS ZAT PROVES ZE MAGIC BATH DEED WORK AFTER ALL, NO?
OH, GREAT. NOW THERE'S MINIATURE AND RAPIDLY AGING ALLIGATORS IN THOSE DAMN SEWERS.
MAMA, DID YOU TAKE AWAY MY GIFT...?
I HAD TO, MAITE. WHEN I LEARNED ABOUT ALL THE PAIN WE HAD CAUSED, I FELT WE DIDN'T DESERVE TO POSSESS SUCH A DIVINE ATTRIBUTE.
YOU MEAN, YOU TOO?
!!!
THAT LAST SNAP OF MY FINGERS MAY HAVE SAVED US ALL.
♫
MADRE DE... GOLDEN GIRL...?
I'M WORKING... I'M WORKING...

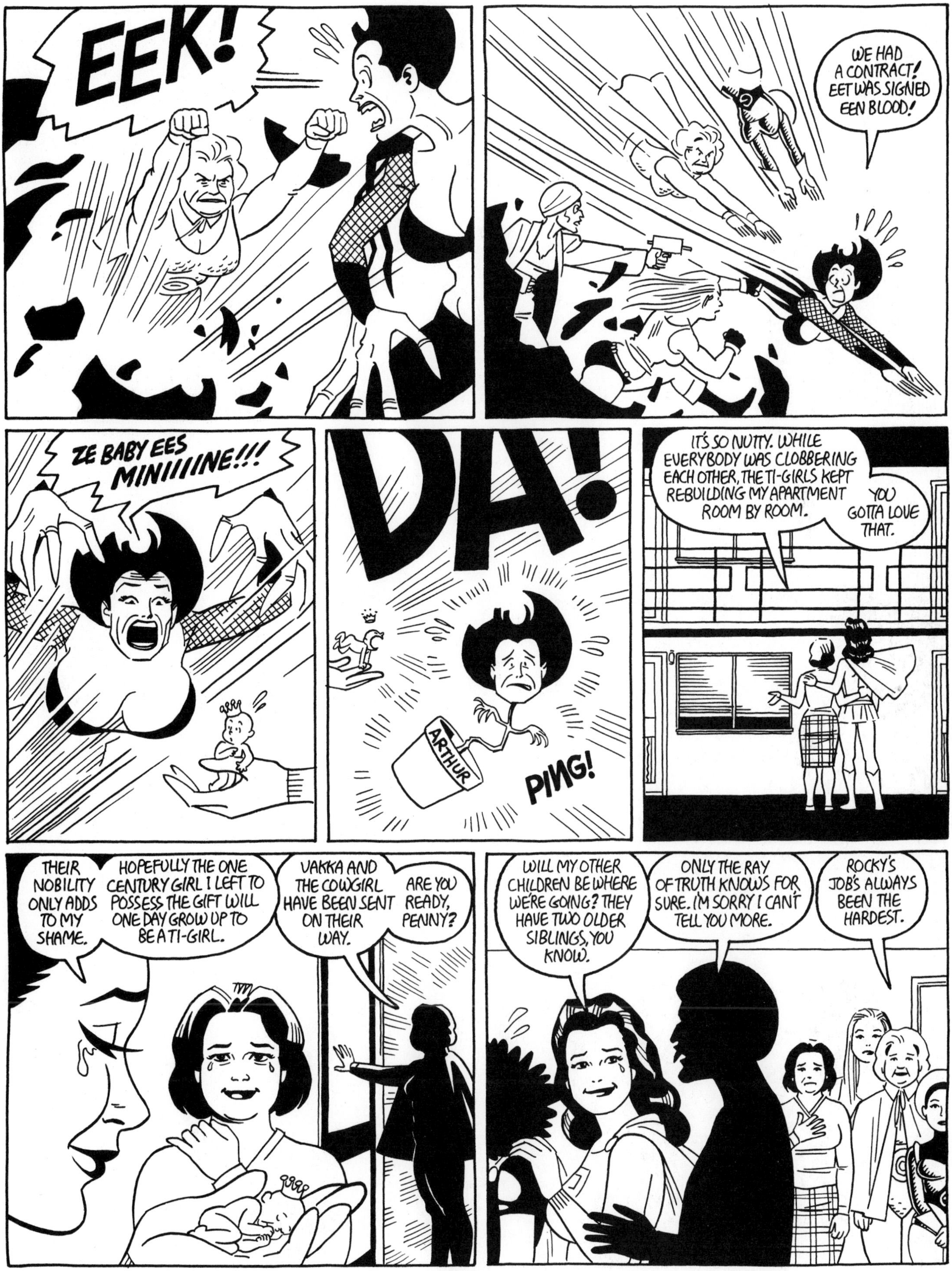
EEK!
WE HAD A CONTRACT! EET WAS SIGNED EEN BLOOD!
ZE BABY EES MINIIIINE!!!
DA!
ARTHUR
PING!
IT'S SO NUTTY. WHILE EVERYBODY WAS CLOBBERING EACH OTHER, THE TI-GIRLS KEPT REBUILDING MY APARTMENT ROOM BY ROOM.
YOU GOTTA LOVE THAT.
THEIR NOBILITY ONLY ADDS TO MY SHAME.
HOPEFULLY THE ONE CENTURY GIRL I LEFT TO POSSESS THE GIFT WILL ONE DAY GROW UP TO BE A TI-GIRL.
VAKKA AND THE COWGIRL HAVE BEEN SENT ON THEIR WAY.
ARE YOU READY, PENNY?
WILL MY OTHER CHILDREN BE WHERE WE'RE GOING? THEY HAVE TWO OLDER SIBLINGS, YOU KNOW.
ONLY THE RAY OF TRUTH KNOWS FOR SURE. I'M SORRY I CAN'T TELL YOU MORE.
ROCKY'S JOB'S ALWAYS BEEN THE HARDEST.

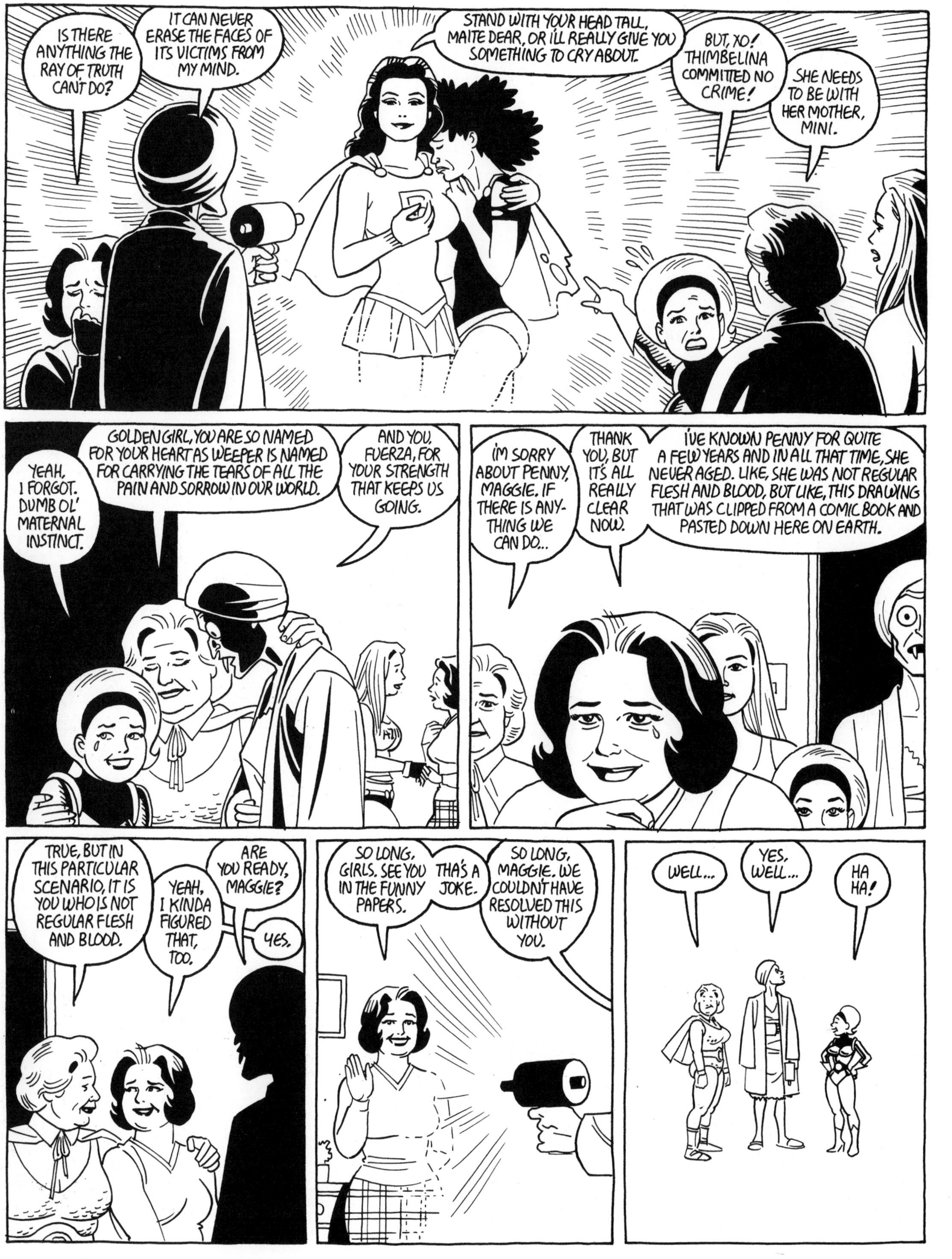
IS THERE ANYTHING THE RAY OF TRUTH CAN'T DO?
IT CAN NEVER ERASE THE FACES OF ITS VICTIMS FROM MY MIND.
STAND WITH YOUR HEAD TALL, MAITE DEAR, OR I'LL REALLY GIVE YOU SOMETHING TO CRY ABOUT.
BUT, XO! THIMBELINA COMMITTED NO CRIME!
SHE NEEDS TO BE WITH HER MOTHER, MINI.
YEAH, I FORGOT. DUMB OL' MATERNAL INSTINCT.
GOLDEN GIRL, YOU ARE SO NAMED FOR YOUR HEART AS WEEPER IS NAMED FOR CARRYING THE TEARS OF ALL THE PAIN AND SORROW IN OUR WORLD.
AND YOU, FUERZA, FOR YOUR STRENGTH THAT KEEPS US GOING.
I'M SORRY ABOUT PENNY, MAGGIE. IF THERE IS ANY-THING WE CAN DO...
THANK YOU, BUT IT'S ALL REALLY CLEAR NOW.
I'VE KNOWN PENNY FOR QUITE A FEW YEARS AND IN ALL THAT TIME, SHE NEVER AGED. LIKE, SHE WAS NOT REGULAR FLESH AND BLOOD, BUT LIKE, THIS DRAWING THAT WAS CLIPPED FROM A COMIC BOOK AND PASTED DOWN HERE ON EARTH.
TRUE, BUT IN THIS PARTICULAR SCENARIO, IT IS YOU WHO IS NOT REGULAR FLESH AND BLOOD.
YEAH, I KINDA FIGURED THAT, TOO.
ARE YOU READY, MAGGIE?
YES.
SO LONG, GIRLS. SEE YOU IN THE FUNNY PAPERS.
THA'S A JOKE.
SO LONG, MAGGIE. WE COULDN'T HAVE RESOLVED THIS WITHOUT YOU.
WELL...
YES, WELL...
HA HA!

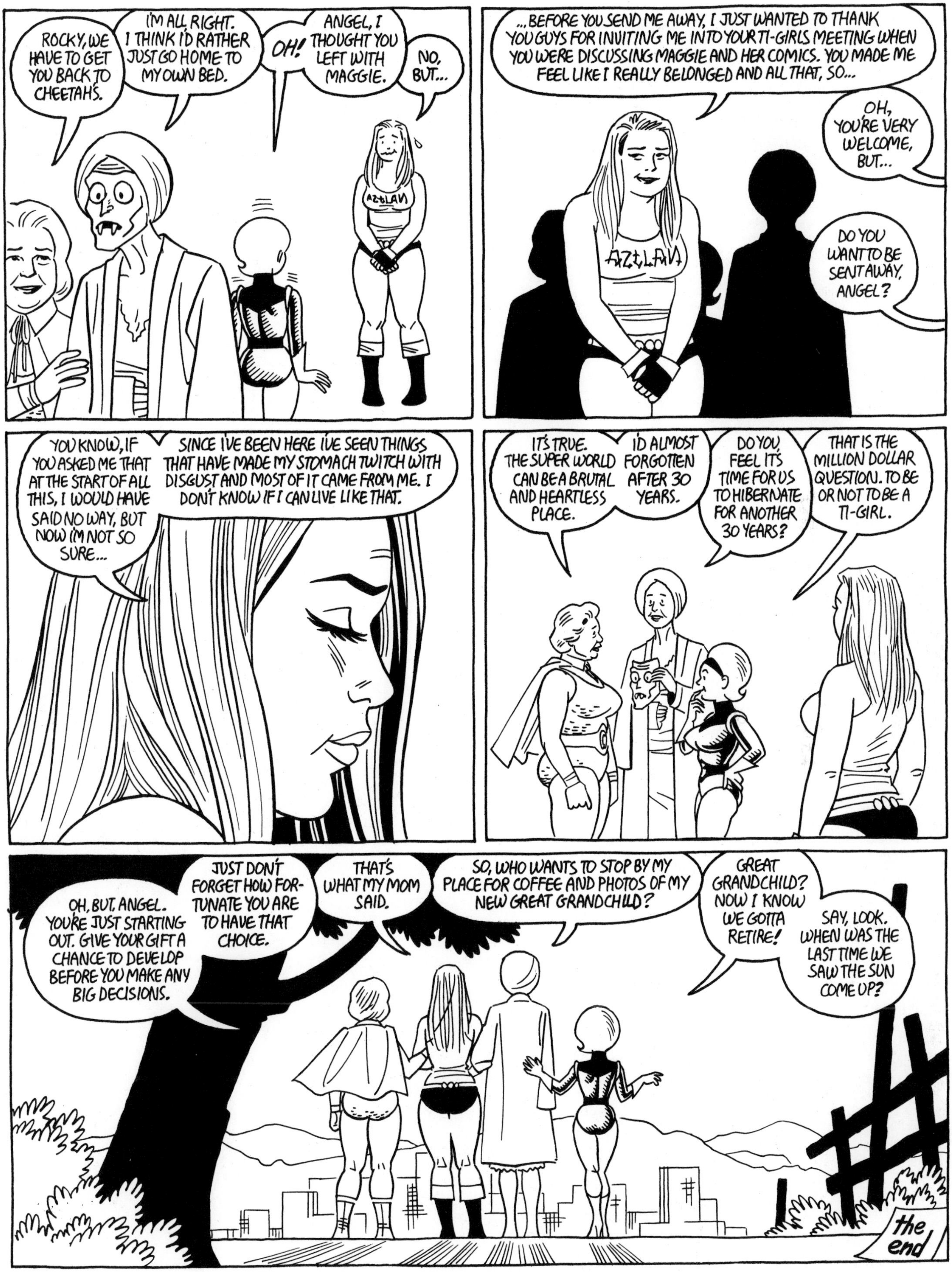

ROCKY, WE HAVE TO GET YOU BACK TO CHEETAH'S.
I'M ALL RIGHT. I THINK I'D RATHER JUST GO HOME TO MY OWN BED.
OH!
ANGEL, I THOUGHT YOU LEFT WITH MAGGIE.
NO, BUT...
AZTLAN
...BEFORE YOU SEND ME AWAY, I JUST WANTED TO THANK YOU GUYS FOR INVITING ME INTO YOUR TI-GIRLS MEETING WHEN YOU WERE DISCUSSING MAGGIE AND HER COMICS. YOU MADE ME FEEL LIKE I REALLY BELONGED AND ALL THAT, SO...
OH, YOU'RE VERY WELCOME, BUT...
AZTLAN
DO YOU WANT TO BE SENT AWAY, ANGEL?
YOU KNOW, IF YOU ASKED ME THAT AT THE START OF ALL THIS, I WOULD HAVE SAID NO WAY, BUT NOW I'M NOT SO SURE...
SINCE I'VE BEEN HERE I'VE SEEN THINGS THAT HAVE MADE MY STOMACH TWITCH WITH DISGUST AND MOST OF IT CAME FROM ME. I DON'T KNOW IF I CAN LIVE LIKE THAT.
IT'S TRUE. THE SUPER WORLD CAN BE A BRUTAL AND HEARTLESS PLACE.
I'D ALMOST FORGOTTEN AFTER 30 YEARS.
DO YOU FEEL IT'S TIME FOR US TO HIBERNATE FOR ANOTHER 30 YEARS?
THAT IS THE MILLION DOLLAR QUESTION. TO BE OR NOT TO BE A TI-GIRL.
OH, BUT, ANGEL. YOU'RE JUST STARTING OUT. GIVE YOUR GIFT A CHANCE TO DEVELOP BEFORE YOU MAKE ANY BIG DECISIONS.
JUST DON'T FORGET HOW FORTUNATE YOU ARE TO HAVE THAT CHOICE.
THAT'S WHAT MY MOM SAID.
SO, WHO WANTS TO STOP BY MY PLACE FOR COFFEE AND PHOTOS OF MY NEW GREAT GRANDCHILD?
GREAT GRANDCHILD? NOW I KNOW WE GOTTA RETIRE!
SAY, LOOK. WHEN WAS THE LAST TIME WE SAW THE SUN COME UP?
the end

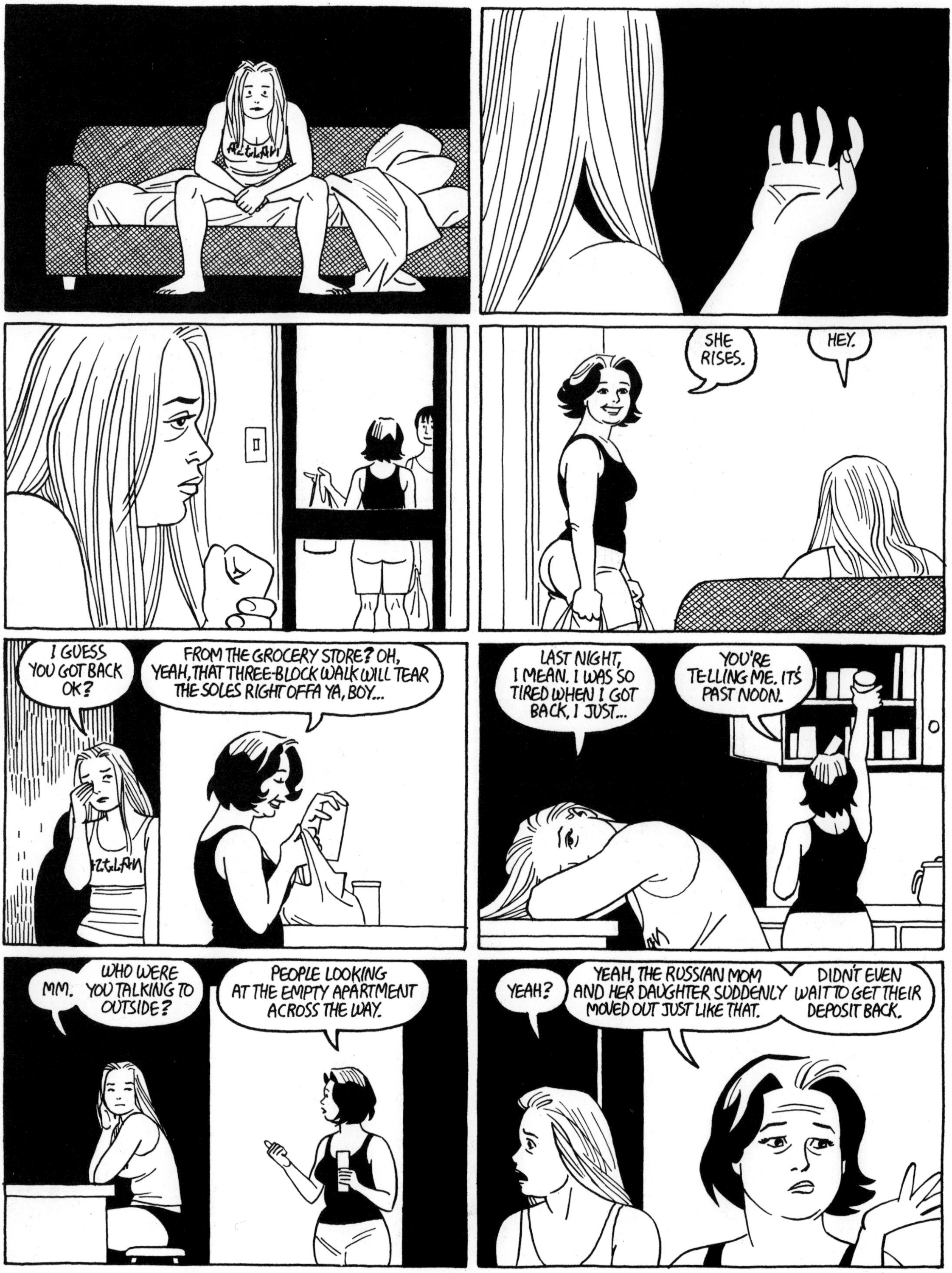
SHE RISES.
HEY.
I GUESS YOU GOT BACK OK?
FROM THE GROCERY STORE? OH, YEAH, THAT THREE-BLOCK WALK WILL TEAR THE SOLES RIGHT OFFA YA, BOY...
LAST NIGHT, I MEAN. I WAS SO TIRED WHEN I GOT BACK, I JUST...
YOU'RE TELLING ME. IT'S PAST NOON.
MM.
WHO WERE YOU TALKING TO OUTSIDE?
PEOPLE LOOKING AT THE EMPTY APARTMENT ACROSS THE WAY.
YEAH?
YEAH, THE RUSSIAN MOM AND HER DAUGHTER SUDDENLY MOVED OUT JUST LIKE THAT.
DIDN'T EVEN WAIT TO GET THEIR DEPOSIT BACK.

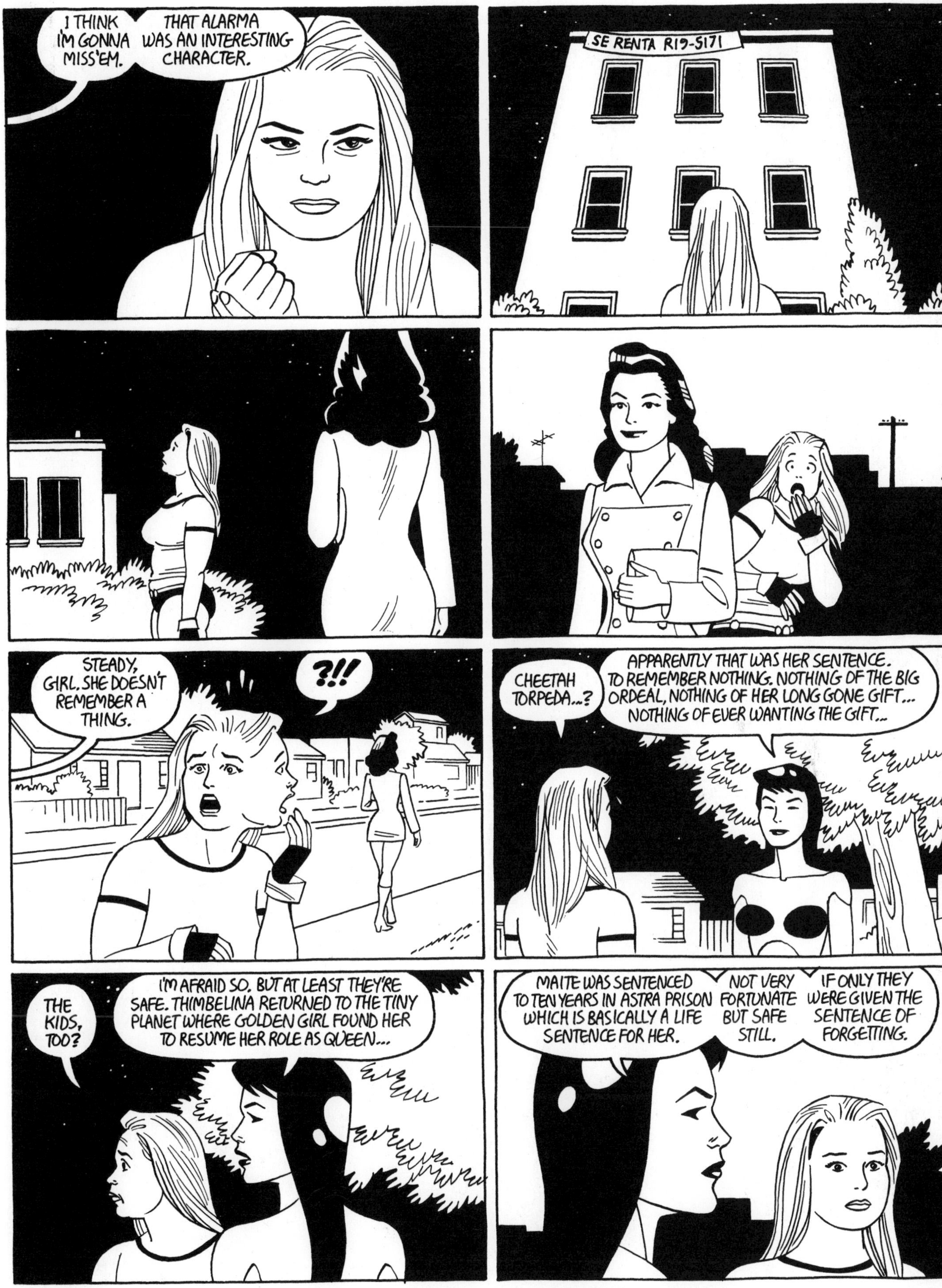

I THINK I'M GONNA MISS'EM.
THAT ALARMA WAS AN INTERESTING CHARACTER.
SE RENTA R19-5171
STEADY, GIRL. SHE DOESN'T REMEMBER A THING.
?!!
CHEETAH TORPEDA...?
APPARENTLY THAT WAS HER SENTENCE. TO REMEMBER NOTHING. NOTHING OF THE BIG ORDEAL, NOTHING OF HER LONG GONE GIFT... NOTHING OF EVER WANTING THE GIFT...
THE KIDS, TOO?
I'M AFRAID SO. BUT AT LEAST THEY'RE SAFE. THIMBELINA RETURNED TO THE TINY PLANET WHERE GOLDEN GIRL FOUND HER TO RESUME HER ROLE AS QUEEN...
MAITE WAS SENTENCED TO TEN YEARS IN ASTRA PRISON WHICH IS BASICALLY A LIFE SENTENCE FOR HER.
NOT VERY FORTUNATE BUT SAFE STILL.
IF ONLY THEY WERE GIVEN THE SENTENCE OF FORGETTING.

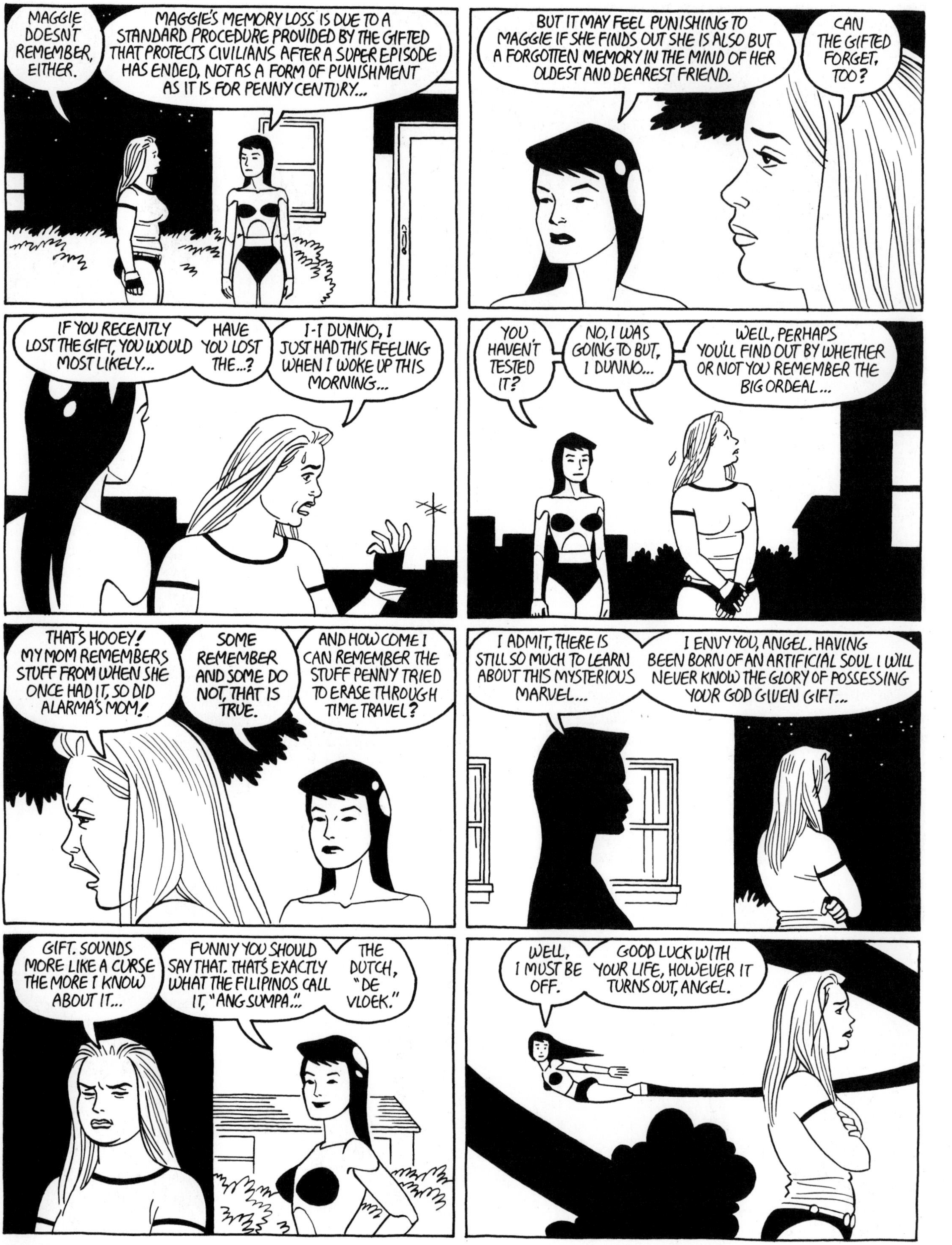
MAGGIE DOESN'T REMEMBER, EITHER.
MAGGIE'S MEMORY LOSS IS DUE TO A STANDARD PROCEDURE PROVIDED BY THE GIFTED THAT PROTECTS CIVILIANS AFTER A SUPER EPISODE HAS ENDED, NOT AS A FORM OF PUNISHMENT AS IT IS FOR PENNY CENTURY...
BUT IT MAY FEEL PUNISHING TO MAGGIE IF SHE FINDS OUT SHE IS ALSO BUT A FORGOTTEN MEMORY IN THE MIND OF HER OLDEST AND DEAREST FRIEND.
CAN THE GIFTED FORGET, TOO?
IF YOU RECENTLY LOST THE GIFT, YOU WOULD MOST LIKELY...
HAVE YOU LOST THE...?
I-I DUNNO, I JUST HAD THIS FEELING WHEN I WOKE UP THIS MORNING...
YOU HAVEN'T TESTED IT?
NO, I WAS GOING TO BUT, I DUNNO...
WELL, PERHAPS YOU'LL FIND OUT BY WHETHER OR NOT YOU REMEMBER THE BIG ORDEAL...
THAT'S HOOEY! MY MOM REMEMBERS STUFF FROM WHEN SHE ONCE HAD IT, SO DID ALARMA'S MOM!
SOME REMEMBER AND SOME DO NOT, THAT IS TRUE.
AND HOW COME I CAN REMEMBER THE STUFF PENNY TRIED TO ERASE THROUGH TIME TRAVEL?
I ADMIT, THERE IS STILL SO MUCH TO LEARN ABOUT THIS MYSTERIOUS MARVEL...
I ENVY YOU, ANGEL. HAVING BEEN BORN OF AN ARTIFICIAL SOUL I WILL NEVER KNOW THE GLORY OF POSSESSING YOUR GOD GIVEN GIFT...
GIFT. SOUNDS MORE LIKE A CURSE THE MORE I KNOW ABOUT IT...
FUNNY YOU SHOULD SAY THAT. THAT'S EXACTLY WHAT THE FILIPINOS CALL IT, "ANG SUMPA."
THE DUTCH, "DE VLOEK."
WELL, I MUST BE OFF.
GOOD LUCK WITH YOUR LIFE, HOWEVER IT TURNS OUT, ANGEL.

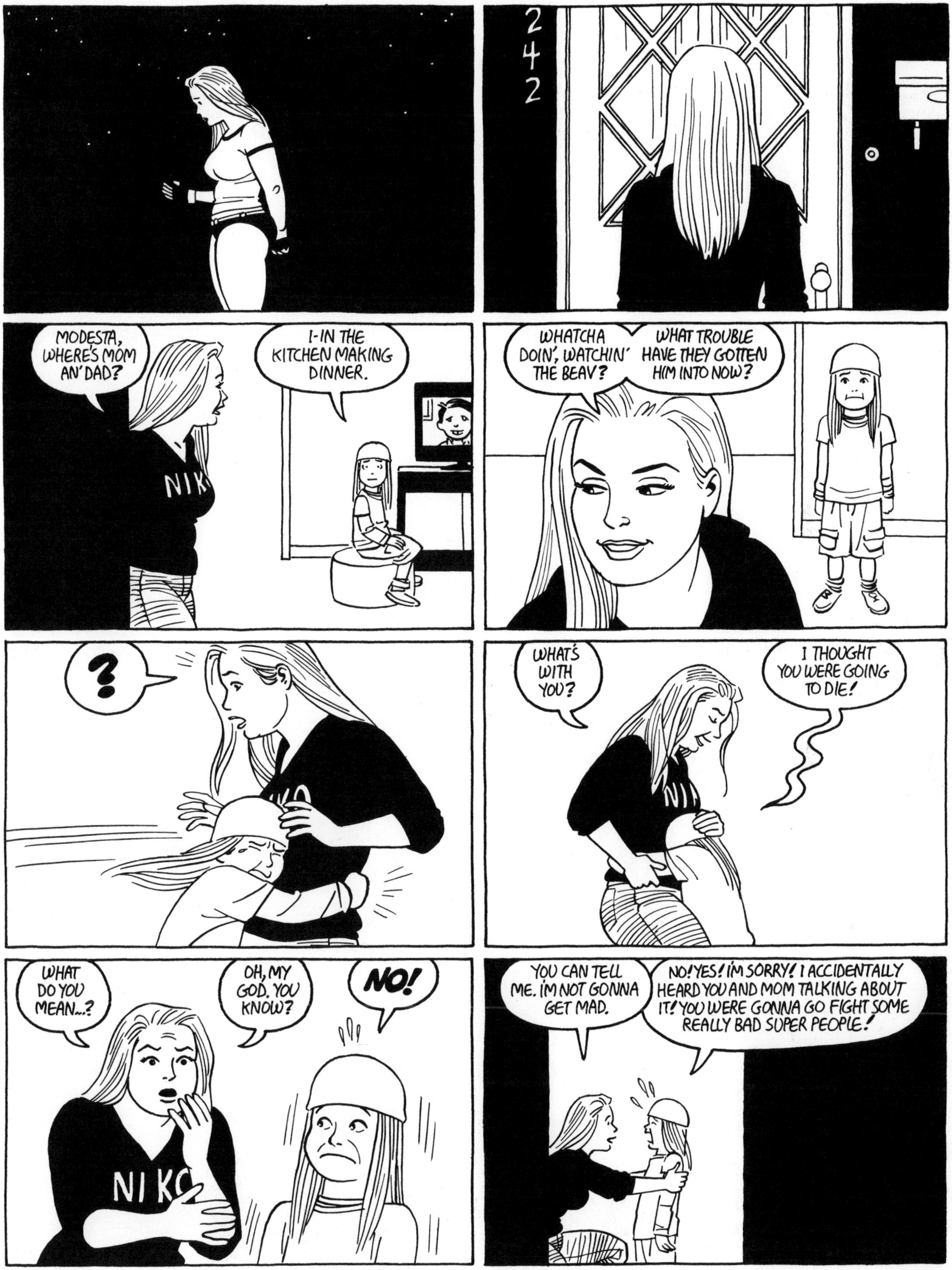
2
4
2
MODESTA, WHERE'S MOM AN' DAD?
I-IN THE KITCHEN MAKING DINNER.
WHATCHA DOIN', WATCHIN' THE BEAV?
WHAT TROUBLE HAVE THEY GOTTEN HIM INTO NOW?
?
WHAT'S WITH YOU?
I THOUGHT YOU WERE GOING TO DIE!
WHAT DO YOU MEAN...?
OH, MY GOD. YOU KNOW?
NO!
YOU CAN TELL ME. I'M NOT GONNA GET MAD.
NO! YES! I'M SORRY! I ACCIDENTALLY HEARD YOU AND MOM TALKING ABOUT IT! YOU WERE GONNA GO FIGHT SOME REALLY BAD SUPER PEOPLE!

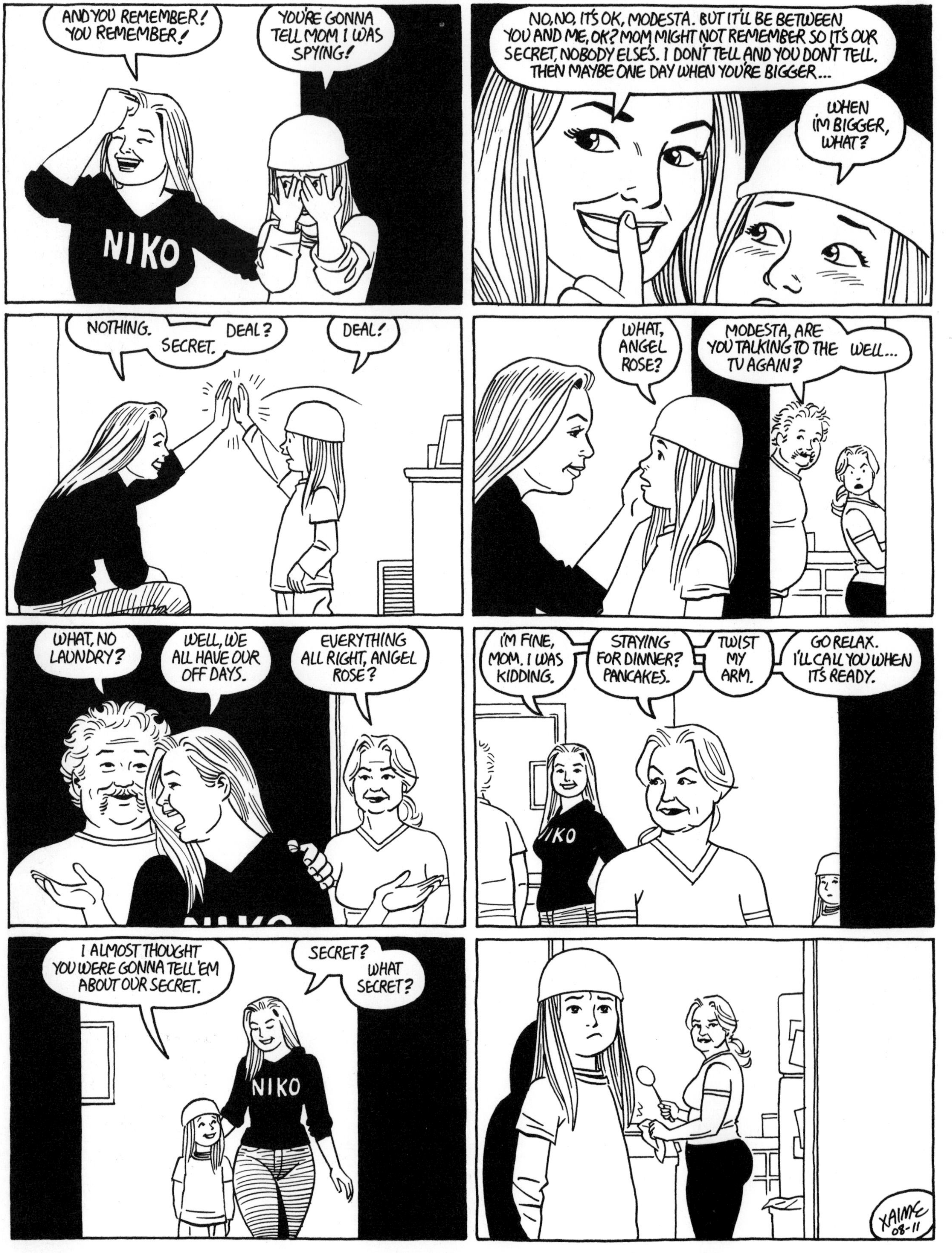
AND YOU REMEMBER! YOU REMEMBER!
YOU'RE GONNA TELL MOM I WAS SPYING!
NO, NO, IT'S OK, MODESTA. BUT IT'LL BE BETWEEN YOU AND ME, OK? MOM MIGHT NOT REMEMBER SO IT'S OUR SECRET, NOBODY ELSE'S. I DON'T TELL AND YOU DON'T TELL. THEN MAYBE ONE DAY WHEN YOU'RE BIGGER...
WHEN I'M BIGGER, WHAT?
NOTHING.
SECRET.
DEAL?
DEAL!
WHAT, ANGEL ROSE?
MODESTA, ARE YOU TALKING TO THE TV AGAIN?
WELL...
WHAT, NO LAUNDRY?
WELL, WE ALL HAVE OUR OFF DAYS.
EVERYTHING ALL RIGHT, ANGEL ROSE?
I'M FINE, MOM. I WAS KIDDING.
STAYING FOR DINNER? PANCAKES.
TWIST MY ARM.
GO RELAX. I'LL CALL YOU WHEN IT'S READY.
I ALMOST THOUGHT YOU WERE GONNA TELL 'EM ABOUT OUR SECRET.
SECRET? WHAT SECRET?
XAIME 08-11